BROOKLANDS
BOOKS

BMW
2002
1968-1976

Compiled by
R.M. Clarke

ISBN 0 948207 83 3

Distributed by
Brooklands Book Distribution Ltd.
'Holmerise', Seven Hills Road,
Cobham, Surrey, England
Printed in Hong Kong

BROOKLANDS BOOKS

BROOKLANDS BOOKS SERIES
AC Ace & Aceca 1953-1983
AC Cobra 1962-1969
Alfa Romeo Alfasud 1972-1984
Alfa Romeo Alfetta Coupes GT.GTV.GTV6 1974-1987
Alfa Romeo Giulia Berlinas 1962-1976
Alfa Romeo Giulia Coupés 1963-1976
Alfa Romeo Spider 1966-1987
Allard Gold Portfolio 1937-1958
Alvis Gold Portfolio 1919-1967
Aston Martin Gold Portfolio 1972-1985
Austin Seven 1922-1982
Austin A30 & A35 1951-1962
Austin Healey 3000 1959-1967
Austin Healey 'Frogeye' Sprite Collection No. 1
Austin Healey Sprite 1958-1971
Avanti 1962-1983
BMW Six Cylinder Coupés 1969-1975
BMW 1600 Collection No. 1
BMW 2002 1968-1976
Bristol Cars Gold Portfolio 1946-1985
Buick Automobiles 1947-1960
Buick Riviera 1963-1978
Cadillac Automobiles 1949-1959
Cadillac Automobiles 1960-1969
Cadillac Eldorado 1967-1978
Camaro 1966-1970
Chevrolet Camaro & Z-28 1973-1981
High Performance Camaros 1982-1988
Chevrolet Camaro Collection No. 1
Chevrolet 1955-1957
Chevrolet Impala & SS 1958-1971
Chevelle & SS 1964-1972
Chevy II Nova & SS 1962-1973
High Performance Corvettes 1983-1989
Chrysler 300 1955-1970
Citroen Traction Avant 1934-1957
Citroen DS & ID 1955-1975
Citroen 2CV 1948-1988
Cobras & Replicas 1962-1983
Cortina 1600E & GT 1967-1970
Corvair 1959-1968
Daimler Dart & V-8 250 1959-1969
Datsun 240Z 1970-1973
Datsun 280Z & ZX 1975-1983
De Tomaso Collection No. 1
Dodge Charger 1966-1974
Excalibur Collection No. 1
Ferrari Cars 1946-1956
Ferrari Dino 1965-1974
Ferrari Dino 308 1974-1979
Ferrari 308 & Mondial 1980-1984
Ferrari Collection No. 1
Fiat-Bertone X1/9 1973-1988
Fiat Pininfarina 124+2000 Spider 1968-1985
Ford Automobiles 1949-1959
Ford Fairlane 1955-1970
Ford Falcon 1960-1970
Ford RS Escort 1968-1980
High Performance Escorts MkI 1968-1974
High Performance Escorts MkII 1975-1980
High Performance Mustangs 1982-1988
Honda CRX 1983-1987
Hudson & Railton Cars 1936-1940
Jaguar Cars 1957-1961
Jaguar Cars 1961-1964
Jaguar XK120 XK140 XK150 Gold Portfolio 1948-1960
Jaguar MK2 1959-1969
Jaguar E-Type Gold Portfolio 1961-1971
Jaguar E-Type 1966-1971
Jaguar E-Type V12 1971-1975
Jaguar XJ6 1968-1972
Jaguar XJ6 Series II 1973-1979
Jaguar XJ6 & XJ12 Series III 1979-1985
Jaguar XJ12 1972-1980
Jaguar XJS Gold Portfolio 1975-1988
Jensen Cars 1946-1967
Jensen Cars 1967-1979
Jensen Interceptor Gold Portfolio 1966-1986
Jensen Healey 1972-1976
Lamborghini Cars 1964-1970
Lamborghini Cars 1970-1975
Lamborghini Countach Collection No. 1
Lamborghini Countach & Urraco 1974-1980
Lamborghini Countach & Jalpa 1980-1985
Lancia Stratos 1972-1985
Land Rover 1948-1973
Land Rover Series II & IIa 1958-1971
Land Rover Series III 1971-1985
Land Rover 90 & 110 1983-1989
Lotus Cortina 1963-1970
Lotus Elan Gold Portfolio 1962-1974
Lotus Elan Collection No. 2
Lotus Elite 1957-1964
Lotus Elite & Eclat 1974-1981
Lotus Turbo Esprit 1980-1986
Lotus Europa 1966-1975
Lotus Europa Collection No. 1
Lotus Seven 1957-1980
Lotus Seven Collection No. 1
Marcos Cars 1960-1988
Maserati 1965-1970
Maserati 1970-1975
Mazda RX-7 Collection No. 1
Mercedes 190 & 300SL 1954-1963
Mercedes 230/250/280SL 1963-1971
Mercedes 350/450SL & SLC 1971-1980
Mercedes Benz Cars 1949-1954
Mercedes Benz Cars 1954-1957
Mercedes Benz Cars 1957-1961
Mercedes Benz Competition Cars 1950-1957
Metropolitan 1954-1962

MG TC 1945-1949
MG TD 1949-1953
MG TF 1953-1955
MG Cars 1957-1959
MG Cars 1959-1962
MG Midget 1961-1980
MGA Collection No. 1
MGA Roadsters 1955-1962
MGB Roadsters 1962-1980
MGB GT 1965-1980
Mini Cooper 1961-1971
Morgan Cars 1960-1970
The Morgan 3-Wheeler Gold Portfolio 1910-1952
Morgan Cars Gold Portfolio 1968-1989
Morris Minor Collection No. 1
Oldsmobile Automobiles 1955-1963
Old's Cutlass & 4-4-2 1964-1972
Oldsmobile Toronado 1966-1978
Opel GT 1968-1973
Packard Gold Portfolio 1946-1958
Pantera 1970-1973
Pantera & Mangusta 1969-1974
Plymouth Barracuda 1964-1974
Pontiac Fiero 1984-1988
Pontiac GTO 1964-1970
Pontiac Firebird 1967-1973
Pontiac Firebird and Trans-Am 1973-1981
High Performance Firebirds 1982-1988
Pontiac Tempest & GTO 1961-1965
Porsche Cars 1960-1964
Porsche Cars 1964-1968
Porsche Cars 1968-1972
Porsche Cars in the Sixties
Porsche Cars 1972-1975
Porsche 356 1952-1965
Porsche 911 1965-1969
Porsche 911 1970-1972
Porsche 911 1973-1977
Porsche 911 Carrera 1973-1977
Porsche 911 SC 1978-1983
Porsche 911 Turbo 1975-1984
Porsche 914 Gold Portfolio 1969-1976
Porsche 914 Collection No. 1
Porsche 924 Gold Portfolio 1975-1988
Porsche 928 1977-1989
Porsche 944 1981-1985
Reliant Scimitar 1964-1986
Riley 1½ & 2½ Litre Gold Portfolio 1945-1955
Rolls Royce Silver Cloud 1955-1965
Rolls Royce Silver Shadow 1965-1980
Range Rover Gold Portfolio 1970-1988
Rover 3 & 3.5 Litre 1958-1973
Rover P4 1949-1959
Rover P4 1955-1964
Rover 2000 + 2200 1963-1977
Rover 3500 1968-1977
Rover 3500 & Vitesse 1976-1986
Saab Sonett Collection No. 1
Saab Turbo 1976-1983
Studebaker Hawks & Larks 1956-1963
Sunbeam Tiger and Alpine Gold Portfolio 1959-1967
Thunderbird 1955-1957
Thunderbird 1958-1963
Thunderbird 1964-1976
Toyota MR2 1984-1988
Triumph 2000-2.5-2500 1963-1977
Triumph Spitfire 1962-1980
Triumph Spitfire Collection No. 1
Triumph Stag 1970-1980
Triumph Stag Collection No. 1
Triumph TR2 & TR3 1952-1960
Triumph TR4.TR5.TR250 1961-1968
Triumph TR6 1969-1976
Triumph TR6 Collection No. 1
Triumph TR7 & TR8 1975-1982
Triumph GT6 1966-1974
Triumph Vitesse & Herald 1959-1971
TVR Gold Portfolio 1959-1988
Volkswagen Cars 1936-1956
VW Beetle 1956-1977
VW Beetle Collection No. 1
VW Golf GTi 1976-1986
VW Karmann Ghia 1955-1982
VW Scirocco 1974-1981
VW Bus-Camper-Van 1954-1967
VW Bus-Camper-Van 1968-1979
VW Bus-Camper-Van 1979-1989
Volvo 1800 1960-1973
Volvo 120 Series 1956-1970

BROOKLANDS MUSCLE CARS SERIES
American Motors Muscle Cars 1966-1970
Buick Muscle Cars 1965-1970
Camaro Muscle Cars 1966-1972
Capri Muscle Cars 1969-1983
Chevrolet Muscle Cars 1966-1972
Dodge Muscle Cars 1967-1970
Mercury Muscle Cars 1966-1971
Mini Muscle Cars 1961-1979
Mopar Muscle Cars 1964-1967
Mopar Muscle Cars 1968-1971
Mustang Muscle Cars 1967-1971
Shelby Mustang Muscle Cars 1965-1970
Oldsmobile Muscle Cars 1964-1970
Plymouth Muscle Cars 1966-1971
Pontiac Muscle Cars 1966-1972

BROOKLANDS ROAD & TRACK SERIES
Road & Track on Alfa Romeo 1949-1963
Road & Track on Alfa Romeo 1964-1970
Road & Track on Alfa Romeo 1971-1976
Road & Track on Alfa Romeo 1977-1989
Road & Track on Aston Martin 1962-1984
Road & Track on Auburn Cord & Duesenberg 1952-1984

Road & Track on Audi 1952-1980
Road & Track on Audi 1980-1986
Road & Track on Austin Healey 1953-1970
Road & Track on BMW Cars 1966-1974
Road & Track on BMW Cars 1975-1978
Road & Track on BMW Cars 1979-1983
Road & Track on Cobra, Shelby &
  Ford GT40 1962-1983
Road & Track on Corvette 1953-1967
Road & Track on Corvette 1968-1982
Road & Track on Corvette 1982-1986
Road & Track on Datsun Z 1970-1983
Road & Track on Ferrari 1950-1968
Road & Track on Ferrari 1968-1974
Road & Track on Ferrari 1975-1981
Road & Track on Ferrari 1981-1984
Road & Track on Fiat Sports Cars 1968-1987
Road & Track on Jaguar 1950-1960
Road & Track on Jaguar 1961-1968
Road & Track on Jaguar 1968-1974
Road & Track on Jaguar 1974-1982
Road & Track on Jaguar 1983-1989
Road & Track on Lamborghini 1964-1985
Road & Track on Lotus 1972-1981
Road & Track on Maserati 1952-1974
Road & Track on Maserati 1975-1983
Road & Track on Mazda RX7 1978-1986
Road & Track on Mercedes 1952-1962
Road & Track on Mercedes 1963-1970
Road & Track on Mercedes 1971-1979
Road & Track on Mercedes 1980-1987
Road & Track on MG Sports Cars 1949-1961
Road & Track on MG Sports Cars 1962-1980
Road & Track on Mustang 1964-1977
Road & Track on Peugeot 1955-1986
Road & Track on Pontiac 1960-1983
Road & Track on Porsche 1951-1967
Road & Track on Porsche 1968-1971
Road & Track on Porsche 1972-1975
Road & Track on Porsche 1975-1978
Road & Track on Porsche 1979-1982
Road & Track on Porsche 1982-1985
Road & Track on Porsche 1985-1988
Road & Track on Rolls Royce & Bentley 1950-1965
Road & Track on Rolls Royce & Bentley 1966-1984
Road & Track on Saab 1955-1985
Road & Track on Toyota Sports & G T Cars 1966-1986
Road & Track on Triumph Sports Cars 1953-1967
Road & Track on Triumph Sports Cars 1967-1974
Road & Track on Triumph Sports Cars 1974-1982
Road & Track on Volkswagen 1951-1968
Road & Track on Volkswagen 1968-1978
Road & Track on Volkswagen 1978-1985
Road & Track on Volvo 1957-1974
Road & Track on Volvo 1975-1985
Road & Track Henry Manney at Large & Abroad

BROOKLANDS CAR AND DRIVER SERIES
Car and Driver on BMW 1955-1977
Car and Driver on BMW 1977-1985
Car and Driver on Cobra, Shelby & Ford GT40
  1963-1984
Car and Driver on Datsun Z 1600 & 2000
  1966-1984
Car and Driver on Corvette 1956-1967
Car and Driver on Corvette 1968-1977
Car and Driver on Corvette 1978-1982
Car and Driver on Corvette 1983-1988
Car and Driver on Ferrari 1955-1962
Car and Driver on Ferrari 1963-1975
Car and Driver on Ferrari 1976-1983
Car and Driver on Mopar 1956-1967
Car and Driver on Mopar 1968-1975
Car and Driver on Mustang 1964-1972
Car and Driver on Pontiac 1961-1975
Car and Driver on Porsche 1955-1962
Car and Driver on Porsche 1963-1970
Car and Driver on Porsche 1970-1976
Car and Driver on Porsche 1977-1981
Car and Driver on Porsche 1982-1986
Car and Driver on Saab 1956-1985
Car and Driver on Volvo 1955-1986

BROOKLANDS MOTOR & THOROUGHBRED & CLASSIC CAR SERIES
Motor & T & CC on Ferrari 1966-1976
Motor & T & CC on Ferrari 1976-1984
Motor & T & CC on Lotus 1979-1983

BROOKLANDS PRACTICAL CLASSICS SERIES
Practical Classics on Austin A 40 Restoration
Practical Classics on Land Rover Restoration
Practical Classics on Metalworking in Restoration
Practical Classics on Midget/Sprite Restoration
Practical Classics on Mini Cooper Restoration
Practical Classics on MGB Restoration
Practical Classics on Morris Minor Restoration
Practical Classics on Triumph Herald/Vitesse
Practical Classics on Triumph Spitfire Restoration
Practical Classics on VW Beetle Restoration
Practical Classics on 1930S Car Restoration

BROOKLANDS MILITARY VEHICLES SERIES
Allied Military Vehicles Collection No. 1
Allied Military Vehicles Collection No. 2
Dodge Military Vehicles Collection No. 1
Military Jeeps 1941-1945
Off Road Jeeps 1944-1971
V W Kubelwagen 1940-1975

BROOKLANDS BOOKS

CONTENTS

ACKNOWLEDGEMENTS

Almost five years ago to the day we dispatched to our printers "BMW 2002 Collection No. 1' our first book on this marque. It was well received and went out of print a few months ago. Instead of reissuing it we decided to update it firstly by dropping some stories and replacing them with others and secondly by adding a further thirty pages.

Our original introduction still seems quite appropriate, it went as follows:

"In 1966 BMW introduced one of its most successful models, the 1600 sports sedan. It quickly gained an enviable reputation, especially in the U.S. and it helped revive the German company's flagging financial position.

By 1968 the new emission control regulations were beginning to bite, the big Austin-Healeys were an early victim and BMW realised that if they were to meet the specifications and maintain a sporty performance they would need to increase the capacity of their power unit. They fitted the 2 litre engine from the 2000ti model which had similar exterior dimensions to the 1600 and so was born the BMW 2002.

The rest of the story is contained within these covers. For readers who wish to study the development of its sister model the 1600, a second book is available – BMW 1600 Collection No. 1."

The Brooklands series now exceeds 250 titles, their purpose is to inform and help second and subsequent owners of interesting cars by making available once again the best contemporary articles that were written about their vehicles. The views of three continents have been included in this anthology and I am sure BMW enthusiasts will wish to join with me in thanking the publishers of Autocar, Autosport, Car and Car Conversions, Car and Driver Classic and Sportscar, Motor, Motor Manual, Motor Racing and Sportscar, Motor Trend, Practical Classics, Road Test, Road & Track and Sports Car World for allowing their valuable copyright material to be included here.

R.M. Clarke

BMW 2002

It's the 1600 sedan with the 2-liter engine— but where did the extra horsepower go?

THE BMW 1600-2, introduced last year, made a splash. In the home market, Germany, it enabled Bayerische Motoren Werke AG to increase total sales for the year in the face of an overall decline in the German car market. In the U.S. it put BMW "on the map" by more than tripling the make's sales rate.

BMW had nearly gone under, little more than five years ago. After the war the company had concentrated on large V-8 cars that were ill-suited for the German market, and had even squandered its money on developing and marketing an exciting sports car with the V-8—the illustrious 507, certainly one of the all-time classics. But sales are needed to keep a firm alive, and while BMW engineers were developing a new 1.5-liter car that stood a chance in the marketplace, BMW managers were finding financial backing to produce the car. They found the backing; the car appeared in early 1963, was an immediate success and put BMW on the road to recovery.

The 1500, as it was called, was a straightforward 4-door sedan powered by a refined 4-cyl, single overhead cam, 1.5-liter engine and engineered to be a really high-quality car of its type with fully independent suspension, disc brakes in front, a very strong body/chassis unit and fairly luxurious fittings. In successive years the engine grew to 1.6 and then to 1.8 and finally to a full 2 liters. When the 2000 was introduced, the whole line—1600, 1800 and 2000 and the variations thereof—got revised rear suspension with the springs moved to a position just over the axle shafts from the earlier position well forward of the axles. A luxurious 2000 coupe was added to the top of the line. And then came the new 1600-2 (2 for 2-door), with the entire 1600 mechanical package stuffed into a smaller, lighter and plainer new body. With the 1600-2 it was suddenly possible to have the (by then) familiar BMW virtues for $2600 instead of $3000; the importer, Max Hoffman, knew this was his chance and put on a healthy

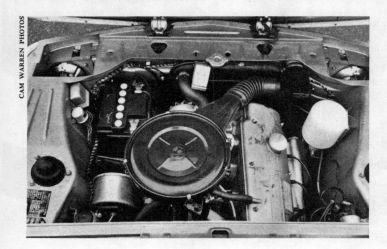

CAM WARREN PHOTOS

BMW 2002
AT A GLANCE

Price as tested.............................$3510
Engine..........4-cyl, inline, sohc, 1990 cc, 113 bhp
Curb weight, lb.............................2210
Top speed, mph................................108
Acceleration, 0–¼ mi, sec....................17.6
Average fuel consumption, mpg.................24
Summary: More flexible and quicker than 1600 ...
usual BMW traits of quality, handling, ride ... modern
sports-car performance for 4 passengers at a reasonable
price.

advertising campaign to tell the general American public about the new car.

The success of the 1600-2 is well known now to R&T readers, but just to refresh the memory, we found it to be one of the best automotive values to be had from any country—brimming with handling, ride, finish, refinement of running and even good style. It was only natural that BMW should then expand on the -2 theme, and last year the company came up with the predictable TI version of it (Touring International) with the engine souped up to 118 bhp @ 6200 rpm (from 96 @ 5800), and an identifying trim change here and there. But by this time BMW saw some handwriting on the wall: that they would not be able to make this highly tuned, dual carburetor 1600 engine comply with the upcoming U.S. emission-control law. So the engineers were given a new project: to drop in the existing 2-liter engine in place of the 1600 TI unit. The 1600 engine, at 1573 cc or 96 cu in., falls just under the 100-cu-in. dividing point in the emission regulations and is entitled to 410 parts of unburned hydrocarbons per million parts of exhaust (ppm) and 2.3% carbon monoxide concentration. But apparently it's easier to meet the 350-ppm, 2.0%-CO requirement for engines of 100-140 cu in. with the 1990-cc (121.5-cu-in.) 2000 engine and a single carburetor. This 2-liter engine is externally the same, and the existing drive-train is the same as that used in the larger cars, so it was mostly a matter of just substituting one for the other.

The resulting car, the 2002, weighs 2210 lb at the curb, which is 160 lb or about 8% heavier than the 1600. With 26½% more displacement and 27½% greater torque, we expected a goodly performance gain over the 1600 even though the gearing is about 10% taller with 3320 rev/mi vs. the

1600's 3675. The gain is there, though our initial tests of the car (which happened to have the wrong flywheel and hence incorrect ignition timing) almost led us to believe it was no quicker than the 1600. The 2002 gets through the standing-start ¼-mile 0.6 sec faster than the 1600, to 60 mph 1.2 sec faster; its top speed is 108 mph vs. the 1600's even 100. It's also likely to go farther between overhauls with its less revvy gearing. And it appears that the emission control—by air injection—doesn't steal performance, as our test car lived up to claims for the European version.

Strangely enough, the 2002—despite its 8-counterbalance crankshaft (the 1600 has four weights) and taller gearing, is also noisier than the 1600 and feels somewhat undergeared at high cruising speeds. On the positive side, the engine revs quite freely (to well beyond its 6000-rpm redline), idles well at 750 rpm, gets excellent fuel economy and has few of the bothersome foibles—such as backfiring—that we've found in many air-injection engines. The noises, from the enthusiast's viewpoint, are all pleasant ones—from the characteristic BMW camdrive whine heard at low speeds to the sound of a healthy engine sailing right past its redline without a clatter.

One comment that engineers always make about BMWs is that the cars seem to have rubber everywhere. This isn't a derogatory comment at all: it seems to be in all the right places. In particular, it's in the shift linkage, making for a soft and smooth "feel" to the gearchange. The BMW gearbox is itself smooth and quiet; its synchronizers—Porsche design—powerful though a little obstructive. An interesting note on the Porsche synchronizer design here: on all cars using it we've found that it's possible to beat the 1st-gear synchronizer by letting the engine idle in neutral, push-

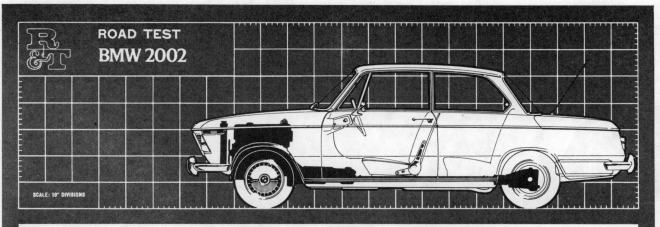

BMW 2002

SCALE: 10" DIVISIONS

PRICE

Basic list. $2988
As tested. $3510

ENGINE

Type. . . . . 4 cyl inline, sohc
Bore x stroke, mm. . . . . 89.0 x 80.0
  Equivalent in. . . . . 3.50 x 3.15
Displacement, cc/cu in. 1990/121.5
Compression ratio. 8.5:1
Bhp @ rpm. . . . . 113 @ 5800
  Equivalent mph. 108
Torque @ rpm, lb-ft. . . 116 @ 3000
  Equivalent mph. 54
Carburetion. . . . one Solex 40 PDSI
Type fuel required. . . . . . . premium

DRIVE TRAIN

Clutch diameter, in. 7.9
Gear ratios: 4th (1.00). 3.64:1
  3rd (1.35). 4.91:1
  2nd (2.05). 7.46:1
  1st (3.84). 13.95:1
Synchromesh. . . . . on all 4
Final drive ratio. 3.64:1

CHASSIS & BODY

Body/frame: unit steel construction
Brake type: 9.4-in. disc front,
  7.9-in. drum rear.
  Swept area, sq in. 243
Wheels. . . . . . steel disc, 13 x 4½J
Tires. . . . . Michelin XAS 165SR-13
Steering type. . . . . . worm & roller
  Overall ratio. 17.6:1
  Turns, lock-to-lock. 3.5
  Turning circle, ft. 34.1
Front suspension: MacPherson
  struts, lower A-arms, coil springs,
  tube shocks
Rear suspension: semi-trailing
  arms, coil springs, tube shocks

OPTIONAL EQUIPMENT

Included in "as tested" price: optional paint, AM/FM radio, sun
roof, radial tires, Skai upholstery,
power brakes, bumper guards,
reclining seats, exhaust pipe tip.

ACCOMMODATION

Seating capacity, persons. . . 4 + 1
Seat width, front/rear 2 x 20.5/51.0
Head room, front/rear. . 40.0/38.0
Seat back adjustment, deg. 90
Driver comfort rating (scale of 100):
  Driver 69 in. tall. 90
  Driver 72 in. tall. 85
  Driver 75 in. tall. 85

INSTRUMENTATION

Instruments: 120-mph speedometer, water temp, fuel level,
99,999 odometer with 9999 trip
meter, clock
Warning lights: directional signals,
high beam, oil pressure, genera-
tor, brake fluid loss

MAINTENANCE

Engine oil capacity, qt. 4.2
  Change interval, mi. 4000
Filter change interval, mi. . . . 4000
Chassis lube interval, mi. . . . 4000
Tire pressures, psi. 26/26

MISCELLANEOUS

Body styles available: 2-door sedan
  (as tested)
Warranty period, mo/mi. 12/12000

GENERAL

Curb weight, lb. 2210
Test weight. 2565
Weight distribution (with
  driver), front/rear, %. . . . 55/45
Wheelbase, in. 98.4
Track, front/rear. . . . 52.4/52.4
Overall length. 166.5
  Width. 62.6
  Height. 54.0
Frontal area, sq ft. 18.8
Ground clearance, in. 6.3
Overhang, front/rear. . . . 29.0/39.1
Usable trunk space, cu ft. . . . 9.5
Fuel tank capacity, gal. 12.1

CALCULATED DATA

Lb/hp (test wt). 22.7
Mph/1000 rpm (4th gear). . . 18.1
Engine revs/mi (60 mph). . . 3320
Piston travel, ft/mi. 1740
Rpm @ 2500 ft/min. 4760
  Equivalent mph. 88
Cu ft/ton mi. 106
R&T wear index. 58
Brake swept area sq in/ton. . . 189

ROAD TEST RESULTS

ACCELERATION

Time to distance, sec:
  0–100 ft. 3.3
  0–250 ft. 6.1
  0–500 ft. 9.6
  0–750 ft. 12.4
  0–1000 ft. 14.9
  0–1320 ft (¼ mi). 17.9
Speed at end of ¼ mi, mph. . . . 75
Time to speed, sec:
  0–30 mph. 3.5
  0–40 mph. 5.8
  0–50 mph. 8.0
  0–60 mph. 11.3
  0–70 mph. 15.5
  0–80 mph. 20.7
  0–100 mph. 44.5
Passing exposure time, sec:
  To pass car going 50 mph. . . 5.9

FUEL CONSUMPTION

Normal driving, mpg. 22–27
Cruising range, mi. 265–325

SPEEDS IN GEARS

4th gear (5770 rpm), mph. . . . 108
3rd (6000). 82
2nd (6000). 53
1st (6000). 29

BRAKES

Panic stop from 80 mph:
  Deceleration, % g. 75
  Control. . . . . excellent
Fade test: percent of increase in
  pedal effort required to maintain
  50%-g deceleration rate in six
  stops from 60 mph. 21
Parking brake: hold 30% grade. yes
Overall brake rating. . . . very good

SPEEDOMETER ERROR

30 mph indicated. . . . . actual 29.0
40 mph. 37.5
60 mph. 55.0
80 mph. 73.7
100 mph. 93.2
Odometer, 10.0 mi. . . . actual 9.70

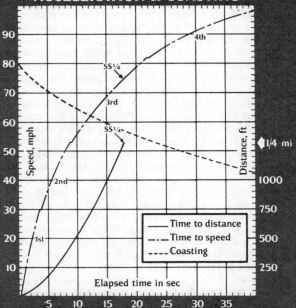

ACCELERATION & COASTING

Time to distance
— · — Time to speed
— — — Coasting

BMW 2002

ing down the clutch and immediately shifting to 1st. The reason for this is that the designers neglected to provide for "upshifting" into 1st (by omitting one small part in the 1st synchro), and this operation is the equivalent of an upshift!

First gear seems a little short-winded, giving 29 mph at 6000, but all the others seem just right. Another characteristic BMW noise—a whump-whump from the clutch throwout bearing when shifting—remained in our 2002 test car, but we're told by the factory that this has been corrected by a new throwout bearing that went into production in January. Our car had a slight final-drive noise on the overrun.

BMW chassis philosophy is based on an extremely rigid body, an absolutely horizontal roll axis, small camber changes in the suspension, and a relatively rigid steering mechanism. The results are always impressive. The 2002 leans quite a lot in hard corners—anti-roll bars are optional and not particularly needed—but a good camber pattern and the test car's optional Michelin XAS tires make fast cornering enjoyable and impressive. The car understeers moderately up to its limit, at which point the inside rear wheel lifts and lets everyone know that's all there is. In normal fast driving the driver will never encounter wheel lift and he'll find himself covering ground rapidly, no matter what the surface. This wheel lift, and the BMW characteristic of violent wheel hop when "popping" the clutch for acceleration runs, are apparently the results of very light shock control . . . which does not, however, create a sloppy ride.

The test car came from the factory with hard brake pads, but the distributor changed these back to the current 1600 material. There was still some squeal from the front discs when they were cold, but their fade resistance is better than that of the early 1600 we tested. The 80-mph panic stop gave a reading of 24 ft/sec/sec, not outstanding but acceptable and with excellent control. Pedal efforts are rather heavy for a vacuum-assisted system, requiring 43 lb for the first ½-g stop from 60 mph. The handbrake, located between the front seats, holds easily on the 30% test hill.

In the matter of ride, that rubber feeling comes out again. In spite of the rigid body, there's no harshness and the overall ride is quite good. No road rumble either, though there was some wind noise from around the left door. The steering wheel is a little high and horizontal and the accelerator a little too upright for some drivers. Fore-and-aft seat travel is generous and adjustable seatbacks are standard, although the test car had optional fully reclining seats. Instrumentation is minimal, like the 1600, and readable; somehow we had expected a tachometer in the 2002, though—and one is optional.

Flow-through ventilation is pretty ineffective, but if the pivoted rear side windows are opened the flow of fresh air through the 2002's interior is outstanding. A quiet 2-speed blower augments air flow for low speeds; the whole system seems better than it was in the earlier 1600.

Some changes have been made in the passenger room to conform it to the safety regs: the padding, and the contour of the lower portion that extends all the way across, have been altered; the steering wheel is simpler in design and has a depressed center; on the other hand, BMW needed to make no changes in their doorknobs to conform. An amusing touch is a safety ignition key—its back end pivoted so as to present no protrusion from the switch. The test car had a fairly common form of 3-point seat belt, with the diagonal portion hooking onto the lap portion, and we felt it to be rather awkward to use.

The 2002, like all BMWs, has many touches that make it seem more expensive than it is—like covering for the underside of the dash, ashtrays for rear passengers, the careful finish throughout. The 1600 was a big bargain at $2613 when it first appeared; emission control and safety equipment have edged it up to $2730 now, and at $2988 the 2002 is still a good buy. Hoffman continues to order all of them with power brakes ($45), vinyl upholstery ($45), and a couple of minor items, and our test car had an excellent Blaupunkt AM/FM radio ($140), radial tires ($59), sunroof ($135) and fully reclining seats ($48). The paint job —a metallic gray—even costs extra, which seems a bit much to ask. Most prospective buyers will leave out many of these items, of course, as standard equipment is comprehensive.

There are two ways of looking at the BMW 2002 as a value in the automotive marketplace: at about $3000 it is fully comparable in performance, handling, ride and finish with sports cars costing as much as $2000 more—although it has a rather unpretentious sedan body. On the other hand, if you're thinking in terms of a sedan already, just consider the 2002, or the 1600 at $258 less, the best sedan buys in the world. They're almost too good to be true, and if too many Americans happen to find this out the Bayerische Motoren Werke may not be able to supply the demand.

BMW 2002

SPORTS CAR WORLD · ROAD TEST

MUNICH'S SUPER CAR

IN a sense I suppose this 2-door, 2-litre, 2+2 machine is Munich's answer to American super cars. Built at least in part to suit US foibles, the 2002 is big on bore, svelte of shape — and low on emissions, need we add. It has the old, freeway on-ramp torque and cruising pace of a marathon winner, plus — and here they added a little pure Bavarian beer and bratwurst — the handling to go gravel-bashing in the rally woods.

It all came about like this. First BMW built the 1600-2: the best-balanced fun package of the decade on its 98.4 in. wheelbase. All cars from BMW are right but some are righter than others. Once you have a singing sedan (sold on some markets as a coupe — draw your own conclusions on rear-seat space) which handles like a sport car, the next logical step is more power. Specially if you earn the daily brot under the sign of a blue-and-white quartered circle.

Enter the 1600 TI, a wildcat in sedan form, fed by two gulping dual-throat carbs. TI owners buy 105 DIN hp at 6000 rpm, a torque peak up around 4500 rpm and a good deal of fuss with carb jets, temperamental plugs and the trickiest cold starts since the high school boy tried to date the burlesque queen.

A dauntless tribe like BMW had no intention of losing anything as good as a 105 mph-plus sedan. Looking over the old corral they noticed that

2000 engine of four-door fame putting out 100 DIN hp on a mere 8.5:1 (TI = 9.5) and best of all using a single, modest Solex. So it wouldn't wind as tight; torque came on like Jack the Bear way down at 3000 rpm (116 lb/ft at that, as against 96 for a TI). That should give a 2100 lb sedanette sufficient urge, nicht wahr?

They were so right. The 2002 may give away 3 mph in top to a TI, doing a "mere" 106.3 mph, but despite a taller back axle (3.64 to the TIs 3.9) it accelerates faster to about 80 from whence TI revs come on to level peg the pair. Covering a classic 0-60 drag the 2002 needs 9.8 sec against 10.1 for the TI.

Meanwhile the big one drinks less — right up to 105. Covering more test ground than ever before — like 3000 miles in three weeks, half of that in three days — we registered a neat 22.9 overall using every available rev. Flat out on an Austrian autobahn for several 100-plus hours the damage was still only 18.3 mpg and 30 is easily on at 70-ish cruising speeds.

Oil consumption for the same period — any brisk engine which doesn't burn some oil at such speed worries me — came out under 1.5 quarts for 3000 miles.

Easy gait and clean exhaust were not solely responsible for BMW's 2002 decision. The '68 European Touring Car title will go to a Group 5 car,

Some call it a coupe. The BMW 2002 shows good balance of space in engine, passenger cabin and boot. Part matt grille, fog lights and Bavarian hat are all extra. Note the big back window.

It doesn't really matter whether your choice is a six-lane highway or a rutted, ox-cart byway, the latest effort from Bavaria is the hairy-chested stallion to please.

BMW only put the insignia on the back. They figured that's the only place it would be seen anyway — by all the other motorists it passed.

Facia is plain, yet essentially designed to work and not to just sit there looking pretty. It features — of all things — a clock instead of tachometer. Wood-rimmed wheel is a little bit too slick.

Engine compartment of the BMW 2002 is tidy and uncluttered. Engine has one carburettor with long inlets. Air intake is from cool air up front of compartment rather than hot air under hood.

which means that while the block must at least look moderately familiar to the man who designed it, most of the rest of the engine is free. Porsche, for example, uses a Carrera 6-powered 911 boosted from 210 to around 230 hp.

A works BMW 2002 has now beaten these quasi-private Porsches twice running — partly because it is homologated 220lb lighter and partly because the factory admits to 207 hp, while rivals insist it must have a minimum of 230. Either way this indicates a fair old reliability margin for the 100 hp road engine.

This, in fact, is the kind of forgiving car your wife will enjoy driving. Mine, who only gets the wheel when we have two cars to shuttle about, did a blithe 100 down a fairly crowded autobahn. She wouldn't touch the TI with two ski poles tied together last winter. Too nervous; all those carb throats to keep clear and the touchy plugs . . .

A fast 200 miles across Germany on two-lane roads only bolstered my growing faith in the big engine/small shell concept and BMW does that better than most. This 2002 proved the most relaxed rapid point-to-point car yet devised. Previous holder of the honor was the firm's 1600-2.

The entire line of two-door BMWs is noted for handling to sports car standards. Your 2002 now comes standard with anti-roll bars front and rear and braced tread tyres so the basic chassis remains a couple of steps ahead of its power. Michelin's new XAS goes admirably with angled A arms in back and neutral basic handling too.

All these comments came from highway use including one 600-mile, almost non-stop day on the inept autobahns of its native heath. Conversation in normal tones at 100 and three full-bore hours without a murmur or twitch from the engine are one side of the 2002 coin.

Then came eight hours of playing chamois along rutted, wooded byways where Martha of Vienna held their recent rally. I used the BMW as a training hack. (When we all drew for cars on rally day somebody else got the 2002 — and won.)

As race iron the BMW is ideal. Broadsliding a downhill gravel hairpin on full opposite lock you can make some pertinent comment like "mark this one first gear," and never lose your place in the script. Not even weak shocks in the test car could spoil this fun — it still handled better than many new, taut sedans.

Okay. Both cruising and fir-bashing are meat and drink to a 2002, but what is it like for day-to-day compatibility?

Two people, of any size up to basketball centres, will thrive on this one, assuming they shell out an extra 40 to 50 dollars for reclining seats which should be included in the price to begin with. Normal-size drivers, who like to run with arms fairly outstretched, will find it is a two-seater.

Yet we travelled four-up on half-hour trips without tears. And the boot is exceptional for a 167 in. body.

Dials and controls, held to a practical minimum, are well clustered. They didn't even provide a tenth wheel on the re-settable odometer but small storage items may be tucked into a glove box, console bin, full-width shelf or two seat-back pockets.

All trim, right down to full carpeting, is done with Teutonic precision but BMW eschewed frills like a passenger grab handle. Really helpful items, like a blade on the driver's wiper to prevent lifting, or a truly powerful washer, are self-understood around Munich.

One feature every sporty driver asks for in the first five minutes is an rpm counter. After five hours you forget it, like as not. Not nearly the high-winder their 1.6-litre mill is, the 1990 cc kind need never go over 5500 (power peak). But if it does, briefly, nothing breaks. A normal ear for mechanicals and red marks on the speedometer to indicate maximum shift points are more than enough. I'd have preferred more oil/amps type of info to a tach.

As for the gears, third takes you to 80 mph for effortless overtaking. One and two go to 30 and 50 respectively so that a tach is as redundant as a close-ratio box when your engine will pull cleanly from 25 in top. 90 mph requires only 5000 rpm, reached in well under 25 sec.

Driver controls are BMW standard, a pleasure to use but sometimes self-willed, like the high-rise clutch. Steering at 3.5 turns is just right for parking but wholly sensitive at speed. Since the big engine only weighs some 11 lb more than a 1.6 unit balance is not affected.

Effort saved winding the steering wheel may be applied to running your windows up and down. Seven turns top to bottom is just not the good life and you need a lot of "up" and "down" because dash vents don't provide high-summer ventilation — even with the pivoting rear windows open. At low speeds side window air is vital; at high speed you can't hear yourself think with them open. Also the frameless glass flutters at maximum chat.

Under the bonnet, hinged in front and all-enveloping, they carry a passion for availability to great lengths. Even the dip stick falls readily to hand, while the exceptionally tidy compartment is full tribute to thoughtful engineering.

Spread over something like the same area of pavement as say a 1500 VW Fastback the 2002 would certainly be named more "fittingly" in America where the super-car concept gained first fame. There must be a predatory cat not discovered by Detroit minions. That is precisely what we have here — a tabby-about-town with the open-road instincts of a cheetah. #

Turn Your Hymnals to 2002– David E. Davis, Jr. Blows His Mind on the Latest from BMW

As I sit here, fresh from the elegant embrace of BMW's new 2002, it occurs to me that something between nine and ten million Americans are going to make a terrible mistake this year. Like dutiful little robots they will march out of their identical split-level boxes and buy the wrong kind of car. Fools, fools! Terrible, terrible, I say. Why are you blowing your money on this year's too-new-to-be-true facelift of the Continental/Countess Mara/Sprite/Sprint Status Symbol/Sting Ray/Sex Substitute/ Mainliner / Belair / Newport / Overkill / Electra / Eldorado / Javelin / Toad / GTO / GTA/GTB/GTS/GTX/Reality Blaster/ Variant/Park Lane/Park Ward/Ward-Heeler/XK-E/Dino/Dud car when you should be buying a BMW 2002, I ask.

Down at the club, Piggy Tremalion and Bucko Penoyer and all their twit friends buy shrieking little 2-seaters with rag tops and skinny wire wheels, unaware that somewhere, someday, some guy in a BMW 2002 is going to blow them off so bad that they'll henceforth leave every stoplight in second gear and never drive on a winding road again as long as they live.

In the suburbs, Biff Everykid and Kevin Acne and Marvin Sweatsock will press their fathers to buy HO Firebirds with tachometers mounted out near the horizon somewhere and enough power to light the city of Seattle, totally indifferent to the fact that they could fit more friends into a BMW in greater comfort and stop better and go around corners better and get about 29 times better gas mileage.

Mr. and Mrs. America will paste a "Support Your Local Police" sticker on the back bumper of their new T-Bird and run Old Glory up the radio antenna and never know that for about 2500 bucks less they could have gotten a car with more leg room, more head room, more luggage space, good brakes, decent tires, independent rear suspension, a glove box finished like the inside of an expensive overcoat and an ashtray that slides out like it was on the end of a butler's arm—not to mention a lot of other good stuff they didn't even know they could *get* on an automobile, like doors that fit and seats that don't make you tired when you sit in them.

So far as I'm concerned, to hell with all of 'em. If they're content to remain in the automotive dark, let them. I know about the BMW 2002, and I suspect enthusiasts will buy as many as those pink-cheeked Bavarians in their leather pants and mountain-climbing shoes would like to build and ship over here. Something between nine and ten million squares will miss out on this neat little 2-door sedan with all the *cojones* and *brio* and *elan* of cars twice its size and four times its price, but some ten thousand keen types will buy them in 1968, so the majority loses for once.

The 2002 is BMW's way of coping with the smog problem. They couldn't import their little 1600 TI, because their smog device won't work on its multi-carbureted engine. So they stuffed in the smooth, quiet 2-liter (single carburetor) engine from the larger 2000 sedan and—SHAZAM—instant winner!

To my way of thinking, the 2002 is one of modern civilization's all-time best ways to get somewhere sitting down. It grabs you. You sit in magnificently-adjustable seats with great, tall windows all around you. You are comfortable and you can see in every direction. You start it. Willing and un-lumpy is how it feels. No rough idle, no zappy noises to indicate that the task you propose might be anything more than child's play for all those 114 Bavarian superhorses.

Depress the clutch. Easy. Like there was no spring. *Snick*. First gear. Remove weight of left foot from clutch. Place weight of right foot on accelerator. The minute it starts moving, you know that Fangio and Moss and Tony Brooks and all those other

PHOTOGRAPHY: J. BARRY O'ROURKE

big racing studs retired only because they feared that someday you'd have one of these, and when that day came, you'd be indomitable. They were right. You are indomitable.

First stoplight. I blow off aging Plymouth sedan and 6-cylinder Mustang. Not worthy of my steel. Too easy. Next time. Big old 6-banger Healey and '65 GTO. GTO can't believe I'm serious, lets me get away before he opens all the holes and comes smoking past with pain and outrage all over his stricken countenance. Nearly hits rear-end of truck in panicky attempt to reaffirm virility. Austin-Healey a different matter. Tries for all he's worth, but British engineering know-how and quality-craftsmanship not up to the job. I don't even shift fast from third to fourth, just to let him feel my utter contempt.

Nobody believes it, until I suck their headlights out. But nobody doubts it, once that nearly-silent, unobtrusive little car has disappeared down the road and around the next bend, still accelerating without a sign of the brake lights. I learn not to tangle with the kids in their big hot Mothers with the 500 horsepower engines unless I can get them into a tight place demanding agility, brakes, and the raw courage that is built into the BMW driver's seat as a no-cost extra.

What you like to look for are Triumphs and Porsches and such. Them you can slaughter, no matter how hard they try. And they always try. They really believe all that jazz about their highly-tuned, super-sophisticated sports machines, and the first couple of drubbings at the hands of the 2002 make them think they're off on a bad trip or something. But then they learn the awful truth, and they begin to hang back at traffic signals, pretending that they weren't really racing and all. Ha! Grovel, Morgan. Slink home with your tail between your legs, MG-B. Hide in the garage when you see a BMW coming. If you have to race with something, pick a sick kid on an old bicycle.

But I don't want you to get the notion that this is nothing more than a pocket street racer. The BMW 2002 may be the first car in history to successfully bridge the gap between the diametrically-opposed automotive requirements of the wildly romantic car nut, on one hand, and the hyperpragmatic people at *Consumer Reports,* on the other. Enthusiasts' cars invariably come off second-best in a CU evaluation, because such high-spirited steeds often tend to be all desire and no protein—more Magdalen than Mom.

CU used to like the VW a lot, back when it was being hailed as the thinking man's answer to the excesses of Detroit, but now that the Beetle has joined Chevrolet at the pinnacle of establishment-acceptance, it's falling from CU's favor. But the BMW 2002 is quite another matter. It is still obscure enough to have made no inroads at all with the right-thinking squares of the establishment. It rides like a dream. It has a surprising amount of room inside. It gets great gas mileage. It's finished, inside and out, like a Mercedes-Benz, but it doesn't cost very much. All those qualifications are designed to earn the BMW a permanent place in the *Consumer* hall of fame. But for the enthusiasts—at the same time, and without even stepping into a phone booth to change costume—it goes like bloody hell and handles like the original bear. No doubt about it, the BMW 2002 is bound to get Germany back into the CU charts, to borrow a phrase from the pop vernacular.

If it wasn't already German, I'd be tempted to say it could be as American as Mom's apple pie or Rapp Brown's carbine. Not American in the same sense as the contemporary domestic car, with all its vast complexity and *nouveau riche* self-consciousness, but American in the sense of Thomas Edison and a-penny-saved-is-a-penny-earned and Henry Ford I (before his ego overloaded all the fuses and short-circuited his mind and conscience). The 2002 mirrors faithfully all those basic tenets of the Puritan ethic on which our Republic was supposedly based. It does everything it's supposed to do, and it does it with ingenuity, style, and verve.

In its unique ability to blend fun-and-games with no-nonsense virtue, this newest BMW also reflects another traditional American article of faith—our unshakable belief that we can find and marry a pretty girl who will expertly cook, scrub floors, change diapers, keep the books, and still be the greatest thing since the San Francisco Earthquake in bed. It's a dream to which we cling eternally, in spite of the fact that nobody can recall it ever having come true. But, as if to erase our doubts, along comes an inexpensive little machine from Bavaria that really can perform the automotive equivalent of all those diverse domestic and erotic responsibilities, and hope springs anew.

I'll be interested to see who those 10,000 owners of the 1968 BMW 2002 actually turn out to be. The twits won't buy it, because it's too sensible, too comfortable, too easy to live with. The kids won't buy it because it doesn't look like something on its way to a soft moon-landing and it doesn't have three-billion horsepower. BMW buyers will—I suspect—have to be pretty well-adjusted enthusiasts who want a good car, people with the sense of humor to enjoy its giant-killing performance and the taste to appreciate its mechanical excellence.

They will not be the kind who buy invisible middle-of-the-line 4-door sedans because that's what their friends and neighbors buy, nor will they be those pitiful men/boys who buy cars and use them as falsies for fleshing out baggy jockstraps. Good horses don't like bad riders, and it's doubtful if the 2002 will attract too many of the timid or confused fantasy-buyers. It's too real.

That last phrase is kind of a key to the whole BMW bag. It is too real. For a couple of years now, "unreal" has been a big word with the semi-literate savages of hot rodding. It's supposed to be a high compliment, but it turns out to be an unwittingly incisive comment on the whole metalflake-angel hair-Batmobile scene. LSD is a drag, not a drug, for that group. Gurus like George Barris and Ed Roth were blowing their minds on fiberglass and tuck-and-roll upholstery while the Indians still thought peyote nuts were something you put on chocolate sundaes.

Let me tell you there's nothing unreal about the 2002. Give it a coat of pearlescent orange paint and surround the pedals with lavender angel hair and it would just naturally die of shame. Like a good sheep dog, it is ill-suited for show competition, only becoming beautiful when it's doing its job. It is a devoted servant of man, delighted with its lot in life, asking only that it be treated with the respect it deserves. You can't knock that . . .

The Germans have a word for it. The German paper *Auto Bild* called the 2002 *Flüstern Bombe* which means "Whispering Bomb," and you should bear in mind that the German press speaks of bombs, whispering and otherwise, with unique authority. They, too, saw something American in the car's design concept, but only insofar as BMW had elected to stuff a larger, smoother engine into their smallest vehicle.

But that's really pure BMW, when you think about it. The current 2000 series started life in 1962 as a 1500, then it became an 1800 and finally a full two liters—going from 94 to 114 horsepower in the process. The current 1600 was introduced about a year-and-a-half ago, and BMW-ophiles everywhere began to think of that glorious day in the future when the factory would decide to put in the 2-liter engine. Well, sports fans, the glorious day has arrived, and the resulting automobile is everything the faithful could have been hoping for.

The engine cranks out 114 hp at 5800 rpm, and the way it's geared it just seems to wind forever—it'll actually turn 60 mph in second, and an easy 80 mph in third. Top

Continued on page **82**

GERMAN CARS

Long distance sprinter

Motorway mile eater, sports car and town potterer all rolled into one well engineered package

SO BMW have now joined the shoehorn bandwagon, the fashionable habit of putting your larger engine into a smaller chassis; and what admirable transport this makes the 2002, the cross between the 1600/2 coupé body and the 2000 engine. You pay £1,600 for what is essentially a two-door four-seater, but the one design embodies so many different features which are better than single features of more specialised examples; the performance for most of the range, and economy are better than the very fast Cortina Lotus, ride and general comfort are in the Triumph 2000 class, and the roadholding and general behaviour on all dry surfaces are matched by very few other saloons or mass production sports cars.

But despite this build-up which suggests quite correctly that the 2002 is very much a driver's car, it is also very much a touring car, quiet and docile to drive, its controls smooth and light, and it is just as happy in the suburban shopping centre as on one's favourite highway. Drawbacks lie in details only; not everyone liked the driving position with the high steering wheel and the pedals are not only too far from the floor but with the brake pedal in good adjustment it is difficult to heel and toe. On one car we cured this fault with a block of wood on the accelerator, but we understand that later cars will have pedals arranged so that you

Price: £1,249 plus £348 8s. 2d. PT equals £1,597 8s. 2d.
INSURANCE: AOA Group rating, 6; Lloyds, 7

shouldn't need to lift heels off the floor. The only other complaint is the door seals; they seem to be so strong that it requires a lot of effort to shut the doors—too much, in fact, for more than one inside doorhandle—a change is on the way again. But at least they keep the noise out.

When the 2-litre engine was first rumoured for the smaller body, many expected that the 2000TI unit would be used as a basis for competition, but in fact the basic 2-litre engine gives quite enough performance for normal use and the essential competition bits are all homologated extras. As with all BMW units starting is instantaneous with full choke and is accompanied by the characteristic whine of the chain driven overhead camshaft; it takes about two miles of gentle driving for running temperature to come up and the engine to pull with its customary strength; top gear performance is particularly good and doesn't begin to flag until nearly the 100 mark. The power/weight ratio is around 100 b.h.p. per ton with one occupant and the 2002 makes particularly good use of it; helped by a flat torque curve and very suitable gear ratios, getaway is very impressive. With a squeak from the tyres and a minor graunchy protest from the rear suspension it leaps away to reach 50 m.p.h. in under 7 seconds and by holding 2nd gear to an unstrained 6,700 r.p.m. 60 m.p.h. in 9.2 seconds against the 8.3 and 11.8 seconds for the 1600. By 100 m.p.h. it is beginning to drop behind the more powerful Cortina Lotus and the best lap speed on our banked circuit was 106 m.p.h. A mean

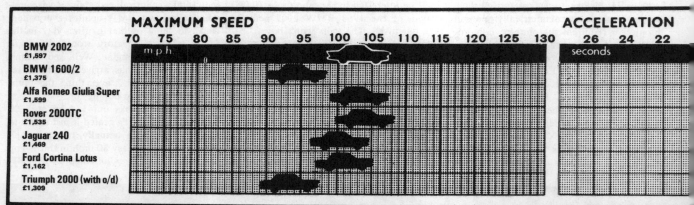

	MAXIMUM SPEED	ACCELERATION
	70 75 80 85 90 95 100 105 110 115 120 125 130	26 24 22
BMW 2002 £1,597	m.p.h.	seconds
BMW 1600/2 £1,375		
Alfa Romeo Giulia Super £1,599		
Rover 2000TC £1,535		
Jaguar 240 £1,469		
Ford Cortina Lotus £1,162		
Triumph 2000 (with o/d) £1,309		

Performance

Performance tests carried out by *Motor's* staff at the Motor Industry Research Association proving ground, Lindley.

Test Data: World copyright reserved; no unauthorised reproduction in whole or in part.

Conditions

Weather: Dry, light winds up to 5 m.p.h.
Temperature 44°-48°F. Barometer 29.70 in. Hg.
Surface: Dry concrete and tarmacadam.
Fuel: Premium 98 octane (RM) 4 star rating.

Maximum speeds

	m.p.h.
Mean maximum speed	107.4
Mean lap banked circuit	106.0
Best one-way ¼-mile	111.1
3rd gear	93.0
2nd gear } at 6,800 r.p.m.	61.0
1st gear	33.0

"Maximile" speed: (Timed quarter mile after 1 mile accelerating from rest)

	m.p.h.
Mean	105.4
Best	107.1

Acceleration times

m.p.h.	sec.
0-30	3.1
0-40	4.8
0-50	6.8
0-60	9.2
0-70	13.3
0-80	17.6
0-90	24.7
0-100	37.4
Standing quarter mile	17.3

m.p.h.	Top sec.	3rd sec.
10-30	—	5.7
20-40	7.6	5.3
30-50	7.4	5.3
40-60	7.7	5.6
50-70	8.8	6.5
60-80	9.8	7.9
70-90	12.5	11.3
80-100	20.3	—

Fuel consumption

Touring (consumption midway between 30 m.p.h. and maximum less 5% allowance for acceleration) .... 27.5 m.p.g.
Overall .... 24.0 m.p.g.
(=11.8 litres/100 km.)
Total test figure .... 1,680 miles

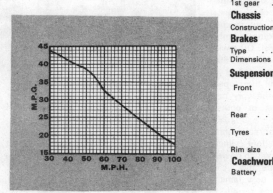

Specification

Engine

Cylinders	4
Bore and stroke	80 mm. x 89 mm.
Cubic capacity	1,990 c.c.
Valves	single o.h.c. and rockers
Compression ratio	8.5 : 1
Carburetter	Solex 40 PDSI twin choke
Fuel pump	Solex mechanical
Oil filter	Fram full flow
Max. power (net)	100 b.h.p. at 5,500 r.p.m.
Max. torque (net)	116 lb.ft. at 3,000 r.p.m.

Transmission

Clutch	Fichtel and Sachs
Top gear (s/m)	1.000
3rd gear (s/m)	1.345
2nd gear (s/m)	2.053
1st gear (s/m)	3.835
Reverse	4.180
Final drive	Hypoid bevel 3.64 : 1

M.p.h. at 1,000 r.p.m. in:—

Top gear	18.5
3rd gear	13.7
2nd gear	9.0
1st gear	4.8

Chassis

Construction	Unitary

Brakes

Type	Disc/drum servo assisted
Dimensions	9½ in. disc, 8.0 in. drums

Suspension and steering

Front	Independent by Macpherson struts, lower wishbones, coil springs and anti-roll bar
Rear	Independent by semi-trailing arms, coil springs and anti-roll bar
Tyres	165—13 radials (German Dunlop SP's on test car)
Rim size	4½J—13

Coachwork and equipment

Battery	12v neg. earth, 44 a/h cap. Otherwise as 1600 specification.

speed observed on MIRA's three straights averaged 107.4 m.p.h. so the true maximum on straight roads should approach 110 m.p.h. which, like our standing start figures, is rather better than BMW claim.

We brought one 2002 back from Munich as part of its running-in; despite cruising easily at a (permitted) 80-90 m.p.h. we still returned 30 m.p.g. over the 750 odd miles to London via Luxembourg. Back in this country with a different fully run-in car we used much more throttle and the consumption dropped to 23 m.p.g. during the period which included testing, rising to 26 m.p.g. for more normal but still spirited use. On the car tested the touring consumption was only 27.5 m.p.g. but the car we first used would certainly have returned over 30.

With the extra power, BMW have added a higher final drive ratio than with the 1600 which gives pleasantly long legged touring and really useful maxima in the gears; the excellent gearbox encourages constant use as the lever slides around with silky precision through well chosen ratios and with a smooth clutch it was difficult to get a jerky change however fast. Two of our staff developed a pet hate against the rough surfaced gear lever knob but that is a very personal and minor detail.

Roadholding on the 1600 is of a pretty high order but on the 2002 it is even better; the addition of anti-roll bars at both ends and minor spring rate adjustments have stopped the inside rear wheel lifting rather prematurely, and the car is generally better balanced, moving smoothly through neutral steer characteristics at speeds many saloons wouldn't even look at, to a gentle final oversteer which is easily countered on well geared and not too heavy steering. This gives good feel in the wet, but the German SP tyres fitted to our test car were not good in these conditions; cornering grip was low and it was rather too easy to get wheelspin under power which of course tended to provoke the rear end prematurely, if still safely.

Good damping control keeps the car on a pretty even keel even on the limit with no lurching or sudden movements as you change from one lock to another in an S-bend. This also keeps the ride on the firm side, but still pitch free and with a degree of comfort which is enhanced by the seats. You can sense the car moving on irregular surfaces but occupants don't seem to mind and four adults can be quite comfortable for long distances—the large fuel tank range allows around 300 miles between stops which on a German autobahn might be covered in 3½ hours non-stop.

That is another side of the 2002's character—the long distance runner. Few cars manage to have quite such a character variation but play each part so well; we thought it an outstanding car.

M

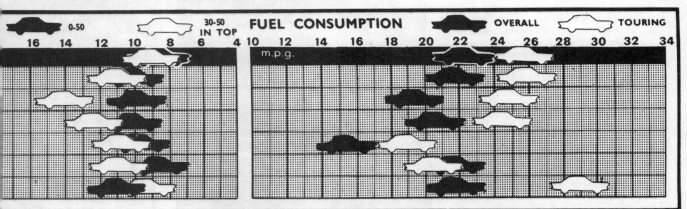

In a class of its own– the BMW 2002

If your ideal high performance saloon car has a matt black bonnet, go-faster stripes and mock alloy wheels you will be disappointed by the BMW 2002. The only concessions it makes to 'performance styling' are discreet black grille bars and a very luxurious highly polished wood rim steering wheel. Otherwise it is outwardly identical to the BMW 1600, and that hardly looks like a racing car. And yet the 2002 can see off virtually all the stripes-and-noise brigade and all but the very best 2 litre sports cars. At a price, of course. Actually £1,597 tax paid.

BMWs have a reputation for solid, fast, *very German* quality saloons. The four cylinder single overhead camshaft engine which powers their complete range started life five years ago as a 1,500 cc unit in the now familiar four-door bodyshell. It has since grown to 1,800 and 2,000 cc, and last year a 1,600 cc version was introduced in a smaller, lighter two-door body. The performance market has been catered for by the 1800 and 2000 TI models which have been available for some time; a 1600 TI is also marketed in Germany. But with basically the same unit in every model it was not surprising that BMW should follow the current trend of popping the largest engine into the smallest body. Like the 1600, the resulting 2002 is called a Coupe in Britain, although it clearly isn't one in the accepted sense of the word. In Germany there's a proper 1600 GT Coupe (derived from the Glas which BMW bought up a while back) so it's all very confusing.

The 1,990 cc engine has a single down-draught twin-choke Solex when fitted to the 2002 and gives 113 gross bhp, about 100 net (for comparison, the 1600 gives 85 bhp). According to the handbook the maximum permitted revs are 6,200 but the test car was not fitted with a rev counter (production models are) and we found that speeds well in excess of the little red marks on the speedo could be attained without any sign of mechanical unrest. This is a very flexible power unit, but in any case the gear ratios are well spaced and the four speed gearbox with Porsche-type synchromesh all round proved delightfully smooth, although it could be difficult to engage first gear from rest.

The acceleration figures are pretty fantastic, an indicated 50 mph coming up in 6.4 seconds from a standing start, making this one of the fastest saloons of any size or price. Even the 0-100 time makes a lot of sports cars look pretty silly. For once the manufacturer's figures are quite a lot down on ours. This is partly because of German laws, which are much tougher than ours on advertised claims (so every car in a batch must be able to attain

Performance

Acceleration:

0-30 mph	2.9 sec
0-40 mph	4.5 sec
0-50 mph	6.4 sec
0-60 mph	8.5 sec
0-70 mph	11.5 sec
0-80 mph	15.1 sec
0-90 mph	20.0 sec
0-100 mph	26.9 sec

Speeds in the gears:

1st	33 mph
2nd	71 mph
3rd	94 mph
4th	110 mph

Overall fuel consumption on test: 26.1 mpg.
Anticipated average consumption in normal use: 27.5 mpg.

Specification

Body-chassis: All-steel unitary construction.
Engine: Four-cylinder, in-line, water-cooled. Bore 89 mm, stroke 80 mm, displacement 1,990 cc. Compression ratio 8.5 to 1. Maximum power 113 bhp (SAE) at 5,800 rpm, 100 bhp (DIN) at 5,500 rpm. Maximum torque 115.7 lb-ft at 3,000 rpm. Single overhead camshaft. Single Solex 40 PDSI carburettor fed by mechanical pump.
Transmission: Mechanically operated single-dry-plate, 7.9 inch clutch. Four speed, all-synchro gearbox with floor shift. Ratios: 1st 3.83 to 1 ; 2nd 2.05 to 1 ; 3rd 1.35 to 1 ; 4th 1.00 to 1 ; reverse 4.18 to 1. Hypoid-bevel final drive, 3.64 to 1. (Limited slip differential available.)
Suspension: Front, independent with McPherson struts, lower wishbones, coil springs, telescopic dampers and anti-roll bar. Rear, independent with semi-trailing arms, coil springs with rubber auxiliary springs, telescopic dampers and anti-roll bar.
Steering: Worm and roller, 3.5 turns lock to lock. Turning circle 34 ft 2 in.
Brakes: Front, 9.45 inch discs. Rear, 7.87 inch drums, power-assisted. Total frictional area 243 sq in.
Wheels and tyres: 13 x 4½J pressed steel disc wheels with German Dunlop SP 165 x 13 tyres.
Weights and measures: Approx kerb weight 18 cwt ; length 166.5 in ; width 62.5 in ; height 55.5 in ; wheelbase 98.4 in ; ground clearance 6.3 in ; fuel tank capacity 10.1 gallons.

any published figures) and partly because BMW are anxious not to upset owners of the slower 1600 TI which isn't sold here.

The suspension, like the 1600, is by struts and wishbones at the front and semi-trailing arms with coil springs at the back, both springs and shock absorbers having been reset for the additional urge. Anti-roll bars are fitted front and rear. The car is quite lightly sprung and well damped, and understeers mildly, allowing fast, safe cornering which is not drastically upset by changes in road surface. The transition from understeer to oversteer is progressive and occurs at relatively high speeds. When pushed to the limit the inside back wheel lifts, and violent take-offs, such as during our acceleration tests, generated a good deal of wheel hop. This also showed up in the wet, but even so its cornering speeds under these conditions on the standard German Dunlop SP radials were still impressive. The servo-assisted brakes proved powerful and the steering precise, with just the right amount of 'feel'. All in all it is a very well balanced and 'forgiving' motor car.

The 2002 has the sort of styling that looks neat and right without being particularly fashionable or particularly dated. The test car was silver, a colour which always seems to suit BMWs well, and had a completely black interior. Visibility is excellent with deep screen and side windows and very thin pillars.

The purposeful theme is carried through to the driving compartment. The front seats are generously large, shaped and fully adjustable for rake. The dished wood rim steering wheel, with its oversize padded horn boss, is placed quite high but most people had no trouble finding a comfortable driving position.

The facia is somewhat Rover 2000-like with a full length open shelf on which the instrument binnacle rests. The instruments consist of three matching dials—a central speedometer, a combined fuel and water temperature gauge which incorporates all the usual warning lights, and on our test car, an enormous clock where the rev counter is to be ('12.45 in 3rd, old boy'). Double push-pull switches for lights, wipers and fan blower are arranged round the instruments ; these proved difficult to reach when strapped in. One column stalk operates the dipswitch and flasher, the other, indicators and washers (which automatically operate the wipers for a few strokes).

BMW have paid a lot of attention to safety. Everything seems to be made of rubber—the switches, window winders, even the gear lever knob is moulded rubber. The ventilation and heating system is quite sophisticated, with demister ducts not only to the screen but also to the side windows, and extractor slots along the back window. There are no face-level vents though, and this is an annoying omission since the considerable wind noise when the quarter lights are open spoils what is otherwise a very quiet car.

It is difficult to know how to classify this car. Although it is a full four seater, with the front seats well back there isn't a lot of rear leg room. The boot is spacious, and with an over 100 mph cruising speed (where it's allowed) it makes a tremendous touring car for two people with a lot of luggage. It is compact, economical and quiet. Whether you think of it as an over-expensive hot saloon or a poor man's Porsche depends on the value you put on those matt black bonnets and go-faster stripes. The 2002 may be difficult to classify but it forms a very good class of its own.

BMW 2002

Model Number Or Target Date For Detroit?

by Bill Sanders

With sublime adroitness and a straight face, BMW deftly puts down Detroit by masquerading their newest bomb as a "Family Sedan." It's got "Family Sedan" comfort, luxury and convenience — but the similarity ends in the first corner.

Attention Messrs. Virgil Boyd, Roy Chapin, Ed Cole and Bunkie Knudsen: if the inner sanctums in that citadel of Great American Industry, Detroit, Mich., are astir with tension over rising import sales, that tension may soon turn to outright panic. An audacious new protagonist has just been unleashed on the automotive scene by the Bayerische Motoren Werke AG, of Munich, Germany.

Latest offering from the Bavarian craftsmen is the BMW 2002, and it's such a rugged contender, in any class, rumor has it even *Ring Magazine* and *The Sporting News* dig it for the image rub off. Esthetically, it's rather ungainly, and, from the outside it will be dismissed by many of our countrymen as just another compact. Lucky for us, gentlemen. Because, everyone who gets behind the wheel, even for a few blocks, asks the same question: why can't they build an American car like this? In performance, handling, ride, comfort and — the list grows too long – every other automotive characteristic, the BMW 2002 deals from the top of

the deck, and, in most instances, outshuffles cars costing much more bread.

Imported car sales in 1967 were up 17% over 1966. So far this year they are cornering approximately 10% of the total U.S. new car market, compared to 9% in 1967, and time for concern is upon us. GM and Ford are now both working on compact cars in an attempt to stem the tide, and that brings us full cycle to our original thesis: will they, can they, turn out a street machine engineered as well as the BMW 2002 and compete in the 3 grand range? What about it, gentlemen?

Powertrain & Performance

BMW arrived at the 2002 as a result of several coincidental occurrences. Their 1600 was, and is, immensely successful in the U.S. With the advent of the 1600-2 (2-door), and the 2-carburetor TI option, BMW was moving into the rarified atmosphere of high-performance, superb handling machinery, while remaining in a competitive price market. Americans were discov-

ering this phenomenon and digging it. Then: Smog Control. The 2-jug mill couldn't pass inspection so the next best thing became a substitute, the 2-liter (1990cc) powerplant with one carburetor. Coupled to a 3.64:1 rear end, performance remains typically BMW; vigorous and potent. No complaints are ever heard from the 2000 engine, even when subjected to the roughest treatment. Lug it down in high gear or down shift at high rpms to 3rd or 2nd; you'll never get a whine or growl from engine or drivetrain. We found we could practically run in any gear or down shift at high rpms to 3rd wind it out in 2nd or 3rd to some far out reaches of engine endurance. Still with no outcry. Our test car wasn't equipped with a tach, an option we highly recommend with the 2002. An engine so vehemently responsive invites overrevving, and when no protest is felt or heard, that tendency easily becomes habitual. Plenty of power always seems to be waiting in reserve, in any gear, except when lugging down in high.

A test of the reclining bucket seats and who wants to read further? Trunk is large with spare hidden under floor panel. Under hood, new air induction system is visible. Large diameter steering wheel is positioned at awkward angle for efficient handling in tight spots.

PERFORMANCE

Acceleration (2 aboard)

0-30 mph	3.2 secs.
0-45 mph	6.8 secs.
0-60 mph	11.0 secs.
0-75 mph	18.1 secs.

Passing Speeds

3rd gear 40-60 mph	7.2 secs.	527.04 ft.
4th gear 40-60 mph	9.2 secs.	673.44 ft.
3rd gear 50-70 mph	7.1 secs.	624.80 ft.
4th gear 50-70 mph	9.0 secs.	792.0 ft.

Standing Start ¼-mile:

75 mph	18.8 secs.

Speeds in Gears:

1st	27 mph @ 6000 rpm
2nd	50 mph @ 6000 rpm
3rd	77 mph @ 6000 rpm
4th	101 mph @ 6000 rpm

MPH per 1000 RPM: 16.9 mph

Stopping Distances:

from 30 mph	34 ft.
from 60 mph	121 ft.

Mileage Range	17.7-26.8 mpg
Average Mileage	23.5 mpg

SPECIFICATIONS

Engine: 4 cyl in-line sohc. **Bore & Stroke:** 3.50 x 3.15 ins. **Displacement:** 121.5 cu. in. **Horsepower:** 113 @ 5800 rpm. **Torque:** 116 lbs. ft. @ 3000 rpm. **Compression Ratio:** 8.5:1. **Carburetion:** 1 Solex 40 PDSI. **Transmission:** 4-speed synchromesh. **Final Drive Ratio:** 3.64:1. **Steering:** worm and roller. **Steering Ratio:** 17.6:1. **Turning Diameter:** 34.1 ft. curb-to-curb, 3.5 turns, lock-to-lock. **Tires:** Michelin XAS 165SR-13. **Brakes:** 9.4-in. disc front, 7.9-in. drum rear. **Suspension:** Front: MacPherson struts, lower A-arms, coil springs, tube shocks. Rear: Semi-trailing arms, coil springs, tube shocks. **Body/Frame:** unit steel construction. **Dimensions, Weights, Capacities:** Overall Length: 166.5 ins. Overall Width: 62.6 ins. Overall Height: 54.0 ins. Wheelbase: 98.4 ins. Front Track: 52.4 ins. Rear Track: 52.4 ins. Curb Weight: 2210 lbs. Fuel Capacity: 12.1 gals.

Whether cornering on a road course (far left) or making panic brake stops (above), the sports car that masquerades as a family sedan unabashedly displays its noble heredity. Credit for such superb handling must be given to costly independent rear suspension that features diagonal trailing arms. Wheels are sloped to negate constant track and camber changes, so common to cross-shaft, rigid axles. Coil springs and tube shocks (see above) aid in giving comfortable ride.

BMW 2002 *continued*

BMW meets smog emission controls by using an air injection system on the 2002. It is set up in an ordinary way with adjustments to carburetor and distributor. Engine configuration is a basic sohc BMW design, with 5-main bearings, but with 8 balance weights compared to 4 on the 1600. And, the oil pump is driven off the crankshaft by a chain drive, as on other BMWs, rather than conventionally off the camshaft.

Handling, Steering & Stopping

You keep telling yourself: The 2002 is basically a family sedan, not a sports car. If you can remember that fact when it comes to handling, the credibility gap is a little easier to understand. Cornering is fantastic. On a winding, tight, rugged mountain road the car has no peer in its class. On an actual road racing course it performs with some race machines — up to a point. You still have to remember it's a sedan! One of the two bad features (that's all we could find) on the 2002 is the steering wheel. It's much too large for good handling, and is positioned at a bad angle, a situation one never fully gets used to. In actuality, the 2002 has a slight understeer when engaged in the usual, spirited driving it was designed for, but the large wheel often creates the sensation of oversteering. On a mountain road with many tight turns, we noticed a slight, temporary oversteer when entering an extremely sharp turn in 4th gear at high speed — 60 to 70 mph — but this can be corrected by downshifting and judicious use of the throttle. On the road course, excessively hard cornering brought the inside rear wheel slightly off the road, but that situation never develops even under the most rugged highway or street driving. Some wheel hop is also evident during extremely fast acceleration. Our test car was equipped with optional Michelin XAS radial tires and we recommend them for the additional price as they make a tremendous difference in ride and handling. Independent suspension at all four wheels adds immeasurably to the handling characteristics of this car, and we ask repeatedly, in vain it seems, why can't our own companies, with their vast resources, develop an independent suspension like this for the family sedan?

Shift lever on the 2002 is in an ideal spot for quick, easy-to-manipulate shifts. BMW pedals still go through the floor rather than being suspended, as is the case on most new cars. This seems to necessitate less pedal pressure and makes operation easier. Pedals are an adequate size although the accelerator could be a little larger and at a less steep angle. Brake and accelerator are positioned for easy heel and toeing. Braking is also an excellent characteristic of the car. Some swerve was noticed when stopping from 60 to 0 mph, with only a slight tendency to lock up. Front discs pull down quite evenly and straight. Brake swept area to weight ratio is quite good.

Comfort, Convenience & Ride

Even with 4-wheel independent suspension and sports car handling, the 2002 lays a comfortable, though pleasingly firm, ride on you. Big, bucket seats are well designed and, with an extensive front/rear adjustment, give an excellent seating location for the shortest chick or tallest guy. Front/rear adjustment, coupled with multiple reclining position backs, seem to give the two front 2002 seats more positions than a 6-way power seat system. Visibility is expansive all around, with low window sills and high windows. Dimmer switch and high beams are incorporated into a lever located on the left side of the steering column. Turn indicator is on the right. The only other bad feature of the 2002 has the turn indicator and windshield washer/wiper combined on the same lever. Often, while attempting to flick the turn indicator without removing the right hand from the wheel, you manage to have the windshield washed and wiped also — unintentionally.

An extremely quiet ride is an attribute not usually found on a small car. Disturbances from wind and road are at an absolute minimum with windows up. Vent window handles are actually knobs and easy to operate for precise window adjustment. Ventilator fan is effective, although rear windows need to be opened slightly on inordinately hot days. Opting for the well designed, useful sunroof will compensate for any lack of cooling and we recommend that extra also. With sunroof open at high speeds, wind disturbance and buffeting was insignificant.

Ignition switch is recessed and located at a spot on the steering column that makes it difficult to reach. If you happen to be a heavy smoker, you may also find the ashtray too small. This BMW body is endowed with good trunk space and tire and tool kit location under floor panels makes packing easy and keeps luggage clean. High liftover makes loading somewhat difficult, especially for women. Quality control is ultra fastidious for a car in this price range, giving one more gold star to a faultless machine.

Americans who accidentally stumble into a BMW dealer and test drive the 2002 are in for a surprise. Keep your fingers crossed, fellas—maybe the word won't get around right away, say until about the year 2002.   /MT

photos by George Foon, Gerry Stiles

BMW 2002—15,000 miles

A smooth, superbly engineered road-burner

By Graham Robson

● LONG TERM ASSESSMENT

In the author's opinion, this is probably the finest dual-purpose car in Europe. Smaller 1600 body combined with 2000 engine gives four-seat family comfort and splendid performance. Famous BMW ohc engine, fine engineering and sports-car-like road holding: 14,000 miles in six months with complete reliability, the car still as good as new. No flashy styling, but what much-travelled businessman could ask for more? Even faster 120 bhp version now available—the 2002TI.

JUST a year ago, if anyone had said that much of my 1968 motoring would be in a fast roadworthy sports saloon costing over £1,600, I would have smiled cynically and replied that such good things never happened to me. If he had gone farther and prophesied that there would be a choice of two such cars I would have doubted his sanity! Yet this all came to pass in April, when Geoffrey Howard and I had to decide between an Alfa Giulia Super and a BMW 2002; this was soon settled, as Geoff had already "owned" two BMW's, so he took the Alfa instead.

In my two previously published assessments, on the Renault 16 and the Vauxhall Victor 2000, I longed for more performance in each case, both for safety and enjoyment. The BMW provided more than I could have hoped, and completely captivated me from the start. It's not going too far to say that this is the most satisfying car I have ever possessed, and is likely to be unbeaten in the near future. My own business needs call for a long-legged car which will take me many hundreds of miles up and down motorways, across country, or even scooting about Europe to sporting assignments, and the 2002 filled the bill admirably. If I had to pay all the expenses it would also be nice to have the creditable fuel economy (about 25 mpg), complete reliability, and to note the heavy demand for second-hand versions when the time came to sell. Mine has covered over 15,000 miles in only eight months, and is still on top of its form; we hope to keep it for some time yet and experience BMW's legendary long-life qualities.

The new thinking in BMW saloons began in 1961, with the Michelotti-styled 1500. This basic body shell is still in production for the current 1800 and 2000. The engine was then a brand-new ohc four-cyl design, canted over at 30deg in the car, bore and stroke being 82mm and 71mm. Later the engine grew to 1600, then 1800 and finally to a 2000; actually 1,990 c.c. with bore and stroke of 89mm and 80mm. Only two years ago BMW announced a smaller, two-door body shell, fitted with the 1600 engine and known locally as the 1600-2. The obvious thing happened, but not until this spring, when BMW married the 1600 body shell to the 2000 engine, added front *and* rear suspension anti-roll bars, and dubbed the new road-burner a 2002. For some months this was definitely *the* BMW to buy, but BMW have now achieved the ultimate by slotting in the higher-tuned 2000TI engine to evolve the 2002TI. Timo Makinen is due to drive a works 2002TI on the Monte next month; if the weather is not too snowy the results could be worth watching!

Road-burner extraordinary; the BMW 2002, distinguished by its black radiator grille

The 2002, then, is a true sports saloon, with 100 bhp from its lightly-tuned 2-litre engine, and a weight of only 2,060 lb—which compares closely with 110 bhp and 2,027lb for the Cortina-Lotus; unladen power-weight ratios are 92 bhp/ton (BMW) and 99 bhp/ton (Cortina-Lotus). Like the Ford it is a two-door, four seater saloon (wrongly named a coupé by its importers) though not quite as roomy in spite of being a bit longer. There is a really nice bonus in the form of fully-independent rear suspension, but a big penalty in the high price tag of £1,632, because of the high import duties from the Common Market. In Germany, of course, it is a very different story. In Germany, of course, it is a very different story. In Germany, of course, it is a very different story. The 2002 costs under £1,000.

Nice things about the BMW's engineering include the well-laid-out independent suspension and fine handling, the sweetly smooth ohc engine, and the many inclusive "extras" such as reclining front seats, wooden steering wheel and combined wiper-washer controls.

My car was delivered by road all the way from BMW in Munich, so that the running-in could be complete on arrival. In fact running in is a bit of a joke for this car; we were allowed 80 mph (4,300 rpm) for the first 250 miles, then up to 100 mph (not much below maximum speed!) for the rest of the way. For normal running-in, 75 mph in top gear is allowed from the start. Steady speed *autobahn* cruising kept stresses down, but may also have delayed the general loosening-up process a bit. As collected, its speedometer read 99,979 (usually they read 99,969 so that pre-delivery running will bring up the zero for customer-collection). Soon after the car got back to England, with 1,474 miles on the clock, I took delivery and was allowed to use full throttle from then on. The car kept its German export plates for a while, which was very good indeed when I needed parking immunity, but bad in traffic, where we British tend to lean on foreigners; it did not collect its British registra-

tion until 3,475 miles. Our experience in the next 13,000 miles has been almost undiluted pleasure and satisfaction; literally the only two things to go wrong have been a broken driver's door pull—this happened very early—and a broken throttle pedal, of which more later. The car has been off the road only for routine service—even with the throttle problem I could keep going—and has not missed a beat for the whole eight months.

We have made three modifications. The first was to re-position the brake and clutch pedals (by re-shaping and welding the shafts) so that they were nearer the floor; right-hand-drive 2002s have pendant pedals, their pads an excessive $7\frac{1}{2}$in. off the floor, but left-hand-drive cars have them sprouting from the floor—inexplicable. Fitting my Radiomobile was complicated, at the time, by there being no fitting kit for this particular bodyshell. My local specialist—Gordon March of Coventry—solved the problem neatly by using the complete pod from my Renault 16, which slotted into the central storage bin as if the two had been designed together. Even now I hear that there's no kit, but Gordon March tells me he is using parts of a BMC 1100/1300 kit which fit even more easily. Because both the bonnet and boot lids are full-length, getting an aerial on to the car is nearly impossible. My car has the gutter fitting which is really too small for perfect reception, but this seems to be the only solution.

Front seat belts are compulsory, of course; mine are Britax with BMW decals. Finally we fitted a wooden gear lever knob to replace the horrid rubber variety which is common to the 1600. My car was shod with German Dunlop SP tyres, rather coarse-treaded and known as doggie-bones in the trade; I always kept them well blown up to 30 psi for a reasonable balance between ride, comfort and stability.

I fell in love with the car almost at once. Even in traffic it was obvious that there was lots of performance, superb handling, and that inde-

The bonnet, heavily sound proofed with polyurethane foam, hinges well out of the way. The box on the end of the air cleaner trunking selects hot or cold air, depending on the season

A plywood floor covers the spare wheel well; the single-skin boot sides are very prone to damage from loose items sliding about inside. The "porthole" by the right-hand hinge is part of the ventilation exhaust system

BMW LONG TERM . . .

finable "something" that is an aura of fine engineering where price takes a back seat in development—this all added up to a most pleasurable whole. I'm a long-distance motorist, possibly covering more miles in a year than anyone else on the staff, and need this *rapprochement* with a car to make me content. The Renault 16 had character but lacked performance, while with the Victor it was the other way round.

At first, the car wasn't as loose-limbed as expected, probably because the *autobahn* delivery service had retarded running-in, but a sample set of figures taken against the road test 2002 (our issue of 16 May 1968) showed there wasn't a lot of difference. By 4,000 miles all was well, and the car has continued to feel good ever since. The fact that our performance check, carried out only last week, shows performance to be slightly down at 16,000 miles, merely proves that BMW make cars to production tolerances, which do deteriorate slightly with age and that our car wasn't "fiddled" in any way for long term press use. I had occasion, some weeks ago, to make a visual check against another 2002, when I was "jumped" by AY 1 just getting on to M1 at Hendon. For the

next 60-odd miles I confirmed that his car seemed to have more snap from medium speeds, but that there was precious little in it. The driver of AY 1 seemed to enjoy himself, and so did I.

On one occasion, the car did lose quite a lot of its zest, and in the most unusual way. The throttle set-up on these cars has a true organ-pedal control, the usual type with a steel blade encased in rubber. Perhaps the combination of over-enthusiastic foot-to-the-floor and a sub-standard pedal helped, but after a time the pedal began to bend, just below the roller fixing to the rest of the linkage. I had to leave for France and the Alpine Rally with the pedal in this condition, one that worsened as we swept down French *autoroutes* and caused maximum cruising speeds to drop back. Before Marseille the metal blade had broken inside the rubber, leaving me with only an uncomfortable half-throttle to use, a maximum speed of 90 mph and a splendid overall fuel consumption for the trip of 28 mpg! A new pedal cured the problem on return, performance is back to normal and fuel consumption to a more believable 25 mpg.

Cynics who might believe I think the car is perfect may now learn of minor gripes. On a car of this price I would have expected the wiper arcs to be matched to r.h.d., but they're not and they leave a nasty blind spot above and to the

right of my eye-line. I find minor switches difficult to reach when wearing belts, and they have sharply uncomfortable edges. It's a constant bore to have to lock both doors from the outside with a key as neither will slam-lock, and I don't like the unprotected flanks of the boot compartment, easily damaged by sharp objects from within. It would be nice to have a bigger fuel tank than 10 gallons, but I must have been spoiled by 12 in the Victor.

The car is now on its second set of Dunlop tyres, the "doggie bones" having been exchanged for a brand new set of Dunlop SP "aquaspurts" at 11,868 miles. The German Dunlops were not swopped round at all—the spare being unused—and calculations of life rendered meaningless by a very expensive tyre burning session in North Wales when I got the car stuck facing the wrong way down a very steep hill with unmade surface. When removed, the front tyres still had 5mm of their 8mm unused—this indicating a probable 28,000 miles to the legal limit; but only 2mm remained at the rear, quite a bit of the spent rubber being not too far from Nefyn in North Wales! Let's make an estimate of 20,000 miles if they'd all been swopped round and cared for. It's quite certain that the rears would wear out first anyway; there is certainly enough power to squeak the tyres on a full-blooded take off, and

Above: The radio fitting kit came straight from the Renault 16 and fits neatly in the central cubby. The wooden gear lever knob replaces the standard rubber one

Left: The paler parts of the brake and clutch pedals show where they have been heat treated to give better location. This type of pedal will be fitted to all 2002s next month

Below: As both boot and bonnet "decks" are hinged, a gutter-mounted aerial was fitted. BMW usually fit theirs either on the roof or in the centre of the rear boot lid

the inside rear wheel sometimes lifts and spins when I take advantage of the formidable cornering power. The "aquaspurts" grip even better than the German tyres, especially in the wet when the renowned jets in the tread remove phenomenal amounts of water from the road. They show few signs of wear just yet and will certainly last out until we have to sell the car next year.

One of the things that appeals strongly is the feeling of having a real Q-car. Only the *cognoscenti* smile knowingly when they see the BMW and 2002 badges, for even in its rich red colour with the fashionable black grille, the car looks like a very modest and sedate family saloon. One can only suppose that BMW's "Move Over" advertising campaign for the car is to educate everyone who might unwittingly get in the way. . . .

As with Alfas and most expensive GT cars, I feel that BMW *must* employ a "sensations" engineer, one who can build in the right noises and responses after development engineers have done their job. Nothing else could really explain that subdued but characteristic whine from the ohc camshaft drive, the silky gear-change that feels as if it isn't connected to vulgar gear wheels at all, and the responsive and delicate handling that flatters a driver so much.

Speaking now as a road tester, I am suspicious of an engine tune which doesn't need any choke even for cold starts (though mpg figures are well up to scratch) and I think the steering wheel is much too big. It is, of course, a very fast car on our crowded roads, whether for thrusting across country, or for cruising along motorways. There's absolutely no temperament from the docile 2-litre engine, which always gives the impression of being throttled down rather than tuned up, and I get very idle over gear changing at times. Speed-limited cruising at 70 mph is ludicrously slow for the 2002—I know that on the Continent one is regularly passed by other 2002s wafting along at speeds up to 100 mph. It's the most high-geared of all BMW's (with an axle ratio of 3.64), so 70 mph is only 3,800 rpm. Helped by the fat Dunlops, and the stiffened suspension, the handling is truly superb, especially as the steering is so light and precise, and with ultimate grip several degrees better than my personal bravery index I'm hardly likely to run it out of road. Understeer or over-steer means little with this sort of car; it's finely enough balanced usually, and I suppose power-on oversteer with a spinning rear wheel would represent the limit.

It is nice to have the ultra-solid BMW bonnet locking handle by the passenger's legs. This must be closed positively to lock the bonnet,

which hinges at the front to reveal all when service is needed. Also nice is the combined, typically German, wiper-washer stalk on the steering column which is sadly missing from domestic products. One would like better heating and ventilation, especially in the methods of getting used air out of the car, and for my money there should be more instruments, particularly an oil pressure gauge and a clock. I suppose one can't have everything, for a clock on German 2002s is replaced by the so-useful rev-counter for British-market cars. The front seats give ample lounging room, and enough location for me without excessive bucketing. The car is frankly too small to be considered a true four-seater, and with my driving seat in its usual way-back position I wouldn't like to inflict a long journey on any adult passenger behind me.

This assessment reads like a saga of contentment, and so it should. When I bade a sad goodbye to my Renault 16 at the end of last year, my closing words were, "almost any new staff car will be less comfortable, less cleverly sprung and less distinctive . . .". Let's just say that the BMW has equalled it and beaten it by really spirited road manners that I will never fail to appreciate. Most motoring writers would vote the 2002 as one of 1968's "in" cars; count me among them.

PERFORMANCE CHECK

Maximum speeds

Gear	mph		kph		rpm	
	R/T	Staff	R/T	Staff	R/T	Staff
Top (mean)	107	103	172	166	5,800	5,600
(best)	110	103	177	166	5,960	5,600
3rd:	89	89	143	143	6,500	6,500
2nd:	59	59	95	95	6,500	6,500
1st:	31	31	50	50	6,500	6,500

Standing $\frac{1}{4}$-mile R/T: 17.4 sec 77 mph
Staff: 18.7 sec 73 mph
Standing kilometre, R/T: 32.8 sec 96 mph
Staff: 34.9 sec 89 mph

ACCELERATION

Time in seconds R/T:	3.5	5.3	7.6	10.6	14.2	18.2	26.4
Staff:	4.0	6.1	8.8	12.3	16.8	23.6	35.9
True speed mph	30	40	50	60	70	80	90

SPEED RANGE, GEAR RATIOS AND TIME IN SECONDS

mph	Top (3.64)		3rd (4.89)		2nd (7.46)		1st (13.95)	
	R/T	Staff	R/T	Staff	R/T	Staff	R/T	Staff
1—30	—	—	6.4	6.9	3.8	4.0	2.5	2.9
20—40	8.1	8.7	5.6	6.0	3.5	4.0	—	—
30—50	7.6	8.5	5.5	5.9	3.7	4.6	—	—
40—60	8.4	9.0	5.8	6.7	5.1	—	—	—
50—70	8.5	10.4	6.2	8.8	—	—	—	—
60—80	10.2	12.9	8.6	10.6	—	—	—	—
70—90	13.2	20.2	—	—	—	—	—	—

FUEL CONSUMPTION
Overall mpg **R/T:** 25.5 (11.1 litres/100km)
Staff: 25.0 (11.3 litres/100km)
NOTE: "R/T" denotes performance figures for the BMW 2002 tested in Autocar of 16 May 1968.

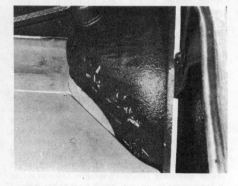

Damage to the unprotected wheel arches in the BMWs boot, caused by sharp-edged luggage crashing about. Some form of trim protection is needed

Brief Specification Resumé
FOUR-CYLINDER front-mounted ohc engine of 1,990 c.c. (89 x 80 mm). Power output 100 bhp (net) at 5,500 rpm.; max. torque 116 lb.ft. at 3,000 rpm. Four-speed, all-synchromesh gearbox; 18.5 mph per 1,000 rpm in top gear. ATE brakes, with 9.5in. front discs and 8 x 1.5in. rear drums. All independent suspension by coil springs, with anti-roll bars at front and rear. Fuel tank 10gal. Kerb weight 2,060 lb. Four-seater saloon body with two doors.

COST AND LIFE OF EXPENDABLE ITEMS

Item	Life in Miles	Cost per 10,000 Miles		
		£	s	d
One gallon of 4-star fuel, average cost today 6s 4d	25	126	13	4
One pint of top-up oil, average cost today 3s 0d	5,000	6	0	
Front disc brake pads (set of 4)	10,000	4	14	8
Rear brake linings (set of 4)	21,000	18	2	
Dunlop SP tyres (front and rear)	20,000	17	10	0
Service (main interval and actual costs incurred to date)	4,000	20	14	8
Total		**170**	**16**	**10**
Approx. standing charges per year				
Depreciation		200	0	0
Insurance		38	0	0
Tax		25	0	0
Total		**433**	**16**	**10**

Approx. cost per mile = 10½d

The BMW 2002 has been available in Britain only since the spring, so depreciation is an estimated figure based on current market prices and on a basis of 10,000 miles per year. The figure quoted for insurance is the sum due after deduction of a 60 per cent no-claims bonus; the writer would also have to agree, for this type of car, to a £25 excess and a "named driver" clause

BMW 2002:

....a controllable urge

BMW's re-entry in 1965 into automobile manufacture must go on record as one of the most successful comebacks at all time.

The impact of the re-appearance of this legendary name was felt almost immediately by many European manufacturers, and now, ever-increasing market acceptance has placed BMW as one of the sales leaders in Germany.

In the last financial year, BMW carved a substantial slice out of the Mercedes Benz share of the home market.

This fact alone gives an insight into what type of car BMW is producing and what segment of the market it is aiming for.

BMW started with a virtually clean sheet when first planning their new range of cars, and every aspect of every vehicle they produce shows evidence of this.

The aim was to produce a car which offered fast, comfortable transport with a strong accent on safety — identical to the Mercedes Benz philosophy.

And not suprisingly, the vehicles which evolved are very similar in many respects to Mercedes Benz — although they fall into a slightly smaller size category.

Limited availability and high prices have kept BMW sales down in Australia, but recent substantial price reductions and a growing band of enthusiastic owners who are constantly singing the marque's praises are doing much to rectify the situation.

Once you have driven a BMW, you begin to understand why the car is making such a mark in European countries, where purchase prices are low enough to bring it within the reach of the average individual.

Any BMW is mechanical evidence of the fact that a car with excellent road holding power need not have firm, harsh suspension, and that a car which is capable of riding smoothly and sure-footedly over roughly corrugated roads need not have a suspension which causes it to lean frighteningly on fast corners.

In the short space of time since their introduction, these cars have shown that the word "compromise" does not exist at Bayerische Motoren Werke.

Initially, the BMW range comprised two basic models sharing the same body shell — the "1800" and the "2000".

Shortly afterwards, the range was expanded to include the "1600", with a smaller, entirely new body and a single overhead camshaft 1600 cc engine, developing 96 bhp SAE at 5800 rpm.

And the latest BMW to reach our shores is the "2002", which can virtually be described as a 1600 with the engine from the 2000 installed under the bonnet.

With this two litre, 113 bhp engine pushing along a body weighing just over 2000 lbs., it can be understood that the 2002 is something of a performer — although it's not quite the rubber burner that some would expect.

Gearbox ratios remain the same as those of the 1600, but final drive ratio has been altered to give economical and relaxed high speed cruising rather than neck-snapping acceleration.

Perhaps the main benefit of the two litre engine is the improved torque which allows the car to accelerate from low rpm strongly and without fuss.

Fuel economy, too, is a big feature of the 2002, and we recorded a figure of 25.5 mpg during testing. Under normal conditions, it would not be hard to exceed 28 mpg.

Apart from the differences already mentioned, there are few other mechanical changes from the 1600,

which gives some idea of the reserves that are built into BMW cars.

Externally, the only way to pick the 2002 from the 1600 is the black-painted grille, anodized hubcaps, and the 2002 motif at the rear.

Inside, there are few obvious differences, apart from the new three spoke steering wheel with its huge padded hub and the addition of a tachometer to the instrument panel.

The safety theme is evident everywhere you look, even down to the heater control levers which on first glance look to be of hard unyielding design, but which do in fact break away on impact.

All-round visibility is excellent, yet the car doesn't make passengers feel conspicuous like some of the mobile glass houses on the road today.

Front seats are designed to make the driver and his companion as comfortable as possible, and fore and aft adjustment is so generous that any driver, regardless of the length of his legs, can achieve a very satisfactory driving position. Those in the back, however, are not as well catered for and if the front seats are pushed right back there just isn't *any* legroom.

As the 2002 is fitted with lap-style safety belts, controls can be reached fairly easily, but I felt that the windscreen wiper switch could be located at a more convenient distance — perhaps it could be incorporated in the column-mounted stalk which operates the washers?

Another small gripe concerns the location of the floor pedals, which are arranged so that operation of the brake pedal requires a definite lifting of the right foot rather than pivoting on the heel. Likewise, the clutch pedal is suspended high off the floor and the driver is forced to adopt a "Knees Up Mother Brown" attitude when gear changing.

Apart from these shortcomings, con-

2000 engine is a snug fit in 1600 engine bay

trols are well placed for relaxed driving.

Gear lever placement is beyond reproach, operation is smooth and positive, and I didn't beat the synchromesh once during 300 miles of testing.

At high cruising speeds, the 2002 is an extremely quiet car and engine noise intruded only under hard acceleration during testing. Suspension noise was hardly discernible over rough roads and even severe corrugations couldn't provoke the tail to hop off line — all credit to the well designed semi-trailing link rear suspension.

The suspension is one of the 2002's biggest features, and part of the secret is the extensive use of rubber to absorb shocks that would normally transmit themselves to the body.

As mentioned before, this suspension is unchanged from the 1600, yet it is capable of containing the extra performance of the 2000 motor with enormous reserves of safety.

Top recorded speed was 111 mph with the engine spinning at 6000 rpm. Even at this high velocity (which betters the claimed factory figure by 5 mph) the car felt well balanced and noise level was low.

This long legged character is one of the 2002's main charms, and there are few cars that can eat up the miles more effortlessly — and none that I can think of with more safety.

The theory at BMW is that to be made as safe as is humanly possible, a car should be designed to avoid accidents in the first place through good braking and handling. In a BMW. if an accident can't be avoided, the front and rear sections will collapse progressively to absorb impact and any protuberances inside the specially strengthened passenger compartment are designed so as not to inflict injury.

All this attention to safety design, and the development and testing that is involved, naturally costs money and the 2002 is priced beyond the reach of many motorists at $4360.

But if safety, comfort and performance count for anything, it's worth every penny of it.

Body design is clean and attractive from any angle. Note good glass area.

DRIVER COMMENTS

BMW 2002

CAR FROM: Grand Prix Motors Pty. Ltd. 208 Riversdale Road, Hawthorn, Vic.

PRICE AS TESTED: $4360 (plus radio, stereo tape)

OPTIONS FITTED: Radio, stereo tape recorder.

ENGINE:

Type	4 cylinder SOHC
Bore and stroke	89x80
Capacity	1990 cc
Compression ratio	8.5:1
Power (gross)	113 bhp @ 5800 rpm
Torque	115.7 lbs. ft. @ 3000 rpm

TRANSMISSION: 4-speed, all-synchro.

CHASSIS:

Wheelbase	98½ inches
Length	166½ inches
Track F	52⅜ inches
Track R	52⅜ inches
Width	62¼ inches
Clearance (minimum)	6¼ inches
Test weight	2068 lbs.
Fuel capacity	10.1 gallons

SUSPENSION:

Front: McPherson struts and rubber mounted lower wishbones, anti-roll bar.

Rear Rubber-mounted semi trailing arms, coil springs, telescopic shock absorbers, anti-roll bar.

BRAKES: Power assisted.

Front: 9.45 inch discs.

Rear: 7.9 inch drums.

STEERING:

Type: Worm and roller.

Turns lock to lock: 3.5

Turning circle: 31 ft. 6 in.

WHEELS/TYRES: 4½ inch steel rims with 165 SR 13 radial ply tyres.

PERFORMANCE:

Zero to

30 mph	3.2 seconds
40 mph	5.2 seconds
50 mph	7.0 seconds
60 mph	9.9 seconds
70 mph	12.8 seconds
80 mph	16.6 seconds
90 mph	22.0 seconds
100 mph	NA

Standing quarter mile 17.5 seconds.

Fuel consumption on test 25.5 mpg. on S fuel.

Fuel consumption (expected) 28 mpg.

Cruising range 283 miles.

SPEEDOMETER ERROR:

Indicated	30	40	50	60	70	80	90	100
Actual	28	37	46	55	64	74	84	NA

MAXIMUM SPEEDS IN GEARS:

First	29 mph
Second	54 mph
Third	82 mph
Fourth	111 mph

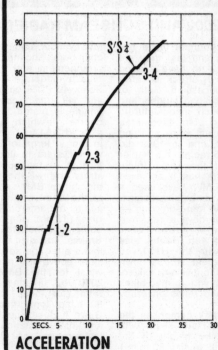

ACCELERATION

ENGINE:

Starting	Good
Response	Good
Vibration	Low
Noise	Low

DRIVE TRAIN:

Shift linkage	Very good
Synchro action	Very good
Clutch action	Good
Noise	Low

STEERING:

Effort	Moderate
Response	Excellent
Road feel	Excellent
Kickback	Low

SUSPENSION:

Ride comfort	Very good
Roll resistance	Very good
Pitch control	Very good

HANDLING:

Directional control	Very good
Predictability	Very good
Resistance to sidewind	Good

BRAKES:

Pedal pressure	Low
Response	Very good
Fade resistance	Very good
Directional stability	Very good

CONTROLS:

Wheel position	Very good
Pedal position	Good
Gearshift position	Very good
Panel controls	Good

INTERIOR:

Ease of entry and exit	Good
Noise level	Low
Front seat comfort	Very good
Front head room	Good
Rear seat comfort	Good
Rear leg room	Poor
Rear head room	Good
Instrument comprehensiveness	Good
Instrument legibility	Good

VISION:

Forward	Very good
Front quarter	Very good
Side	Very good
Rear quarter	Very good
Rear	Very good

CONSTRUCTION:

Sheet metal	Very good
Paint	Very good
Chrome	Very good
Upholstery	Very good
Trim	Very good

GENERAL:

Headlights - highbeam	Good
Headlights - lowbeam	Good
Wiper coverage	Fair
Wipers at speed	Very good
Maintenance accessibility	Good
Luggage space	Very good

Hair on Their Chests

BMW 2002 AND SUNBEAM RAPIER H 120

ON THE face of it there is nothing to connect these two cars whatsoever except for the price and that they are both, loosely, two-door saloons. And yet both have a good deal in common — at least, that's how it struck us after driving the two of 'em in fairly short succession. Both, of course, are hair-on-the-chest versions of existing models and both are good examples of the cars which manufacturers add a bit of muscle to so that they can point them at a slightly wider market. The BMW is an even more sporting version of an already sporting motor-car, and in 1968 did what you might call Rather Well in Group 5 racing; the Rapier is a slightly more elaborate version of the same thing, although in neither normal nor H120 form has it achieved any kind of competition record. Where BMW have used a smallish, lightish shell and dumped in a bigger engine, Rootes have taken the other tack and have got someone — in this case Holbay (whose racing engines have a considerable competition record) — to squeeze a power bonus out of the engine the car is usually fitted with. Rootes also go a little more wild on the finish — with the H120 you get a go-faster paint trim, with zonking great stripes down the sides, plus sexy-looking wheels, without even asking, while the more conservative BMW gives you a matt-black grille, the words 2002 on the blunt end and relies on pretty shattering performance to do the rest.

Looking at them in more detail, the BMW comprises the 1600 two-door body shell, giving the car four seats with rear-seat legroom strictly controlled by the height of the driver. Into this is slotted the oversquare (89 m.m. x 80 m.m.) four-cylinder engine of 1990 c.c. Hemispherical combustion chambers, inclined overhead-valves in an inverted "V" arrangement and operated by a single overhead camshaft, plus a moderate compression ratio of only 8.5 to 1 and a Solex 40 PDSI carb help it to produce 100 b.h.p. at five-five and yet retain commendable flexibility and economy. This engine is mated to a four-speed gearbox — all-synchro, of course — which in turn drives through a high-geared back axle: at 3.64 to 1, the final drive gives 18.5 m.p.h./1000 r.p.m. in top: in terms of British speed limits, the sickening seventy is equivalent to under 4000 r.p.m. The suspension is similar to that of the 1600 — in other words, you get i.f.s. with struts and wishbones, plus an anti-roll bar which is one of the things BMW added for the 2002 version. Independence at the blunt end is by semi-trailing arms, coil springs and, again, an anti-roll bar; standard equipment includes $4\frac{1}{2}$ in. rims (13 in. wheels, by the way) and the list of optional equipment includes a five-speed box and a limited-slip diff. Brakes are disc at the front, drums astern; an alternator looks after the sparks and the body shell includes extractor slots above the rear window with ducts in roof pillars and waist for the BMW version of Aeroflow. Total weight is 2070 lb., unladen, which gives an unladen power/weight ratio (for those too idle to do their own sums) of over 90 b.h.p./ton. Which suggest it oughter go a bit, and by Gawd it does. Inside, you get full carpeting, reclining seats, and instrumentation by means of rev-counter, speedo, water temperature and fuel gauges, plus odd warning lights and things.

There's nothing much to show on the outside; B.M.W. spent all the money on pretty shattering performance and handling.

The H 120 has plenty of exterior goodies, enough urge to be interesting, and excellent finish throughout.

Holbay Racing Engines have never been particularly famous for road conversions, preferring to win their reputation from the successes of their single-seater racing engines. However, the Rootes Arrow power unit didn't give them much trouble, and they have come up with an engine which, again, has a good deal of top-end urge and yet is still tractable enough for traffic use. The normal Rapier 1725 c.c. "four" (81.5 m.m. x 82.5 m.m.) gets a compression increase on its standard alloy head up to 9.6 to 1 and the ports are modified. A pair of 40 DCOE Webers, a free-flow exhaust manifold and a modified cam with more valve lift completes the deal, and all this gives 105 b.h.p. at five-two. It also gets wider section tyres, a noticeably higher final drive ratio (up from 4.22 to 3.89 to 1, giving 17.3 m.p.h./1000 r.p.m. in direct top, and 21.6 in overdrive top), the stripes and so on we mentioned before and a spoiler tail shape. Inside the car is as beautifully and fully equipped as are most Rootes products in the upper price bracket, and you get full instrumentation — including an oil temperature gauge — plus reclining seats and an adjustable steering column: in other respects it is pure Rapier, just as we tested in our September, 1968 issue.

It manages to convey a feeling of luxury which the BMW somehow misses: instinctively we felt the German car had no carpets — which it has, of course: it just feels a little more spartan, somehow. Wind noise has a good deal to do with this, probably; on the Rapier, it is commendably low, even at 90 m.p.h., whereas the same speed in the BMW makes conversation a frustrating thing to attempt. On the other hand, the BMW's steering is outstandingly light and precise, whereas on the Rapier, the change from 155 to 165 section tyres seems to have improved the roadholding but only at the expense of the steering, which is now definitely on the heavy side. And even the Rapier's improved handling is not up to BMW standards: the German car is undoubtedly one of the best in its class — or even out of it — from this point of view. Balance is near perfect, and the very effective i.r.s. provides extremely good traction out of bends although, as you might expect, full urge out of a greasy hairpin will get the inside wheel really spinning. The Rapier, however, needs to be cornered smoothly, and you can't fling it about as you can the BMW, which will just go round corners, as simply as that; the only real indication that you are getting near the limit is an uncomfortable angle of heel as the body rolls further and further. The Rapier is controllable, but inspires less confidence, and the fact that in the wet the front goes first while, on dry surfaces, oversteer is the dominant effect can be a shade off-putting until you get used to it. It's only fair to add, of course, that in the wet

anything over four thousand on the clock means you can boot the tail round to overcome the understeer, and that in the dry the final oversteer is something you don't reach until you're cornering ruddy 'ard, Kipling. The difference between the two cars in a nutshell is that the BMW is highly chuckable, while the Rapier just ain't.

So far as performance is concerned, the BMW has the higher top speed, by quite a margin, reaching a best one-way of 112 m.p.h. and a mean of 110, compared with the Rapier's best figure of 107 and mean of 106, both in overdrive top: in direct top you can get 104 or so. There isn't much to choose between 'em when it comes to the spacing of gear ratios: the BMW gives you 32, 60 and 90 in first, second and third; the Rapier lets you go to 33, 54 and 80, with the ton available in overdrive third. Acceleration figures are comparable: 0-60 wants 10.7 seconds for the Rapier, 9.3 for the BMW; 0-80 figures are 18.1 and 16.8 seconds respectively. Both cars will potter along at thirty in top, but neither is very keen on the idea — the Rapier's handbook, in fact, advises against running at less than two thousand revs in top, and the car doesn't really start happening until the rev-counter is showing around 4000. Similarly, the BMW isn't really happy until you're doing about three-five, while top gear performance is slightly poorer than that of the Rapier: the 70-90 figure in top for the BMW was 13.0 seconds, and for the Rapier — in overdrive top. yet — was 11.4

Fuel consumption is a point on which the BMW scores marginally: we got 25 m.p.g. on this one, compared with 23 for the Rapier. But the Rapier carries more of the go-juice, with a fifteen-gallon tank compared with the ten-gallon effort fitted to the BMW, and this in fact gives the Rapier a slight advantage when it comes to a question of range between fuel stops. And actually buying the cars? Well, your friendly neighbourhood Rootes man will let you have an H120 Rapier for £1,634; the BMW man across the street will sell you a 2002 for exactly forty shillings less. But back home in Germany, Wolfgang can, we're told, buy a 2002 for under a thousand quid — around the price, over here, of, say, a C*rt*n* GT. Makes you think, doesn't it?

Martyn Watkins

PERFORMANCE DATA

	Rapier H120	BMW 2002
Mean maximum speed	106	110
Acceleration— 0-30	3.0	2.7
0-40	5.2	4.2
0-50	7.3	6.6
0-60	10.7	9.3
0-70	13.8	12.6
0-80	18.1	16.8
Fuel consumption	23 m.p.g.	25 m.p.g.

ROAD & TRACK ROAD TEST

BMW 2002 AUTOMATIC

Cars tell you how they want to be driven—
and this one tells you it wants to be driven hard

CARS TELL YOU how they want to be driven. If you're in a big family type car with featherbed suspension, numb steering and have only the vaguest idea where the extremities are, you drive one way. If you're in a tautly suspended small sedan with sharp steering and can see where everything is, you drive another way. In the BMW 2002 Automatic, the car tells you it wants to be driven hard. You can see where you're going, it goes where you direct it, it responds eagerly to your impulses and it stops when it's told to stop.

If you'll permit another generalization, we'll also say that drivers reflect the characteristics of their cars. To most drivers of American cars, BMW drivers rank as impertinent and impatient. Because the car is eager and aggressive, the driver is eager and aggressive. Even our kindly old editor found himself impatient with the great passenger barges basking around in traffic. Ordinarily the gentlest of men, he had to resist the temptation to intrude himself on their normal state of somnolence by flashing his lights and nipping in and out around them.

BMWs want to go. Around corners (because the suspension is excellent), accelerate briskly (because the engine is eager and the gearbox works right), cruise as fast as the road will permit (because it's comfortable going fast) and stop (because the brakes are fully up to the job). BMWs, it seems to us, do everything a car should—and do it better.

Our test car is the BMW 2002 Automatic which is the 2002 equipped with the 3-speed ZF automatic already available in the 2000. This transmission works equally well in the 2002 and while the shifts aren't as silky as with a great U.S.-designed automatic, the engine does have sufficient torque to avoid the ski-slope feeling common to many small-engined automatics where you build up a great stack of revs only to fall into the next gear (and off the torque curve) with a lurch and take forever to get back up again. There's also a safety override on the automatic that prevents over-revving on manually selected downshifts.

You give away a little performance with the automatic, as you would expect. The 4-speed manual we tested earlier covered the standing quarter in 17.6 sec and our automatic took 17.9. It is still plenty lively, of course, and goes about the job with a delightful eagerness.

Other refinements that have been made in the 2002 Automatic include an automatic choke, a worthwhile improvement in convenience. Our test car also had the optional anti-roll bars front and rear, which reduce body lean and give a crisper handling feel. There's still considerable body lean in hard cornering but this is well controlled and upsetting to neither driver nor passengers.

The test car also had the optional Michelin XAS 165-13 tires which increase the sure-footedness but also result in the steering being noticeably heavier.

For some strange reason, the already disgraceful quantity of speedometer error in the 2002 has been added to in the Automatic. In our test car, when the speedometer was reading 60, the actual speed was only 53 and you had to have the needle close to 80 to keep up with 70-mph traffic. The odometer error is also ridiculous in that only 92 actual miles are covered for every 100 recorded on the dial. When BMW engineering does so many things so well, it is disillusioning to find such details ignored.

So far as the driver's comfort is concerned, the ventilation system has good flow but is poorly directed as there is no face-level venting and the fresh air that does come in is directed at the inboard calf. The window winders are tiresomely low-geared—as are the wind wings—and the windows roll down only far enough to leave an uncomfortable ridge for the arm to rest on.

The instruments are well displayed in an attractive black setting and in addition to a drop-down glove box there is a useful parcel tray molded into the padding in front of the passenger's front seat. The seats are very comfortable, fully adjustable, and the buckles of the 3-point seat belts pull down beside the hip where they should be. There isn't much room left in the rear when the front seats are in their normal position but there's adequate space for four when it is necessary to carry that number. The trunk is of a practical size and shape (the spare fits under the floor mat) and the compartment is fully finished off, a nice touch.

The pricing structure of the BMW 2002 is of the variety we find rather distasteful. The basic list of the 2002 Automatic (West Coast POE) is $3340, a bargain figure. But once you go into the showroom, you find that they don't have any cars to sell for this price as the importer orders all of them equipped with radial tires ($59 extra), vinyl upholstery ($45), chrome exhaust tip ($2), reclining seats ($48) and power-assisted brakes ($45). These things, plus the anti-roll bars ($20), tachometer in place of clock ($40) and the dealer preparation charge ($80) result in your basic 2002 Automatic at $3340 having a real price of $3679. And if you decide not to have all these extras, which aren't really extras, you must place your order and await delivery. Most importers long ago abandoned this type of almost-misleading pricing because of the ill-will it created among potential customers. The BMW 2002 Automatic isn't overpriced at its "real" price, so why aggravate the buyer?

BMW 2002 AUTOMATIC
ROAD TEST RESULTS

PRICE
List price.................$3340
Price as tested............$3687

ENGINE & DRIVE TRAIN
Engine.........4-cyl inline, sohc
Bore x stroke, mm....89.0 x 80.0
Displacement, cc/cu in.1990/121.5
Compression ratio..........8.5:1
Bhp @ rpm.........113 @ 5800
  Equivalent mph.............98
Torque @ rpm, lb-ft..116 @ 3000
  Equivalent mph.............52
Transmission type: 3-spd automatic
Gear ratios, 3rd (1.00)....3.64:1
  2nd (1.52)..............5.53:1
  1st (2.56)..............9.32:1
Final drive ratio..........3.64:1

GENERAL
Curb weight, lb............2270
Weight distribution (with
  driver), front/rear, %.....55/45
Wheelbase, in.............98.4
Track, front/rear......52.4/52.4
Overall length............166.5
  Width.................62.6
  Height................54.0
Steering type......worm & roller
  Turns, lock-to-lock........3.5
Brakes.....disc front/drum rear
  Swept area, sq in.........243

ACCOMMODATION
Seating capacity, persons......4
Seat width,
  front/rear.......2 x 20.5/51.0
Head room, front/rear...40.0/38.0
Seat back adjustment. degrees..90
Driver comfort rating (scale of 100):
  For driver 69 in. tall........90
  For driver 72 in. tall........85
  For driver 75 in. tall........85

PERFORMANCE
Top speed, high gear, mph....102
Acceleration, time to distance, sec:
  0–100 ft..................4.0
  0–250 ft..................6.8
  0–500 ft.................10.3
  0–750 ft.................13.2
  0–1000 ft................15.5
  0–1320 ft (¼ mile).......17.9
  Speed at end, mph.........70
Time to speed, sec:
  0–30 mph.................4.9
  0–40 mph.................7.1
  0–50 mph.................9.8
  0–60 mph................13.3
  0–80 mph................25.7
  0–90 mph................39.5

BRAKE TESTS
Panic stop from 80 mph:
  Distance, ft..............380
  Max. deceleration rate, %g...84
  Control............excellent
Fade test: percent of increase in
  pedal effort required to maintain
  50%-g deceleration rate in six
  stops from 60 mph.........33
Overall brake rating.....very good

SPEEDOMETER ERROR
30 mph indicated......actual 28.0
40 mph................36.0
60 mph................53.0
80 mph................71.0

CALCULATED DATA
Lb/hp (test weight).........23.7
Cu ft/ton mi............91.8
Mph/1000 rpm (high gear)... 17.2
Engine revs/mi............3500
Engine speed @ 70 mph.....4120
Piston travel, ft/mi.........1840
R&T wear index..............61
R&T steering index.......1.20
Brake swept area, sq in/ton...182

FUEL
Type fuel required......premium
Fuel tank size, gal..........12.1
Normal consumption, mpg..19.5

ACCELERATION & COASTING

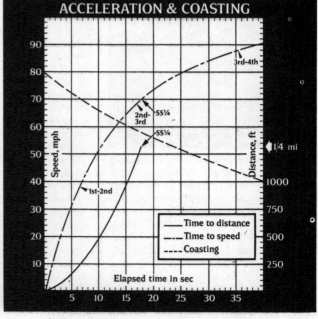

CAR and DRIVER ROAD TEST

BMW 2002

A lot of deutschemarks have gone over the exchange counter since we tagged the BMW 1600 "the world's best $2500 sedan." (February, 1967.) That was back in the days when you could buy all the deutschemarks you wanted for a quarter a piece. Now, after last fall's revaluation, you can't touch a mark for 27 cents, and the same car, well, OK, the same car with 400 more ccs and a handful of options that any "best" car should have, will set you back a solid $3500—if you insist on a radio and an automatic transmission you'll have to unroll about four grand.

As a $3500-sedan the BMW 2002 isn't looking too tall. For all of the things that you seek in a sedan—comfort, room and general convenience of operation—you could do better, for less money, with a Peugeot 504 or a Saab 99 or any number of American intermediates like an Olds Cutlass or a Chevelle. Competition is tough, both in price and in design, in the sedan business, particularly now in a time when smaller, more efficient automobiles are the only high fliers in the marketplace. Considering the delicacies available in the $3000-3500 sedan range, the BMW 2002 is hard pressed to keep its nose above water.

But there are shallower depths in which the 2002 can operate quite happily. Forget about the sedan body and pretend that it's a sports car—a transformation that's almost automatic in your mind anyway after you've driven it a mile or two. With the possible

exception of the new Datsun 240Z (which is not yet available for testing), the BMW will run the wheels off *any* of the under-$4000 sports cars without half trying. It is more powerful and it handles better.

Of course, forgetting about the BMW's sedan body is pure fantasy—the upright, block-like shape is too definite to be conjured or contemplated into something more Italianesque. It is, and always will be, a sedan with all of the attendant styling minuses and convenience pluses that that entails. But, spiritually if not stylistically, it is a sedan with a difference, a sedan that can beat the sports cars at the game they invented. That is the secret of the BMW's uniqueness, and if it continues to flourish in the market at its newly inflated price, it will be for that reason alone.

Although its price is far more jarring than its visual impact, the 2002 is a plainly honest machine, a kind of Bavarian Road Runner without the humorous overlay. It's the absolute hot setup in Germany where over-30 fat-cats bully their way through schools of VWs on the autobahnen with much flashing of lights and cold, sideways glances. Opels and Fords are driven by those who have renounced solid German technology in favor of vogueish, Detroit-inspired sheet metal, and the young man seeking to leave his mark in the well-understood games of traffic saves his money for a BMW 2002, or more likely the vitamin-enriched 2002 TI. From the outside the two seem identical, but the TI generates 22 more horsepower with the aid of a pair of 2-bbl side-draft Solexes and more compression, and its bigger brakes, stronger spindles and wider wheels strongly suggest the purpose of its existence. With the TI, maybe an orange one that sticks out of the somber greys, steel blues and whites of Teutonic traffic like one of the Weathermen at a Police Ball, you are the man to be reckoned with in anything but a top-end dash down the autobahn. And as if the TI wasn't enough, those overkill specialists down in BMW's dyno rooms have just put the finishing touches on the TII The extra "I" denotes fuel injection, with bigger exhaust valves and more compression included as frosting. When last we were in Munich the only TII engine available for testing was not in a 2002 but in the larger 2000 sedan. With 500 pounds extra weight its acceleration wasn't much better than a 2002 TI, but it would crank right past the redline in fourth gear with nonchalance. In the smaller car it will be devastating.

Meanwhile, back in the States, where exhaust emission controls are the law of the land, you have to settle for the plain vanilla 2002—no "T"s or "I"s are permitted. BMW engineers consider the TI a hopeless case when it comes to meeting the emission specs but are optimistic about the injected model —optimistic but non-committal when you ask when. Those same engineers shake their heads in mild disbelief at the thought of Americans classifying the "de-toxed" 1600 and 2002 as high performance automobiles. They feel that the necessary air pump and

35

PHOTOGRAPHY: HUMPHREY SUTTON

BMW 2002

SPIRITUALLY, IF NOT STYLISTICALLY, THE BMW 2002, EVEN WITH AN AUTOMATIC TRANSMISSION, IS A SEDAN WITH A DIFFERENCE—A *SEDAN* THAT CAN RUN THE WHEELS OFF MOST OF THE UNDER-$4000 SPORTS CARS WITHOUT HALF TRYING

restrictions in ignition timing have hobbled the 2002 almost to the level of the European 1600 and rendered the 1600 a total invalid.

The engineers, of course, have numbers to back up their pessimism about the power available in the models imported to the U.S., but the 2002 is still very definitely a performance car, simply because its capabilities are not based solely on engine output. It's an agility specialist with controls that accurately telegraph back to the driver enough about what's going on so that he can comfortably operate near the limits. Its compact dimensions, more than a foot shorter than a Maverick, allow you to squeeze through bottlenecks that no American car could even consider, and the driver's fantastic view of the world around takes the guesswork out of the squeezing operation.

The 2002 is happiest in point A to point B dashes, and the more trying the circumstances the better. The ride is not soft but admirably controlled. The car is sure-footed on rough roads and you'll find yourself upshifting, downshifting, keeping the revs up and angling through corners at speeds that will make passengers wish they had taken a bus and left the driving to anybody but you. If you are at all susceptible to fantasizing, the 2002 will have you believing that every little outing is a special stage of internation-

al rally and prestige of the entire factory rests upon your shoulders. And before you've spent very many miles behind the wheel you'll discover that you can heel-and-toe like you've been doing it all your life. Yes, heel-and-toe, that anatomically impossible operation that has resulted in flat spotted tires and graunched gears every time you've tried it, is as easy as closing a door in the 2002. Such is not the stuff sedans are made of, but then we've already established that the 2002 is not a sedan.

For this test we have a pair of 2002 non-sedans—one with the recently introduced automatic transmission and the other with a standard 4-speed manual. By testing both cars together we could see exactly what effect the automatic has on performance and on the BMW's dashing personality.

In both cases the effect is pronounced. BMW buys the automatic from ZF. It's a 3-speed device, with a torque converter and it performs with noteworthy distinction. Part-throttle upshifts are very smooth, full-throttle upshifts happen at about 6200 rpm, just before the red line, and if you stand on the gas pedal it's smart enough to downshift if it's operating in a speed range that would make that operation at all helpful. And the shift linkage, though not inspired, is simple and accurate

enough so that you are not likely to inadvertently make a wrong selection. But all of this favorable comment notwithstanding, the automatic is little more pleasant than having one foot in quicksand. It changes the 2002's nature from aggressive to passive; changes it from a sports car to a sedan, and that is where the water gets deep. The automatic probably hurts performance less than it hurts the performance "feel." Quarter-mile times were slower by 0.7 seconds with the automatic, most of which is lost at the start because there is not enough torque to spin the wheels, and the trap speed was slower by exactly 2 mph. The manual transmission 2002, even with all of its parasitic emission control devices working away, accelerates through the quarter in 17.1 seconds at 78.6 mph which makes it the top eliminator, by a slight margin, over all of the imported cars in its price class.

The BMW has about the same edge in handling. The test cars both had the optional front and rear anti-sway bars to compliment the traditional MacPherson strut front and semi-trailing arm rear suspension. Peugeot uses a similar arrangement in the 504 and it's the only other sedan, domestic or imported, in this price class that can match the BMW's handling on poorly surfaced roads. When you corner hard on smooth roads the 2002 assumes a mild understeering attitude which is subject to change without notice. With only a hint of its intentions it will hang its tail out in the kind of fat drift angle that dirt trackers live by. To the timid this probably sounds treacherous, and it would be if the BMW was intent on continuing this tail-wag into a spin, but it doesn't. In fact, after a couple of tries you discover you can stay hard on the throttle and use the steering to keep everything pointed in the right direction. That's when it all gets to be fun. The steering has enough feel to be very helpful during these maneuvers, but its slow (3.75 turns lock-to-lock) ratio means that you will be called upon for some occasional arm-winding corrections.

Only one situation can embarrass the BMW's suspension and that is spinning the rear tires. Every BMW we've ever tried, and that includes the 2800 coupe, suffers wheel hop if you lose traction during acceleration. Never mind that the text books say it can't happen—the Germans have found a way.

They've also found a way to make braking performance consistent. Both cars pulled slightly to the left under braking, locked up their front wheels first and required 277 feet (0.77G) to stop from 80 mph. Even though the stopping distances set no records the brakes do merit high marks because of the accuracy with which you can apply them. The power booster is particularly impressive because of its lightning response time which, among other advantages, allows you to pump the brakes very rapidly should a situation demand it.

Continued on page 82

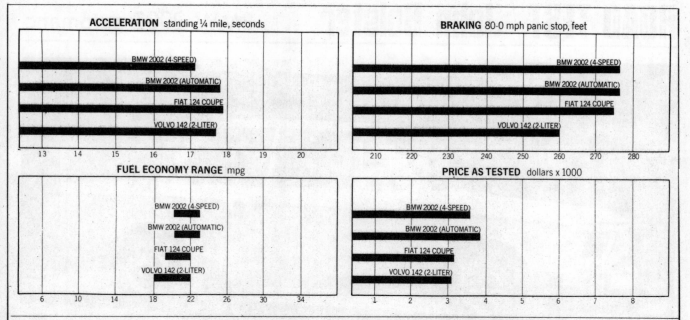

ACCELERATION standing ¼ mile, seconds

BMW 2002 (4-SPEED)	
BMW 2002 (AUTOMATIC)	
FIAT 124 COUPE	
VOLVO 142 (2-LITER)	

Scale: 13 14 15 16 17 18 19 20

BRAKING 80-0 mph panic stop, feet

BMW 2002 (4-SPEED)	
BMW 2002 (AUTOMATIC)	
FIAT 124 COUPE	
VOLVO 142 (2-LITER)	

Scale: 210 220 230 240 250 260 270 280

FUEL ECONOMY RANGE mpg

BMW 2002 (4-SPEED)	
BMW 2002 (AUTOMATIC)	
FIAT 124 COUPE	
VOLVO 142 (2-LITER)	

Scale: 6 10 14 18 22 26 30 34

PRICE AS TESTED dollars x 1000

BMW 2002 (4-SPEED)	
BMW 2002 (AUTOMATIC)	
FIAT 124 COUPE	
VOLVO 142 (2-LITER)	

Scale: 1 2 3 4 5 6 7 8

BMW 2002 4-SPEED (AND AUTOMATIC)

Importer: Hoffman Motors Corporation
375 Park Avenue
New York, N.Y.

Vehicle type: Front engine, rear-wheel-drive, 4-passenger, 2-door sedan

Price as tested: $3599.80 ($3845.80) (Manufacturer's suggested retail price, including all options listed below, Federal excise tax, dealer preparation and delivery charges, does not include state and local taxes, license or freight charges)

Options on test car: Base car, $3159.00; dealer preparation, $35.00; deluxe upholstery, $45.00; power brakes, $45.00; anti-freeze, $3.80; bumperettes, $8.00; Michelin XAS tires, $59.00; sun roof, $135.00

(2002 Automatic, $3475.00; dealer preparation, $35.00; power brakes, $45.00; deluxe upholstery, $45.00; anti-freeze, $3.80; bumperettes, $8.00; exhaust tip $2.00; reclining seats, $48.00; tachometer, $40.00; anti-sway bar, $20.00; Michelin XAS tires, $59.00; special paint, $65.00)

ENGINE
Type: 4-in-line, water-cooled, cast iron block and aluminum head, 5 main bearings
Bore x stroke . . 3.50 x 3.15 in, 89.0 x 80.0 mm
Displacement . . . . 121.4 cu in, 1990 cc
Compression ratio . . . . 8.5 to one
Carburetion . . . . 1 x 1-bbl Solex 40 PDSI
Valve gear . . chain-driven single overhead cam

Power (SAE) . . . . 113 bhp @ 5800 rpm
Torque (SAE) . . . . 115 lbs/ft @ 3000 rpm
Specific power output . . . . 0.93 bhp/cu in, 56.8 bhp/liter
Max recommended engine speed . . . 6400 rpm

DRIVE TRAIN
Transmission . . . . 4-speed, all-synchro (3-speed auto)
(Max. torque converter ratio . . . . . . 2.1 to one)
Final drive ratio . . . . 3.64 to one

			Mph/1000	
Gear	Ratio	rpm	Max test speed	
I	3.84	4.7	30 mph (6400 rpm)	
II	2.05	8.9	57 mph (6400 rpm)	
III	1.35	13.7	88 mph (6400 rpm)	
IV	1.00	18.3	111 mph (6150 rpm)	
I	2.56	7.1	46 mph (6400 rpm)	
II	1.52	12.0	77 mph (6400 rpm)	
III	1.00	18.3	107 mph (5850 rpm)	

DIMENSIONS AND CAPACITIES
Wheelbase . . . . 98.4 in
Track, F/R . . . . 52.4/52.4 in
Length . . . . 166.5 in
Width . . . . 62.6 in
Height . . . . 55.5 in
Ground clearance . . . . 6.3 in
Curb weight . . . . 2260 lbs
Weight distribution, F/R . . . 55.1/44.9%
Battery capacity . . . . 12 volts, 55 amp/hr
Alternator capacity . . . . 420 watts
Fuel capacity . . . . 12.1 gal
Oil capacity . . . . 4.3 qts
Water capacity . . . . 7.0 qts

SUSPENSION
F: Ind., Macpherson strut, coil springs, anti-sway bar
R: Ind., semi-trailing arms, coil springs, anti-sway bar

STEERING
Type . . . . Worm & roller
Turns lock-to-lock 3.75
Turning circle curb-to-curb . . . . 32.6 ft

BRAKES
F: . . . . 9.45-in disc, power assist
R: . . . . 9.05 x 1.57-in drum, power assist

WHEELS AND TIRES
Wheel size . . . . 13 x 4.5-in
Wheel type . . . . stamped steel, 4-bolt
Tire make and size . . Michelin 165 HR 13 XAS
Tire type . . . . Tube type, radial ply
Test inflation pressures, F/R . . . . . . 26/26 psi
Tire load rating . . . . . . 1010 lbs per tire @ 32 psi

PERFORMANCE
Zero to	Seconds
30 mph	2.5 (3.2)
40 mph	4.2 (4.8)
50 mph	6.5 (7.2)
60 mph	9.6 (10.3)
70 mph	13.2 (14.5)
80 mph	17.7 (20.2)

Standing ¼-mile . . . . 17.1 (17.8) sec @ 78.6 (76.6) mph
Top speed (observed) . . . . 111 (107) mph
80-0 mph . . . . 277 ft (0.77 G)
Fuel mileage . . . . . 20-23 mpg on premium fuel
Cruising range . . . . 242-278 mi

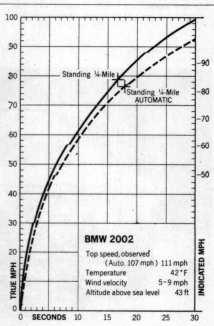

Standing ¼-Mile
Standing ¼-Mile AUTOMATIC

BMW 2002
Top speed, observed
(Auto. 107 mph) 111 mph
Temperature 42°F
Wind velocity 5-9 mph
Altitude above sea level 43 ft

TRUE MPH / SECONDS / INDICATED MPH

The conservative lines of the BMW 2002 belie its performance.

41-5-1

Automatic with a sporting character

It is perhaps not generally realised that the role of the automatic gearbox is changing. The majority of the large cars are now sold in automatic form but, to the uninitiated, the sports car is inseperable from do-it-yourself gear selection. The pioneer work of Chaparral and McLaren made it clear that, far from being confined to non-performing cars for aunties, the automatic gearbox will eventually become a valuable performance-increasing adjunct of racing cars. BMW are aware of this trend, and they are now offering the ZF automatic transmission on the cars of their range which appeal to the more sporting driver.

By the yardstick of 1970, a sports car does not have to be a stark open two-seater. The BMW 2002 consists of the engine from the

2000 series in the compact two-door body shell of the 1600. Set up for fast driving with firm suspension, the resulting car handles in a most sporting manner, the reduced weight also giving the efficient overhead-camshaft 2-litre engine a chance to show what it can really do. Perhaps the most marked characteristic of this unit is its phenomenal torque at low and medium revs, in which respect it can certainly out-perfom all of its competitors. This is just what is required with automatic transmission.

It is unfortunately true that many engines which are used with automatic gearboxes are totally unsuited to the work. Gutless, non-pulling engines, or those lacking flexibility, are a complete waste of time. The transmission has to be set to change up and down

all the time, the result being a noisy, fussy car that exploits none of the real advantages of automatic driving.

The ZF box on the BMW takes advantage of the sports-type engine. It has an instant kick-down which allows the unit to run up to peak revs, and the full-throttle up-changes give a considerable increase in performance. Let us compare a manual 2002 with the automatic model which I have just tested.

I do not change up on full throttle during road tests with a manual box, as this is a somewhat destructive manoeuvre which should be confined to Shelsey and Prescott and which no private owner would habitually employ on the road. The automatic box, on the other hand, is built to do it all the time and that is why it can beat a manual box over certain parts of the acceleration range, in spite of its slightly greater weight. I do use controlled wheelspin at standing starts, which makes the manual car a little quicker off the mark, but the automatic gains by its power-sustained change-up at just over 40 mph, so its 0 to 50 mph is only a tenth of a second longer than that of the hand-change car. At traffic lights the automatic would beat the manual 2002 unless the driver risked the noise and smoke of a wheelspin start.

By staying in third the manual driver can beat the automatic man in the 0-80 mph range, who has changed up at 75 mph, but the automatic can beat the manual over the standing quarter-mile. As for timed maximum speed, it's 108 mph for the manual 2002 and 107 mph for the automatic (when, incidentally, the speedometer cheerfully alleges 115 mph). So one can say that the very small loss of performance with the ZF box may actually amount to an appreciable gain under typical road conditions.

The slightly heavier gearbox has no effect on the handling of the car. It has a neutral characteristic under normal conditions, changing to moderate oversteer when really pressed. There is remarkably little roll, with a delightfully responsive feel to the steering, and the independent rear suspension pays dividends on bumpy corners. Compared with

The car rolls little under hard cornering, the rear suspension paying dividends on bumpy surfaces.

41-5-2

less responsive cars that understeer markedly, the BMW needs more correction in gusty winds at speeds over 100 mph.

The ride is distinctly firm at low speeds, and the car always has a taut feel about it. For fast cruising over bad roads, however, the standard of comfort is higher than would be expected. The brakes are very powerful indeed and the car does not tend to deviate during emergency stops. The hand brake is effective, and there is a parking lock on the transmission quadrant.

The engine is quiet at high cruising speeds, but it tends to be noisy when accelerated up to full revs. The gearbox has an audible whine when the car is going slowly in low gear, but it is silent thereafter. I let the car choose its own change-up speeds when recording acceleration figures, but manual changes can be made and this is useful for holding a lower gear during fast cornering. A safety device prevents bottom gear from being accidentally engaged at speeds which would entail turning the engine at destructively high revolutions, but its influence is not normally felt.

The 2002 feels very refined in normal driving, the flexible engine doing much of its work in top gear, and the machinery only becomes obtrusive when peak revs are required. There is a welcome absence of road noise, and only a little wind noise at maximum speed. It is curious that no eyeball-type fresh air vents are provided on this modern car. The interior is less austere than on previous BMWs, with attractive upholstery and trim; the seats are very comfortable and give quite reasonable lateral location for fast cornering.

Both on the road and on the circuits, the BMW 2002 is a highly respected car. With the collaboration of ZF it is one of the first medium-sized cars to have an automatic transmission that causes no appreciable loss in performance or increase in fuel consumption. I have been a die-hard upholder of manual gearboxes, with a secret leaning towards unsynchronised vintage types, but I enjoyed the automatic BMW so much that I might even be converted!

SPECIFICATION AND PERFORMANCE DATA

Car tested: BMW 2002 two-door saloon with automatic transmission. Price: £1,954 including tax.
Engine: Four cylinders, 89 mm x 80 mm, 1990 cc. Single chain driven overhead camshaft operating inclined valves in light alloy cylinder head. Compression ratio 8.5 to 1. 100 bhp net at 5500 rpm. Downdraught Solex carburetter.
Transmission: ZF automatic gearbox with torque converter, ratio 0 to 2.11 to 1, and three-speed epicyclic train, ratios 1.0, 1.52 and 2.56 to 1. Divided propeller shaft to hypoid final drive, ratio 3.64 to 1. Driveshafts with constant velocity joints to rear hubs
Chassis. Combined steel body and chassis. Independent front suspension by MacPherson struts and lower wishbones with anti-roll bar, ZF-Gemmer worm and roller steering gear. Independent rear suspension by semi-trailing arms and anti-roll bar. Coil springs and telescopic dampers all round. Twin-circuit servo-assisted disc front and drum rear brakes. Bolt-on disc wheels fitted 165-SR13 radial-ply tyres.
Equipment: 12-volt lighting and starting with alternator. Speedometer, rev counter, water temperature and fuel gauges. Cigar lighter, heating, demisting and ventilation system. Windscreen wipers and washers. Flashing direction indicators.
Dimensions: Wheelbase, 8 ft 2½ in; track, 4 ft 4 in; overall length, 13 ft 10½ in; width, 5 ft 2½ in; weight, 18 cwt 2 qrs.
Performance: Maximum speed, 107 mph; standing quarter-mile, 17.4 s. Acceleration: 0-30 mph, 3.9 s; 0-50 mph, 6.9 s; 0.60 mph, 10.4 s; 0-80, 21.4 s.
Fuel consumption: 23 to 27 mpg.

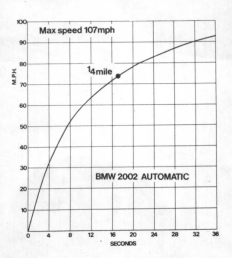

The automatic 2002's performance is scarcely inferior to that of the manual version. 41-5-3

The interior is plain and simple, but well-finished (above). The familiar single-cam 2-litre engine develops 100 bhp net (below). 41-5-4 41-5-5

2 CAR TEST

Fiat 124 Coupe

BMW 2002

SOMETIMES, a particular type of car becomes fashionable. At the moment, fashion favours the sporting four-seater. From the multitude of cars in this class, two stand out as direct competitors, of great interest (judging by letters) to many of our readers. These are the BMW 2002 and the Fiat 124 Coupé 1600. Recent price increases on both sides have still left them well within striking distance of each other—the BMW is the more expensive by £77, a difference of just over 4 per cent. They are both more expensive than the Ford Capri–Opel Manta–Sunbeam Rapier group which offers the same sort of image. The Alfa GTV, on the other hand, costs a good deal more than the Fiat or BMW and in any case doesn't give as much back seat room.

We are therefore left with the BMW, which is no more or less than the little 1600 saloon with a bigger engine and stiffer suspension; and the Fiat, based on the floorpan and suspension of the ordinary 124 saloon but with a new coupé body shell, twin-cam engine and five-speed gearbox. What separates these two from their lower-priced equivalents could be broadly described as driver appeal; engine response, steering and handling. Even more than usual, therefore, our two-car test technique of convoy driving, turn and turn about, is the most likely way of finding which is the better car.

Description—BMW 2002

Fitting a larger (but not more heavily tuned) engine into an originally smaller capacity car has nearly always made a pleasant ideal.

Several manufacturers have lately tried their hands at it, but few have succeeded as well as BMW with the 2002. It first appeared at the 1968 Geneva Show, being in effect the two-year-old 1600 two-door close-coupled four-seater with the standard 2-litre engine from the bigger, squarer-bodied BMW 2000.

The engine follows classic BMW design—a chain-driven single ohc aluminium cross-flow head topping notably over-square cylinders (89 x 80 mm, giving 1,990 c.c. capacity). With the comparatively modest 8.5-to-1 compression ratio and a downdraught Solex carburettor, it produces 100 bhp (DIN) at 5,500 rpm, with maximum torque of 116 lb. ft. at 3,000 rpm. Such an engine, put in a body of modest proportions weighing 18½ cwt at the kerb, means excellent performance and flexibility, and a potentially long stride; obviously deciding that acceleration matters more than anything else, BMW slightly under-gear the car overall at 18.5 mph per 1,000 rpm in top. The gearbox is a middling wide-ratio four-speed one.

Suspension is basically the same as the 1600's—on coil springs, with MacPherson struts in front, and semi-trailing arms at the back—with the addition of anti-roll bars at each end. The steering box hides worm and roller gear, and the servo-assisted brakes are as on the 1600, ATE-Dunlop 9½in. discs in front and 8 x 1½in. drums at the rear. Apart from the rev counter that replaces the 1600's clock, equipment is more sensible-family-car than sports-saloon. The price in Britain is £1,874.

Description—Fiat 124 Coupé 1600

At first sight, Fiat's contender in this comparison might not seem the obvious one,

of any make. The BMW's two-door body has been called a coupé, but it isn't really, whereas there can be no argument about the Fiat's title. The 124 coupé first appeared at Geneva a year before the Bavarian car, fitted then with a bigger bore 1,438 c.c. version of the 1,197 c.c. 124 saloon engine; instead of the original pushrod ohv light-alloy cylinder head, a tooth-belt-drive twin overhead camshaft head with single twin-choke Weber carburettor was provided. This engine gave 90 bhp (DIN).

Then last year Fiat put the 1,608 c.c. 80mm bore-and-stroke engine from the 125 saloon into the coupé as an option—though with some alterations, like two bigger Weber carburettors and a higher (9.9-to-1) compression ratio which put the power up to 110 bhp (DIN) at 6,400 rpm with 101 lb. ft. torque at 3,800 rpm. As those figures show, the Fiat power unit is obviously a more highly developed "sporting" engine than its 24 per cent larger rival. It has a 1cwt heavier car to propel via rather lower overall gearing (17.5 mph per 1,000 rpm in top), but a five-speed gearbox instead of only a four-speed.

Also on coil springs, the Fiat has wishbone independent front suspension and a live rear axle located by trailing arms and a Panhard rod, with anti-roll bars at each end. Steering is another worm-and-roller set-up, and the Fiat-Bendix brakes are all discs of just under 9in. dia; Bonaldi servo assistance is standard. Equipment inside the car is comprehensive, the only instrument lacking being an ammeter. The British price is £1,797.

Performance—BMW

Considering the undeniably sporting nature of the car, the BMW's engine and driveline are remarkably "soft". The single-carburettor engine develops peak power at 5,500 rpm, and peak torque at only 3,000 rpm, and with good basic breathing there is plenty of punch and response through the whole speed range from 1,000 rpm onwards. At the same time, the flatness of the power curve means that there is no sensation of being "over the top"; the engine pulls lustily all the way to the red line at 6,500 rpm. Nevertheless, it is as well to remember that the car *is* over its power peak at maximum speed, suggesting that slightly higher overall gearing might be of benefit. The gear ratios are excellently chosen, giving roughly 30, 60 and 90 mph in the three intermediate ratios. The gearchange itself feels slightly sloppy, yet allows very quick changes to be made with very little effort.

In absolute terms the BMW is fast but not electrifying, just failing to break the 10sec mark to 60 mph, despite the fact that a slight overspeed brings it to this point in second gear. It is easy to make a rapid getaway from rest, thanks to the nicely progressive clutch and accelerator linkages. It takes less than half a minute to reach 90 mph from rest, but from there on the acceleration starts to tail off a little. Even so, there is still enough response left when cruising at 100 mph to feel the car trying harder when the throttle is opened.

Perhaps the most impressive aspect of the BMW's performance is its flexibility. Top gear will not quite pull from 10 mph, but third gear returns such good figures from this speed that one only needs to take second gear when seeking the last edge of acceleration. From 20 mph onward, top gear is perfectly satisfactory for all normal driving. In other words, it is open to a BMW driver to be extremely lazy if he so wishes, to avoid changing gear very often.

Performance—Fiat

The Fiat's engine, aspirated by two large twin-choke carburettors and boasting a pretty high compression ratio, is inevitably a taut-feeling unit with a lot of sporting character. Peak power is developed right up at the red line—6,400 rpm—and peak torque is only reached at 3,800 rpm. To make the most of the rather restricted power curve, a five-speed gearbox is standard. This has very close ratios, but they are rather bunched towards the lower and middle speed ranges. First gear will not take the car to 30 mph, nor second gear to 50; third gear is just about good for 70 mph with a little overspeeding.

The mean maximum speed of 109 mph comes a little below the peak power speeds. But it must be remembered that fifth is an overdrive top, and it feels a little like tempting providence to cruise on the yellow line, as is perfectly possible at the moment. By British standards, in fact, the car is rather under-geared.

The Fiat's figure of 10.7sec to 60 mph is slightly misleading, since it includes two gearchanges, one of which is the awkward second-third change, where it is quite easy to

Considering they started with the floorpan of the 124 saloon, the Fiat stylists created something of a classic with their coupe. Because it is much lower than the BMW behind it, the Fiat looks longer. In fact, the German car is bigger all round

TWO CAR TEST...

overshoot into fifth and spoil the run. A more reliable indication of acceleration overall is the 27sec to 90 mph (with the car still in fourth gear). Following the change to the wider-spaced fifth, acceleration becomes much more leisurely.

The gearchange itself is well matched to the character of the engine: taut and precise, but slightly heavy. There is moderate spring-loading towards the third-fourth gate.

Although flexibility is not the Fiat's strong point, third gear will pull it away from 10 mph, and fourth from 20 mph; while it can just be persuaded to pull from 20 mph in fifth gear also. Most of the time, however, the benefits of changing down are sufficiently obvious to ensure that the gearbox gets used a good deal. The synchromesh is extremely strong, even on first gear—which tends to be used for little other than standing starts because it is so low.

Performance differences

The Fiat's engine, giving away nearly 400 c.c. to the BMW unit, has to work a good deal harder to achieve the same results. In consequence, it feels much the more sporting of the two. Against the stopwatch, the two cars are very evenly matched indeed—more so than almost any other pair of cars we have tested in this way. Their standing quarter-mile times are identical, and in the couple of cases where the Fiat appears to lose out, this is because of its over-close bottom-end gear ratios.

At the very top end, the Fiat has something of an edge and is able to pull steadily away from the BMW. This reflects the Fiat's slightly higher maximum speed, probably the result of superior aerodynamic form.

The Fiat is also at a slight advantage in circumstances where it happens to have exactly the right gear, for example when accelerating down a short straight between two corners on a twisty road. Overall, however, the BMW is better placed in this case with its massively spread power band. Our figures show how very much more flexible the German car is.

Handling and ride—BMW

Needing 3.7 turns across lock-to-lock with a compact mean turning circle diameter of 31ft 5in., the steering of the BMW is of about average gearing by modern saloon car standards. It is accordingly fairly light. The quite large steering wheel (15½in.) amplifies play in the worm-and-roller steering gear to an effective 1½in. at the rim; this seems too much if tried when standing still, but in fact is not often noticed when driving. The car responds positively and accurately to whatever you do with the wheel. There seems to be a minimum of damping in the steering itself, so that feel is excellent, though with little kickback. Straight-running stability is fairly good, although one is conscious of having to steer along motorways.

Hurry the BMW through open bends and you find it generally delightful. It doesn't roll too much, and seems pretty well balanced, having no excessive understeer like so many bigger-engined small-ish cars. Play with the accelerator in appropriate places and the tail can be broken away very controllably; on

slippery surfaces the inside back wheel will spin fairly easily, but generally it is both that slide. Roadholding on the German-made Dunlop SP 57 radials, however, is good in all conditions.

As well as roll (not much, as already said) one other sort of attitude must be mentioned when talking about the 2002, and that is the degree of squat exhibited under hard acceleration. It is very much part of the likeable character of the car, fairly noticeable, but not at all objectionable. Ride is quite good. The car feels sure of its feet on a bumpy, joggly English country road without riding harshly; it is well damped and there is little feeling of float at any time. (It is the seating that disappoints here; one is not held much by the too-flat surfaces of the seats, seeming to bob about somewhat relative to the car's motion).

Handling and ride—Fiat

It is often a surprise to an experienced driver to learn that the Fiat has worm-and-roller steering. This is because it has the slightly damped movement and excellent precision and response of a good rack-and-pinion arrangement without any noticeably large amount of the slop found in other steering gear systems involving more than the two links of a rack set-up. There is plenty of feel, and a certain amount of kickback on uneven roads. At three turns of the 15in. steering wheel for a somewhat bulky 35ft 9in. turning circle, it is quite high-geared, a bit heavy when parking, and immediately responsive. Straight running is excellent, except to a small degree on bumpy roads when the car wanders very slightly.

Along winding roads, the Fiat is another car that seems to revel in being driven fast. It does however understeer a lot, more so than its predecessor; there is sometimes a tendency towards spinning the inside rear wheel on accelerating hard out of a slippery corner entered slowly. Rear-end breakaway is not often encountered except in slippery conditions, and then only with the car in the right gear for full power to be applied. Roll is more noticeable than it was before, though still is not at all excessive.

Likewise, ride is softer than before, perhaps at the expense of handling. While there is a suggestion of float over poor going, bumps do come through quite firmly at times.

Handling and ride differences

The BMW's steering is lower-geared, lighter, better-insulated against road-shocks, tighter locked and so in spite of being 4½in. longer the car is the more manoeuvrable. But though certainly good enough, the steering is not as accurate as the Fiat's and not quite so responsive. The 2002 is definitely more tail-happy than the 124, which understeers a lot more and rolls a bit more. Although the BMW's steering feels delightfully free of friction where the Fiat's feels damped in comparison, feel in both is good. But the Fiat's seats, mentioned here for the contribution they make towards handling and ride, are very much better, locating the driver properly. The Fiat apparently runs straighter and is possibly more stable in a side wind. In ride the BMW is slightly softer but better damped and seems to keep better contact with the road.

Fuel consumption

As one might expect, the BMW with its much smaller carburettor area turns out to be the more economical car—although the difference is not unduly great. Since both cars are rather under-geared, one might speculate on how much better they might be with higher overall gearing. As it is, there is undoubtedly more scope for driving the BMW for economy if its owner so wishes—the Fiat is over-choked for

Top to bottom: The Fiat has a sloping back window and a chopped-off tail; the BMW has a much more upright build and more rounded lines at the back. The BMW's bonnet rises sills and all, giving good access; accessibility to most components under the Fiat's bonnet is also good. Both bonnets are front-hinged, for extra safety.

The chunky BMW's styling is based on a very prominent waistline which continues all round the car. The 2002 has a matt-black grille to distinguish it from the smaller-engined 1600. Glass area is exceptionally generous, but visibility in the rain is spoiled for British drivers by the left-handed wiper pattern. The BMW has single headlamps of conventional continental pattern rather than the four tungsten-halogen units fitted to the Fiat

that sort of thing and mildly objects to being trickled along in a high gear for very long. One point worth bearing in mind is that neither car has a very large tank—even the BMW is pushed to make 250 miles between fillings, and the Fiat needs refuelling sufficiently often to be irksome on a really fast run. Neither car uses any oil to speak of.

Brakes

To any driver who is not going to use either car to anywhere near three-quarters of its capability, the brakes of each will seem excellent. Both require very low effort for ordinary stops, (the Fiat especially so) or even for one middling high-speed panic-stop. The Fiat starts to stop almost immediately you begin to press the pedal, and its working movement seems unusually long. If anything, the pads seem almost too willing to work at first, and one soon learns that they are pretty soft (that is, giving lessening retardation as they are heated). On this test Fiat there was a suggestion of an irregularity in a disc as one slowed gently, retardation varying rhythmically.

But attempt to drive either car fast along a give-and-take road involving straights and frequent corners and you encounter serious fade. The Fiat is slightly the worse of the two, in that the necessary increase in brake pedal pressure is the more suddenly experienced. Admittedly both recover quite quickly after fading, but the sort of vastly enjoyable rapid descent (and even ascent) of an Alpine pass which both cars are so ideally meant for would have to be markedly restrained. A surprising state of affairs in either case, the more so with the Fiat, which is built within sight of the Alps.

Noise

The Fiat is overall the noisier of the two, understandably perhaps in view of its more heavily tuned engine, for that is the main source of noise here. But to anyone who likes sporting character this will not matter; the Fiat's intake noise when working hard is not at all unpleasant. In a lengthy traffic jam one is a little conscious of the electric fan switching in and, on the test car, of some gearbox noise in neutral. Whine on drive or overrun is audible but not serious. There is a little more bump-thump on the Fiat, but it isn't bad either, nor is wind-noise.

The BMW engine is more subdued at all times, making a pleasant busy hum when working, and a very slight high-frequency vibration felt in the gearlever from around 5,500 rpm onwards. Bump-thump is quite quiet too; it is the quite loudly buffeting wind noise around the driver's and front passenger's windows that is most noticeable at the car's happy 100 mph cruise.

Fittings and furniture

The BMW and Fiat employ entirely different approaches to interior design. In the Fiat, the interior matches the sporting appeal of the body, with a comprehensive set of instruments and a massive central console. The BMW on the other hand, retains the simple interior of the 1600 saloon from which it was derived.

There are major differences in the driving positions. The relatively tall BMW accommodates a wide range of drivers in comfort. The front seats are quite high, which helps to make the visibility extremely good. Now that BMW have re-worked the pendant pedals in their right-hand drive cars, they are much easier to use. The BMW steering wheel, quite deeply dished, has a rather large-diameter rim with a plain plastic finish.

In the Fiat, the lower-set driving position which is a result of the lower build of the car (it stands nearly four inches lower than the BMW) means that even though fore-and-aft seat movement is quite generous, it is only the

TWO CAR TEST . . .

smaller drivers who can make themselves really comfortable. Taller drivers are also handicapped by the poor wheel-to-pedals relationship, which puts the wheel at full stretch with the pedals still too close. On the credit side, the pedals are well spaced and there is a proper rest for the left foot clear of the clutch. The steering wheel is smaller than that in the BMW and in keeping with the overall character of the car it has a wood-finish rim and matt-black, perforated spokes.

The front seats themselves follow the general trend. In the BMW they are pretty ample devices with a modicum of shaping, with fully reclining backrests. In the course of a long drive they stay pretty comfortable, but they hardly provide enough sideways support during enthusiastic cornering. The Fiat seats are smaller and very positively shaped indeed, especially the cushion. In this way they provide excellent support in all directions, but feel tight for drivers of ample width.

The BMW's back seat is a remarkably plain bench, quite high-set and well angled but,

unexpectedly, lacking a centre armrest. There is noticeably less headroom in the back than there is in the front, where it is better than average. The Fiat's back seat also lacks a centre armrest, but this matters less because the seats themselves are sculptured into two individual places. They are low-set but well angled, with sufficient space for small passengers to make themselves comfortable. They, like those in front, have a very good view; in fact, both cars are notable for their generous area of glass.

Both cars place a speedometer and rev counter in front of the driver, but while the BMW otherwise has only a single combination dial with fuel contents, water temperature and warning lights, the Fiat has four separate dials placed towards the centre of the car. The Italian car has a profusion of controls, while the BMW manages with just four knobs and two column-mounted stalks. While the BMW has two-speed wipers, the Fiat has a single continuous speed with a rheostat variation, plus its very useful intermittent-wipe facility. Both cars have their washers electrically operated; the BMW still has its wipers set up for left hand drive. Where headlamps are concerned, the Fiat with its four-lamp tungsten-halogen system is much the better equipped, although the single units on the BMW are surprisingly good.

Both cars have water-valve heaters, with the BMW system being the easier to control. The Fiat (whose heater controls are on the centre console, aft of the handbrake) tends to produce either hot or cold air, but not warm. The Fiat has much the better ventilation system, with two butterfly-type inlets at the ends of the facia and two others in the centre console. Its air extraction is not very good, however, unless one or both rear windows are opened.

The BMW has a tremendous advantage in boot space, offering more length and, very important, quite a lot more height in its luggage compartment. It also has a very large, wide-opening boot lid, in contrast with the Fiat's restricted boot opening. Both cars have a fairly high sill over which luggage must be lifted, and both bury the spare wheel and tool kit (quite a good kit in both cases, incidentally) beneath the boot floor.

BMW: The front seats are large but not very positively shaped, but there is lots of room for a large driver; the back seat is a plain bench with no dividing armrest but with recessed elbow niches at each side; the boot opening rises complete with the tops of the rear wings. Luggage space is large for the size of car but loading must be done over a high sill

BMW 2002
Price £1,874
(total including purchase tax)

	Maximum speeds	
rpm	mph	
5,800	107	Top
6,500	89	3rd
6,500	59	2nd
6,500	31	1st

	Acceleration	
Ind. mph	sec	mph
33	3:2	0-30
44	5.1	0-40
54	7.3	0-50
64	10.1	0-60
75	14.5	0-70
85	19.5	0-80
96	27.6	0-90
107	43.2	0-100

17.8sec 77mph Standing ¼-mile

Top (3.64)	3rd (4.89)	mph
—	4.1	10-30
7.7	4.3	20-40
7.5	5.0	30-50
8.2	5.5	40-60
9.2	5.9	50-70
10.2	7.0	60-80
12.7	—	70-90
21.2	—	80-100

25.5	Overall mpg
28	Typical mpg
Negligible	Oil consumption

SPECIFICATION
FRONT ENGINE, REAR DRIVE
ENGINE

Cylinders	4, in line
Main bearings	5
Cooling system	Water; pump, fan and thermostat
Bore	89.0mm (3.50in.)
Stroke	80.0mm (3.15in.)
Displacement	1,990 c.c. (121.4 cu. in.)
Valve gear	Single overhead camshaft and rockers
Compression ratio	8.5-to-1. Min. octane rating: 97RM
Carburettor	Solex 40 PDSI
Fuel pump	Solex mechanical
Oil filter	Full flow, renewable element
Max. power	100 bhp (DIN) at 5,500 rpm
Max. torque	116 lb. ft. (DIN) at 3,000 rpm

TRANSMISSION

Clutch	Fichtel and Sachs diaphragm spring, 7.9 in. dia.
Gearbox	Four-speed, all-synchromesh
Gear ratios	Top 1.0; Third 1.34; Second 2.05; First 3.83; Reverse 4.18
Final drive	Hypoid bevel, 3.64-to-1

SUSPENSION

Front	Independent; MacPherson struts, lower wishbones, coil springs, telescopic dampers, anti-roll bar
Rear	Independent; semi-trailing arms, coil springs, telescopic dampers, anti-roll bar

STEERING

Type	ZF-Gemmer worm and roller
Wheel dia.	15.5in.

BRAKES

Make and type	ATE disc front, drum rear
Servo	ATE vacuum
Dimensions	F. 9.5in.; R. 9.0in. dia. 1.57in. wide shoes
Swept area	Total 299 sq. in. (260 sq. in./ton laden)

WHEELS

Type	Pressed steel 4.5in. rim, 4-stud fixing
Tyres—make	Dunlop
—type	SP57 radial-ply tubeless
—size	165-13in.

Fiat 124 Coupé 1600
Price £1,797
(total including purchase tax)

Maximum speeds

	mph	rpm
Top	109	6,200
4th	93	6,400
3rd	68	6,400
2nd	44	6,400
1st	26	6,400

Acceleration

mph	sec	Ind. mph
0-30	3.5	31
0-40	5.3	41
0-50	7.4	51
0-60	10.7	61
0-70	14.4	72
0-80	19.4	82
0-90	27.0	93
0-100	43.1	105

Standing ¼-mile 78mph 17.8sec

mph	3rd (5.85)	4th (4.30)	Top (3.79)
10-30	8.4	—	—
20-40	6.3	10.1	13.6
30-50	5.7	8.9	12.1
40-60	6.2	9.0	11.4
50-70	6.8	9.4	12.3
60-80	—	10.0	14.6
70-90	—	10.6	19.3
80-100	—	—	29.1

Overall mpg	23.6
Typical mpg	26
Oil consumption	negligible

SPECIFICATION
FRONT ENGINE, REAR DRIVE
ENGINE
Cylinders	4, in line
Main bearings	5
Cooling system	Water; pump, electric fan and thermostat
Bore	80.0mm (3.15in.)
Stroke	80.0mm (3.15in.)
Displacement	1,608 c.c. (97.5 cu. in.)
Valve gear	Twin overhead camshafts, direct-acting
Compression ratio	9.9-to-1. Min. octane rating: 98RM
Carburettors	2 Weber 40DIF 10/11
Fuel pump	Fispa mechanical
Oil filter	Fram full flow
Max. power	110 bhp (net) at 6,400 rpm
Max. torque	101 lb. ft. (net) at 3,800 rpm

TRANSMISSION
Clutch	Diaphragm-spring, 7.87 in. dia.
Gearbox	Five-speed, all-synchromesh
Gear ratios	Top 0.83; Fourth 1.0; Third 1.36; Second 2.10; First 3.67; Reverse 3.53
Final drive	Hypoid bevel, 4.3-to-1

SUSPENSION
Front	Independent; double wishbones, coil springs, telescopic dampers, anti-roll bar
Rear	Live axle, trailing arms, Panhard rod, coil springs, telescopic dampers, anti-roll bar

STEERING
Type	Worm and roller
Wheel dia.	15.0in.

BRAKES
Make and type	Fiat-Bendix disc front and rear
Servo	Bonaldi vacuum
Dimensions	F. 8.95in. dia.; R. 8.95in. dia.
Swept area	Total 270 sq. in. (227 sq. in./ton laden)

WHEELS
Type	Pressed steel, 5.0in. rim, 4-stud fixing
Tyres—make	Pirelli
—type	Cinturato CN53 radial-ply tubeless
—size	165-13in.

Personal choice

I can't recall any pair of cars which caused more agony and heart-searching than these two when it came to choosing the better. Our performance figures show them to be incredibly well matched against the stopwatch; the similarity extends to most other aspects of driving as well.

To start with the BMW I find it fits me very well, and I have a great deal of admiration for its tremendous flexibility, its supple ride and its relative quietness, although this is less so when full throttle is used. Its very large boot is also a plus point.

The Fiat offers me a far less comfortable driving position, so it starts off with a deficit. But I can't deny that it has better steering and probably better handling, too, although one eventually comes to terms with the BMW's slight sloppiness and realizes that one is talking of very small margins. The difference is, I think, that the average driver would be able to step into the Fiat and drive it fast straight away, while he would have to spend a bit of time getting used to the BMW.

I admire Fiat's doing the decent thing and providing a five-speed gearbox to go with their rather peaky engine, but I think the ratios are too squashed down towards the bottom end. The BMW's four much wider ratios work very well in practice.

In neither car am I altogether happy with the brakes. Both might give you a few worrying moments at the end of a fast downhill drive, with the Fiat worrying me more because when its brakes fade, they fade more suddenly.

In general, the Fiat has much more of that taut feel which a truly sporting car should have. This is true of the engine, the gearchange, and the steering. At the same time, it is an eminently practical car with a number of clever or helpful features. The fact that it has been given headlamps to match its performance is just one instance.

Even so, on balance, I will take the BMW. Perhaps I admire the two-facedness of the German car. It is easier to drive smoothly and quite fast, yet it takes *more* skill if it is to be driven right up to the limit. In this way, it suits both my driving moods: the relaxed (which is most of the time) and the keen. It is not as pretty a car, but then I can't see the car once I am inside it, so I don't really care.

The thing which really tips the balance for me is the driving position. It is a measure of how closely these two cars are matched that, were I *under* five feet ten (especially four inches under, instead of over as is actually the case), I would plump for the Fiat. I feel sorry for you, seventy-inchers; for you, the choice is one which you are bound to regret—half the time!

Jeffrey Daniels

Personal Opinion

With the strong rider that I'd require distinctly near-adequate braking equipment on both cars, this is a nearly impossible choice. I prefer the Fiat's looks—but the BMW is just as pretty. I prefer the Fiat's gearchange—but the BMW's, once you've bought a decent gearlever knob, is just as delightful. I thoroughly enjoy the very Italian and sporting character of the Fiat's engine—and I revel in the BMW's great spread of good torque. I prefer the Fiat's steering and its straight stability—and I prefer the BMW's handling and its relative lack of understeer. The Fiat makes a pleasant noise, but the BMW's eager yet quieter hum is just as appealing. (Here one must stop to apologise about all these I's: any opinion, for what it is worth, is personal; these two cars arouse strong personal feelings.)

As my colleague Jeffrey Daniels says, one could probably adapt the driving position of the Italian Standard Apeman's Fiat to suit the not-necessarily-so-standard Lesser Armed Longshanked British Ape, with the aid of dished steering wheels and some attention to the seat runners. Even so, I think my frequently lazy nature and stolid British faint distrust of high Italian revolutions over a long period of office would settle for the torquey 2002; not that there is much stolid about that little motor car. But instead of another steering wheel and longer seat runners, I'd have to buy another seat, an oil pressure gauge and an ammeter; assuming that they'd already done something about the brakes.

Michael Scarlett

Fiat: The boot is relatively small and shallow, with a restricted opening and a high sill. The back seats are formed into two individual spaces: there is little width for three in any case; there is no centre armrest but there are rests at the sides. The front seats are very deeply shaped, but their relationship with wheel and pedals is not right for tall drivers

BMW 2002

The 2002 rates at the top of its class in handling capabilities and as its racing record proves, it may be considered a true sports car.

Better choose a color you can live with because you'll want to keep this one a long time!

"The engineers who develop BMW cars are enthusiasts too." This simple statement in the front of the owners manual certainly sets the tone for what follows in the most comprehensive 90-page booklet we've ever seen. It is further amplified after the briefest acquaintance with any BMW automobile.

The *Bayerische Motoren Werke* is as old as the automobile engine itself and is a company that excels in the production of blue-blooded automobiles. Their 2800 series cars are among the most sought-after forms of personal transportation in Europe. Each one offers its owner a satisfying means of covering all sorts of terrain at very high speeds, and with great safety and comfort. Needless to say, they are not cheap automobiles, but worth every penny of their $7,000 plus price tag. Fortunately, BMW also build smaller cars with most of the features of their larger brethren at a price you can take.

The BMW 2002 is not a large car by any standards, but with its 166.5-inch overall length, it still offers ample room for four full-size adults in excellent comfort with enough rear seat space to squeeze

in an extra body if need be. With the ever increasing demand for maximum utilization of road space, BMW are certainly doing their share by producing small cars with roomy interiors—effectively putting a "quart into a pint pot." The 2002 is a spacious family sedan with the performance and handling of a fast touring-type machine.

This model is only available in two-door form, but the large door makes entry simple for the average person. Both seats tilt forward for entry to the rear and the seat backs are released by the small lever located near the top of the seat. No stooping or fumbling for the release near the floor is needed, as on most two doors.

Once seated, the most impressive and immediate feeling one has is the excellent visibility. The roof pillars must be the slimmest we've seen in a long time though they are evidently extremely strong, forming as they do an integral part of the roll-cage passenger compartment. At eye level, there must be at least 95% glass. The instrument binnacle is both simple and functional. In the center is the speedometer with trip odometer. To the right

is a tachometer (a mandatory option on all 2002s), and this is matched to the left with a dial incorporating the fuel and temperature gauges plus the four warning lights for oil pressure, alternator charging, hi-lo beam and turn and flasher signal indicators.

Two knobs at each end of the binnacle are for lights and heater blower on the left and cigarette lighter and wipers on the right. The instrument lights are rheostatically controlled from the light switch for a wide range of intensity to satisfy most night driving needs.

Below the binnacle and on either side of the steering column are the heater and fresh air controls. These can be operated by touch and the system will produce enough air to suit polar bears. Air-conditioning, incidentally, is not a factory option. Defrosting, demisting and the doughty heater are all within easy reach. At the extreme ends of the dashboard are two small ducts that blow air directly on the side windows for demisting purposes.

Two stalks control a multitude of services. The left-hand one operates the hi-lo beam control and the headlight flasher. The right one is the turn signal plus windshield washer and a few sweeps of the blades when pulled toward the driver. A little practice is required in avoiding this

Though BMW's general styling theme is nearly a decade old, the lines remain contemporary because they are functional. Despite flow-through ventilation, vent panes are retained.

Instrumentation lacks gauges for oil pressure and alternator, but the 2002 is one of the few cars where all controls are centered in front of the driver.

control as the first turn one makes with the car can prove mildly traumatic if the wipers and washers start smearing the windshield at the same time.

Another function of the turn signal switch is redundant in this country. In Euope it's a requirement for the off-side parking lights to be lit when a vehicle is parked at night in the street. The U.S. 2002 retains this feature which only operates when the ignition key is removed and the lever is left in either left or right position.

A horn button in each spoke of the leather covered steering wheel completes *all* the controls and instrumentation. It's been quite a while since we've tested a car that puts *everything* in front of the driver, made it easy to see, and arranged it so you can operate all the controls without having to unfasten the safety harness. All driving controls are operated without the hands having to let go of the steering wheel. The feet are for clutch, brake and accelerator only, with no stabbing around to find a floor dip-switch.

A large open tray extends to the right of the instrument binnacle allowing plenty of room for storage of small items. To ensure that nothing slides around, there are small retaining ridges that prevent loose items from piling up in a heap during hard cornering. BMW 2002 power comes from a hot little four cylinder in-line overhead camshaft engine with Hemi-head combustion chambers, a 1,990cc (121.4 cu. in.) cast iron block and an alloy head. Its power output is a healthy 113 hp at 5,800 rpm. The tachometer is red-lined at 6,000 rpm with a safe maximum of 6,200 rpm. The engine is so well balanced that the power comes on with much the smoothness of a rotary or a turbine. Take it easy in 1st as the needle gets round that dial awfully fast. Maximum torque is at 3,000 rpm (115.7 lbs.-ft.) but the curve is practically flat for a good thousand or so rpms on either side of the peak point. The torque drops off towards the 5,500 rpm mark and best shifting for fast times was usually between 5,000 and 5,500 rpm.

The compression ratio is a mild 8.5 to one but this still requires the use of premium gas to satisfy emission modifications. The engine gave a solid 23.4 mpg average under very hard driving during the test and cruising at freeway speeds brought 25 mpg. The car is so much fun to drive up through the gears that most owners will probably go for their jollies by using engine and gears rather than be miserly with the throttle. This car is bought for driving. With that in mind, it is a relatively simple matter to have the engine tweaked to produce a potent ma-

provides the 2002 with very good adhesion and handling. Front suspension is by MacPherson strut with lower wishbones, the spring columns incorporating double-acting hydraulic shock absorbers, coil springs and auxiliary rubber springs. Wheel travel is a healthy seven inches, which is ideal on rough roads. Rear suspension is by trailing arms located by a delta-shaped box section support beam which also locates the final drive assembly. Anti-sway bars front and rear complete the package.

Steering is ZF worm and roller with a ratio of 17.58 to one. Add a set of Michelin XAS radials and the whole becomes a handling machine that will not have many equals on any road and fewer peers, at any price. From the radial tires to the leather-covered steering wheel, an empathetic driver can be completely aware of the car's behaviour at all times. Hard driving inspires confidence and it is exceptionally difficult to get completely out

BMW 1600 and 2002 (pictured) are outwardly identical but the latter is available only as a two-door sedan. Unusual visibility is one of BMW's many plus features.

chine for rallying. The 2002 engine can be stretched to over 200 horsepower for racing purposes with very little work being required on the bottom end.

The overhead cam is Duplex roller chain driven with the usual tensioner and backlash controls. The valves are inclined at a narrow vee angle and with the cross-flow head, there is excellent swirl action in the combustion chambers. Fuel supply is maintained by an engine driven pump at 0.3 psi and the oil pump is chain-driven off the bottom of the crankshaft. A full flow oil filter is standard.

The whole engine is tilted over 30 degrees to the vertical over the front axle assembly and is mounted close to its center of gravity. Two side mounted rubber cushions on the block attach it directly to the front axle cross-member. The rear of the engine bolts directly to the gearbox.

Power is transmitted to the gear box by a hydraulically operated single dry-plate diaphragm-spring clutch, complete with an automatic wear compensator. The four-speed transmission has Porsche synchromesh on all gears and is one of the smoothest units on the road. Speed shifting is a joy because it is impossible to beat the synchromesh.

The ratios in the box are ideally matched with the engine torque. First gear has a 3.835:1, second is 2.053:1, third 1.345:1 and fourth, 1.0:1. Second will turn 60 mph and third will bring up 80 mph on the dial. Varying the shift points slightly in first and second and taking off below 2,500 rpm could produce slight

Anti-roll bars front and rear are a mandatory $40 option on 2002s equipped with a 4-speed transmission. These and the tach ($40 also) can be skipped when an automatic is specified.

variances in the times either way so the above figures should be taken as being on the conservative side. Very possibly, one driver could pick up a second on another in the same car.

Passing with the BMW 2002 is a safe operation, even if only fourth gear is used. Gearing down to third at 50 mph and stepping on it will bring up 70 mph in just under 10 seconds.

That the BMW 2002 is well endowed with power and a great transmission is only part of the picture. The engineers have certainly excelled themselves in the roadholding department. Total performance is a complete entity. You don't add bits at a time. You have to design the whole car from the wheels up, especially if it is to be assessed as a package.

Four-wheel independent suspension

of shape in this car. We never came close.

Having given the owner a going machine, BMW have wisely added a compatible set of anchors to bring it smoothly to a stop in a hurry, and without wobbling all over the highway. The 9.45-inch diameter discs up front provide most of the stopping power and are backed up with 9-inch drums on the rear. The dual-circuit safety system has been standard on BMWs long before the Federal requirements became mandatory. With a weight division of 1,250 lbs. front to 970 lbs. rear, there is a slight tendency to nose down under heavy braking, but the rear end always stayed firmly on the ground, which is good indication of the suspension working well.

While we have stressed the performance of the 2002, remember that this is also a family sedan. For mundane transportation needs, there is a large 15.5-cu.-ft. trunk that will haul a month's worth of groceries. The spare wheel is stowed under the flat floor of the trunk on the left, the right side being the gas tank area. The tool kit is rather spartan compared with the exotic

1. MacPherson strut tower
2. Overhead cam
3. Solex 40 PDSI carburetion
4. Brake fluid reservoir
5. Well-ventilated battery
6. 500-watt alternator
7. Forward opening hood
8. Emission control

BMW 2002 2-DOOR SEDAN

PERFORMANCE AND MAINTENANCE

Acceleration: Gears:
  0-30 mph . . . . .3.0 secs.— I
  0-45 mph . . . . .6.0 secs.— I, II
  0-60 mph . . . . .9.6 secs.— I, II
  0-75 mph . . . . .13.9 secs.—I, II, III
  0-1/4 mile . . . . .16.9 secs. @ 83 mph

Ideal cruise . . . . .70-80 mph
Top speed (est) . . . . .108 mph
Stop from 60 mph . . . . .142 ft.
Average economy (city) . . . . .22.9 mpg
Average economy (country) . . . . .25.0 mpg
Fuel required . . . . .Premium
Oil change (mos./miles) . . . .—/6000
Lubrication (mos./miles) . . . .—/6000
Warranty (mos./miles) 12/12,000
Type tools required . . . . .Metric
U.S. dealers . . . . .225 total

SPECIFICATIONS AS TESTED

Engine . . . . .121.3 cu. in., OHC 4
Bore & stroke . . . . .3.50 x 3.15 ins.
Compression ratio . . . . .8.5 to one
Horsepower . . . . . 113 (SAE gross) @ 5800 rpms
Torque . . . . .115.7 lbs.-ft. @ 3000 rpms
Transmission . . . . .4-speed, manual
Steering . . . . .3.5 turns, lock to lock
                          34.2 ft., curb to curb
*Brakes . . . . .Disc front, drum rear
Suspension . . . . .Coil front, coil rear
Tires . . . . .165 SR x 13, tube-type radial
Dimensions (ins.):
  Wheelbase . . . . .98.5   Front track 52.5
  Length . . . . . . .166.5   Rear track 52.5
  Width . . . . .62.5   Ground clearance 6.3
  Height . . . . .55.5   Weight . . . .2080 lbs.
Capacities: Fuel . . .12.2 gals.   Oil . . .4.25 qts.
  Coolant . . . . .7.3 qts.   Trunk . . .15.5 cu. in.

*Power assisted as tested

RATING

	Excellent (91-100)	Good (81-90)	Fair (71-80)	Poor (60-70)
Brakes	95			
Comfort		89		
Cornering		90		
Details	91			
Finish	93			
Instruments		88		
Luggage		89		
Performance	91			
Quietness		85		
Ride		90		
Room	91			
Steering	95			
Visibility	98			
Overall	91			

BASE PRICE OF CAR

(Excludes state and local taxes, license, dealer preparation and domestic transportation): $3346 at West Coast P.O.E.

Plus desirable options:
$ 160 AM/FM radio
$ 48 Reclining bucket seats
$ 40 Tachometer (replaces clock)
$ 59 Michelin XA5 radial tires
$ 45 Tinted glass
$ 45 Vinyl upholstery
$3753 TOTAL
$1.48 per lb. (base price).

ANTICIPATED DEPRECIATION

(Based on current Kelley Blue Book, previous equivalent model: $201 1st yr. + $252 2nd yr.

Braking by servo-assisted front discs is always controllable. Two types of optional radials are offered, tube-type at $40 and Michelin XAS for $19 more.

Rear window and windshield are almost identical in size and despite the thin pillars, the body structure may be accurately described as containing an integral roll cage.

one in the BMW 2800, but is quite satisfactory for roadside work.

Flow through ventilation is standard and the rear windows open outwards to assist the system. Good nylon carpeting and high-grade vinyl upholstery (optional extra) look like they will stand the hard wear-and-tear of family life.

The 2002 meets all Federal safety and smog requirements and exceeds quite a few. The front and rear body sections are of the crushable variety, and the passenger compartment follows standard European practice in cars of this type by having a rigid-type cage construction. Minimum crash shock is transmitted into the passenger area. Properly strapped in, the odds are against severe injury in city-speed crashes. The door locks have extra safety locks to prevent them opening under impact, helping reduce the risk of ejection for passengers who may not have fastened their seat belts.

We returned the 2002 to its makers reluctantly. It is difficult to find much fault with this car. It's a sports sedan by any interpretation. Criticism degenerates to nit-picking, such as asking for a slightly larger outside mirror. The car abounds with lots of small technical features which are practical and not there purely for gadgetry's sake. Such an item is the inability to depress the inside door locking button down with the door open, making it impossible to lock the keys in the car.

We could find little fault with the quality of the paint, trim or general workmanship. It's rare to find this standard on cars nowadays, and particularly in this price bracket.

Although the car tested ran out at $3,737.00, it still represents excellent value for the money. AM/FM radio is not a must but as this has got to be one of the quieter running cars on the road, one might as well indulge a little and enjoy the benefits of the better radio.

The dealer network is expanding and at the present time, there are 225 nationwide. However, with the overall reliability of the automobile, a long trip should not be cause for concern. The owners manual is so complete that any mechanic worthy of the name should be able to perform quite complicated repairs if required. In fact, the manual is without doubt the best we have ever seen for any automobile and we would highly recommend it as mandatory reading for student drivers because it is so well stocked with excellent driving tips.

If you are contemplating the purchase of a BMW 2002, we would suggest you choose a color you can live with because you'll want to keep this one a long, long time!.

Ken Wright

The 2002 Tii (above) retains the small shell of the 1600 coupé but has Kügelfischer petrol injection for its 2-litre engine (below). Power output installed is 130 bhp.

2002 gets fuel-injection

It is well known that the BMW 2002 consists of a 2-litre ohc engine in the compact 1600 bodyshell. With its small size and light weight, it is a very popular model of more than lively performance. In standard, single carburetter form, it satisfies the requirements of the majority of buyers.

There is, however, a definite demand for a hot 2-litre, and lucky continental motorists have been able to buy a multi-carburetter version of the 2002. In England, unfortunately, we have had to go without for a very simple reason—the right-hand steering goes just where the carburetters should be; an insuperable obstacle. Insuperable, that is, with carburetters, but now an even hotter 2-litre BMW engine has been developed from the competition type, and there are no installation problems because the new unit has fuel-injection.

The well-tried Kügelfischer system is employed and there is no doubt that the engine can easily stand the increased stresses,

as it sustains incredible outputs when turbo-charged for racing. It retains the single overhead-camshaft with rockers and inclined valves that are now found on all BMW engines. The gearbox has been developed with a new type of synchromesh to give faster and smoother changes.

In view of the higher performance potential of this model, the bodyshell has been reinforced to give greater rigidity. This has permitted suspension modifications for increased cornering power, including the use of wider wheels and tyres plus more powerful dampers. Larger brakes have also been adopted.

The result of all this is an 18 cwt car with an overall length of 13 ft 10.5 in and a width of 5 ft 2.6 in, propelled by an engine with a gross output of 147 bhp that develops 130 bhp as installed. It must be emphasised, however, that this 2002 remains a tractable touring car with a four-seater body, though it is sporting rather than luxurious—BMW

luxury cars have six cylinders.

Very sensibly, the makers eschew boy-racer decoration and the car has that unobtrusive appearance which pays dividends when one is in a hurry on police-infested roads. The interior is plain but functional and the driving position is first class, with a good view all round. Everything about the car seems substantial, and there is no sign that any weight saving has been attempted.

The car was placed at my disposal in France during a heatwave and though I was able to cover a useful mileage on typical *Routes Nationales*, there were no *Autoroutes* handy for sustained maximum speed tests when I was driving this particular car.

The makers claim 120 mph, which may well be possible on a long enough straight, but what is much more useful is the rapid acceleration up to 110 mph, a speed that comes up in a remarkably short distance. The car is high-geared and will cruise easily at 100 mph on a very small throttle opening.

The clutch and gearchange handle well and permit the full potential of the engine to be exploited, third gear in particular being ideal for overtaking on French roads. The fuel-injection engine has plenty of torque and there is no necessity to use the lower gears a great deal. The unit is flexible throughout its range and idles evenly, only a scarcely perceptible rhythmic surge on part-throttle acceleration betraying the presence of injection to the experienced observer.

Immediately, one notices that the suspension feels much harder than that of other BMW models. In fact, this is probably more a matter of heavier damping than stiffer springs, as is confirmed by the capacity of the car to absorb bad road surfaces at high speeds without throwing the passengers about. Some road noise is evident under these conditions but it is strictly moderate. Similarly, the engine sounds healthy and unmistakably has four cylinders, but when driven at ordinary touring speeds it is well silenced.

Though the Tii is such a satisfactory every-day touring car, there is the feel of a competition car about it. Very well balanced, it flicks through corners without effort, and it shows its breeding when forced to change its line in the middle or to take an adverse camber in its stride. The independent rear end sticks down extremely well over broken surfaces, while the absence of wheelspin on leaving sharp corners is praiseworthy. Nevertheless, an oversteering condition can be induced by suitable provocation.

The BMW 2002 Tii is not cheap, but it represents remarkable value when its performance is taken into account. You can buy more car for the money but that is not the point. The man who chooses this model will realise the amount of time that can be saved on a journey by small overall dimensions. Fierce acceleration in a ponderous package is not the answer in the traffic of today, but the same performance in a nippy little car certainly takes a lot of beating.

JOHN BOLSTER

Car described: BMW 2002 Tii 2-door saloon, price £2295 including tax.
Engine: Four cylinders 89 mm x 80 mm, 1990 cc. Chain-driven overhead camshaft. Compression ratio 10 to 1. 130 bhp (net) at 5800 rpm. Kügelfischer fuel-injection.
Transmission: Single dry-plate clutch. Four-speed, all-synchromesh gearbox with central change, ratios 1.0, 1.32, 2.015, and 3.767 to 1. Hypoid final drive, ratio 3.45 to 1.
Chassis: Combined steel body and chassis. Independent front suspension by damper struts, coil springs, and lower wishbones, with torsional anti-roll bar. Worm and roller steering gear. Independent rear suspension by semi-trailing arms, coil springs, telescopic dampers, and auxiliary rubber springs, with anti-roll bar. Dual-circuit servo-assisted brakes with front discs and rear drums. Bolt-on disc wheels fitted 165 HR13 radial-ply tubed tyres.
Equipment: 12-volt lighting and starting. Speedometer, rev-counter, fuel and water temperature gauges. Cigar lighter. Heating, demisting and ventilation system. Windscreen wipers and washers. Flashing direction indicators.
Dimensions: Wheelbase 8 ft 2.4 in. Track 4 ft 4.4 in. Overall length 13 ft 10.5 in. Width 5 ft 2.6 in. Weight 18 cwt.
Performance (Maker's figures): Maximum speed 120 mph. Acceleration 0-50 mph 6.2 s.

BMW 2002tii

First test of the fast new fuel-injection model

THE BMW 2002 is one of our favorite cars. After all, we did name it Best in Class in our roundup of the world's best cars earlier this year. But it has been around over three years now, and its basic machinery and body date back to early 1967 when the 1600 2-door was first introduced. So it was time for a little updating. BMW has done just that and at the same time introduced some new variations on the 2-door theme.

For the home market the 2-door line starts with a 1602—the 1600, facelifted—and goes through an 1802 (1.8-liter engine) and the 2002 (2-liter) to the top-of-line 2002tii. There had been a 2-carburetor 2002TI of 120 bhp DIN not available here; the 2002tii uses Kugelfischer mechanical fuel injection to get another 10 bhp and replaces the TI. In the U.S. from henceforth, we'll get only the 2002 and 2002 tii; Hoffman Motors is no longer importing the 1.6-liter model.

But getting the hot model is something new and nice for the U.S., which has been denied the 2-carburetor versions since emission regulations went into effect.

The facelift is mild. There are new, rubber-tipped bumpers which are wider and wrap around to the wheel openings at each end of the car, and a new rubber-faced body molding running between the wheel openings at bumper level (this looks odd, conflicting esthetically with the horizontal chrome strip farther up the body side). The front seats have been reshaped, the instrument panel slightly rearranged and a few minor electrical-accessory changes made. Later in the year a new body variation, the Touring, will be available here in either 2002 or 2002tii form; this is a "hatchback" 2-door sharing the 2-door's basic body but with new roof and open-up rear end.

For now, the important news is the mechanical goodies offered in the 2002tii at approximately $400 over the regular 2002. We hadn't expected to see BMW import this engine with mechanical fuel injection as electronic injection is generally considered best for emissions, but here it is—in U.S. form somewhat detuned with its compression ratio dropped from 10.0:1 to 9.0:1 but still notably more powerful than the 2002. The Kugelfischer system is somewhat similar to

BMW 2002 tii

the Bosch injection long used on Mercedes engines, with a mechanical metering unit furnishing fuel at high pressure to port injectors. As with most such injected engines, the timed delivery of fuel to the ports makes it possible to use more radical valve timing and ram-tuned intake pipes without sacrificing low-speed tractability, and BMW does exactly that to extract the extra horses. The tii's power peak is moved up to 5800 rpm (the 2002 peaks at 5500), but more significantly the torque peak of the injection engine occurs between 4000 and 4700 rpm compared to a mere 3000 for the 2002. That torque peak is also much higher—145 lb-ft vs the 2002's 116—but it's clear that the engine needs to be wound up to get the benefit of it.

There's more than just a hotter engine. The 2002tii inherits the 2002TI's beefier chassis components, with bigger brakes front and rear and 1.4 in. additional track at both ends. Its wheels are wider—though still not very wide at 5.0 in.—and the Michelin XAS tires carry an H rating (130 mph) instead of the 2002's S rating (112 mph). In other words, the chassis has what it needs to handle the additional power; in Germany it has to be that way because people drive their cars as fast as they will go.

Transmission and gearing are also different for the tii. A new 4-speed gearbox with Borg-Warner synchromesh, similar to that used in the 6-cylinder BMWs, is standard and a 5-speed ZF box optional. The final drive ratio is 3.45:1, same as in 2800s. The 4-speed gearbox has slightly taller ratios in the indirect gears and the 3.45 final drive is taller than the 2002's 3.64:1, so the tii is longer-legged all the way.

The engine sounds and feels very much like that of a regular 2002; despite its higher output it's actually a bit quieter and smoother, a fact enhanced by the gearing when one is cruising at Interstate Highway speed. It idles just as nicely as a 2002 and pulls smoothly from low engine speeds in any gear, though of course a driver has to use the gearbox skillfully to get the most out of it. But the difference in performance doesn't show up until 4000 rpm is reached: above that there's definite "on cam" feeling that stays with you up to over 5500 rpm. BMW fans may be disappointed with our acceleration times for the standing ¼-mile and 0-60 mph, as we were; the tii is only 0.3 sec quicker in the quarter and its 0.6-sec-better 0-60 time is aided by the fact that 2nd gear takes it to 63 mph. Two explanations: one, our test car was not fully broken in, and since we journeyed to New York on a tight schedule to test the car there wasn't time to put a few hundred extra miles on it; second, that taller gearing takes its toll. There was particular difficulty getting the 2002tii "off the line" smoothly (BMW rear suspension always lets the wheels patter badly anyway) and when the wheels finally settled down the engine bogged. The real benefit comes at the high end—the tii gets to 100 mph nearly 10 sec quicker than the 2002—which means that the car is geared for top speed, not acceleration. This is a bit curious—we'd expect BMW to select "acceleration" gearing for the U.S. version and would suggest that the 2002's 3.64 gears would have been better. The 5-speed, which uses a 4.11:1 final drive, goes too far in the other direction!

The tii uses more fuel than the very economical 2002, but it still isn't what we call thirsty, doing over 22 mpg in everyday driving. In all the 2002tii offers a good combination of performance, refinement and economy, and our only serious question is about the gearing. The gearbox itself is a delight, with wonderfully smooth synchronizer action of just a slight notchiness as one moves from gear to gear offering a feel

BMW 2002 tii

of precision rather than real resistance. BMW seems to be leaning away from Porsche synchromesh, as used in the 2002 box, and toward the B-W design. We have no strong preference; some staff members prefer the smoothness of the Porsche synchros and others the notchiness of the Borg-Warner.

The throttle and brake pedals are positioned just right for blipping the throttle while downshifting, so the 2002tii is perfectly set up for vigorous driving on winding country roads. Having driven it several laps around the Lime Rock circuit and over some of the lovely roads of rural New England, we can vouch for that.

The responsive engine, nice gearbox and good controls are just part of what makes all BMWs real driver's machines. Then comes handling, and for a rather tall sedan the 2002tii is quite good. Its steering seems somewhat lighter than previous 2002s we've driven, despite the new car's greater weight; it's still not the lightest thing going but is very precise and quite quick enough. The tii comes with anti-roll bars front and rear, which keep body roll down to a moderate level, and the wider track, wider wheels and slightly stiffer tires all conspire to make the tii significantly better-handling than a 2002. Springing seems to be no stiffer. The ride is still fairly soft and smooth over large irregularities, though small ones such as tar strips bring out the harshness of the steel-belted tires. There's lots of suspension travel so that one can negotiate all kinds of evil road surfaces, even with four people aboard, at speed without fear of bottoming. Our test car's body was tight and rattle-free; some owners report that this isn't always the case, however.

The tii's stable understeer, which is moderate but stays with you even at high speeds, gave us the courage to work up our speed at Lime Rock; and this gave the brakes a good workout. They were up to it. Though they smelled strongly after a few laps, they were still effective, and in our fade test they showed no fade at all. The standard 2002's had shown a 21% increase in pedal effort in the 6-stop test, so there's a clear improvement here.

The 2002, tii or otherwise, is a very "upright" car, getting considerable passenger space into a compact overall length by virtue of its height. This means a commanding driving position, and all-around glass gives the driver a commensurate view. So it's a good traffic car. The "vertical" character carries through to an accelerator pedal that seems too upright when one holds it steady at cruising speed. BMW

engineers make good use of steering-column stalks for things like headlight flashing and wipers-washers, but we've never understood why they put the directional-signal stalk on the gearshift side where the hand can be so busy. Instrumentation is minimum: BMW doesn't like oil-pressure gauges or ammeters, so we have to make do with flashing lights (many owners add supplementary gauges) for that information.

Ventilation isn't a strong feature of the 2002 and the hot, humid weather during this test emphasized that BMW might have done some facelifting in this department. The airflow through the system is not bad, though one has to open the swiveling rear side windows to maximize it (thus accepting considerable wind noise), but there are none of the dash vents that are so welcome in contemporary cars—including BMW's own 6-cyl models. Bad marks here for the 2002 and

2002tii. And no factory air conditioning is available—only an add-on kit.

Notwithstanding the weatherproofing deficiency, the BMW 2002tii is a keen sports sedan—a real blast to drive fast and yet practical enough for a small family to use for daily transportation and extended trips. The price is high and getting higher, thanks to the German currency's upward spiral, but the 2002tii is bound to give BMW's little 2-doors a popularity boost. It certainly gave our collective mood a boost—it's nice to know that even with tightening smog regulations it's possible to get more performance in a car that was already strong in that department.

COMPARISON DATA

	BMW 2002 tii	Alfa Romeo 1750 Berlina	Volvo 142E
List price, incl. prep	est. $4000	$3905	$4080
Curb weight, lb.	2310	2484	2696
0-60 mph, sec	9.8	11.0	10.5
Standing ¼-mi, sec	17.3	17.9	17.5
Speed at end	78.5	76	76
Stopping distance from 80 mph, ft	315	n.a.	306
Fade in 6 stops from 60 mph, %	nil	nil	20
Cornering capability, g	0.726	0.692	0.649
Fuel economy, mpg	22.7	20.4	23.7

SCALE: 10" DIVISIONS

PRICE

List price, east coast...est. $4000

IMPORTER

Hoffman Motors Corp., 375 Park Ave., New York, N.Y.

ENGINE

Type.............sohc inline 4
Bore x stroke, mm......89.0 x 80.0
  Equivalent in.......3.50 x 3.15
Displacement, cc/cu in.1990/121.4
Compression ratio.........9.0:1
Bhp @ rpm.........140 @ 5800
  Equivalent mph..........118
Torque @ rpm, lb-ft..145 @ 4500
  Equivalent mph.........91
Fuel injection.......Kugelfischer mechanical
Type fuel required..regular, 91-oct
Emission control....fuel injection, engine mods

DRIVE TRAIN

Transmission.....4-speed manual
Gear ratios: 4th (1.00)......3.45:1
  3rd (1.32).............4.56:1
  2nd (2.02).............6.98:1
  1st (3.76).............13.0:1
Final drive ratio..........3.45:1

CHASSIS & BODY

Layout.....front engine/rear drive
Body/frame...........unit steel
Brake type....10.07-in. disc front, 9.05 x 1.57-in. drum rear; vacuum assisted
  Swept area, sq in.........306
Wheels.......cast alloy 13 x 5J
Tires.....Michelin XAS 165 HR-13
Steering type......worm & roller
  Overall ratio............17.6:1
  Turns, lock-to-lock........3.7
  Turning circle, ft.......31.5
Front suspension: MacPherson struts, coil springs, tube shocks, anti-roll bar
Rear suspension: semi-trailing arms, coil springs, tube shocks, anti-roll bar

INSTRUMENTATION

Instruments: 120-mph speedometer, 8000-rpm tachometer, 99,999 odometer, 999.9 trip odometer, coolant temp, fuel level
Warning lights: oil pressure, brake system, alternator, high beam, directionals

MAINTENANCE

Service intervals, mi:
  Oil change.............4000
  Filter change..........4000
  Chassis lube...........none
  Tuneup................8000
Warranty, mo/mi.......12/12,000

RELIABILITY

From R&T Owner Surveys the average number of trouble areas for all models surveyed is 11. As owners of earlier models of BMW reported 7 trouble areas, we expect the reliability of the BMW 2002 tii to be better than average.

ACCOMMODATION

Seating capacity, persons.......4
Seat width, front/rear...2 x 20.5/ 51.0
Head room, front/rear...40.0/38.0
Seat back adjustment, degrees..90

GENERAL

Curb weight, lb............2310
Test weight................2645
Weight distribution (with driver), front/rear, %....56/44
Wheelbase, in..............98.4
Track, front/rear.......53.8/53.8
Overall length............166.5
  Width...................62.6
  Height..................55.5
Ground clearance...........6.3
Overhang, front/rear....29.0/39.1
Usable trunk space, cu ft......9.5
Fuel tank capacity, U.S. gal..12.1

CALCULATED DATA

Lb/bhp (test weight)......18.8
Mph/1000 rpm (4th gear)....19.8
Engine revs/mi (60 mph)....3020
Piston travel, ft/mi.........1585
R & T steering index........1.13
Brake swept area sq in/ton....242

ROAD TEST RESULTS

ACCELERATION

Time to distance, sec:
  0–100 ft.................4.4
  0–250 ft.................7.0
  0–500 ft................10.0
  0–750 ft................12.6
  0–1000 ft...............14.8
  0–1320 ft (¼ mi)........17.3
Speed at end of ¼ mi, mph...78.5
Time to speed, sec:
  0–30 mph................3.9
  0–40 mph................5.9
  0–50 mph................7.7
  0–60 mph................9.8
  0–70 mph...............13.9
  0–80 mph...............17.9
  0–100 mph..............32.0
Passing exposure time, sec:
  To pass car going 50 mph..5.3

FUEL CONSUMPTION

Normal driving, mpg........22.7
Cruising range, mi........275

SPEEDS IN GEARS

4th gear (5600 rpm).........115
3rd (6400)................95
2nd (6400)................63
1st (6400)................34

BRAKES

Panic stop from 80 mph:
  Max. deceleration rate, % g..87
  Stopping distance, ft.......315
  Control...............excellent
Pedal effort for 50%-g stop, lb..35
Fade test: percent increase in pedal effort to maintain 50%-g deceleration rate in 6 stops from 60 mph....................nil
Parking: Hold 30% grade?.....yes
Overall brake rating.....very good

HANDLING

Speed on 100-ft radius, mph..32.9
Lateral acceleration, g......0.726

SPEEDOMETER ERROR

30 mph indicated is actually...29.5
40 mph....................39.5
50 mph....................50.0
60 mph....................60.0
70 mph....................70.0
80 mph....................80.5
100 mph...................101.0
Odometer, 10.0 mi..........10.0

ACCELERATION

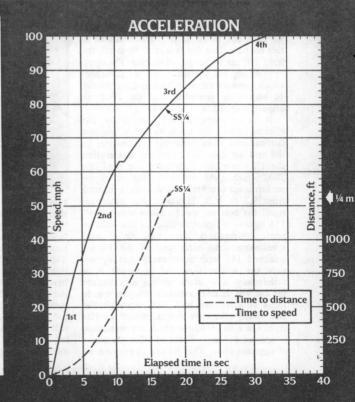

ROAD TEST

BMW 2002 TII

Modern suspension and engine developments have blurred the distinction between sports cars and saloons, many four-seat closed cars now being quicker — round corners as well as on the straight — than ostensibly more sporting soft-topped rivals of similar capacity. This trend is admirably exemplified by the BMW 2002 range of cars which are fast as well as being sufficiently compact for sports car agility and adhesion, yet large enough to seat four adults and carry a good deal of luggage.

Even in its lowest state of tune, as fitted to the ordinary 2002, the 100 net bhp produced by the BMW 2-litre four exceeds the maximum power developed by some similarly sized sports-car engines, though 50 bhp/litre has been reliably attainable for many years. With twin Solex carburetters, however, the output goes up to 120 bhp for the 2002 Ti (Touring International) which we have not tested as it is not available in this country. But the fastest of them all, the 2002 Tii, can be bought in Britain. The extra "i" stands for injection (by Kugelfischer) which gives an extra 10 bhp, making the car 30 bhp more powerful than the 2002 we originally tested in June 1968.

It took several attempts to prove the effectiveness of this extra 30 bhp as our test car suffered from some elusive trouble. In the end we confirmed that on acceleration the Tii is usefully faster than our road test 2002 which itself was at the top end of the performance bracket — 0-60 mph is reduced from 9.2 to 8.2s. However, for maximum speed the best we could achieve was "only" 113 mph — a figure claimed for the 2002 by some journalists who can only read speedometers. In early tests of the Tii we achieved 113 mph quite easily, but by the time the acceleration had improved to a satisfactory level after various adjustments the car was unable to maintain higher speeds for a complete lap at MIRA, although the best timed quarter-mile was as high as 120 mph. On a flat road the predicted maximum is around 117 mph obtained from the mean of opposite runs. This failure to perform as

BMW expect is unusual — normally we better the German company's ultra-conservative claims quite substantially.

Nevertheless the 2002 Tii is a very fast 2-litre as well as a fine sports saloon. Stiffer than the plain 2002, its handling is tauter and its roadholding marginally better, but the ride on broken surfaces is noisier. The absence of proper face-level ventilation, however, is a serious fault on such an expensive car. At nearly £2300 the Tii is £400 more than the 2002.

Performance and economy

There is a lot to be said for the BMW arrangement of a single overhead camshaft operating inclined valves via twin rocker shafts. It certainly doesn't hamper the free-revving Tii engine which is quite happy to go beyond 6000 rpm in the lower ratios without getting at all rough. The camshaft is chain driven (you can hear a sophisticated whine when the unit starts from cold). The injection system has no enriching lever and takes care of cold starts automatically. According to the handbook you are not supposed to touch the accelerator pedal when starting but we found it helped if it was lightly touched since normal tickover — not easily adjustable — can be as low as 400 rpm, a throttle setting which is a little low to "catch" on a cold morning.

Early Tii units used to suffer from a cyclic idling beat from about 400-1000 rpm but this seems to have been cured and the Kugelfischer system is now completely untemperamental. The pull is even from low

revs although the engine isn't as happy to slog from under 10 mph in third as that of the 2002. Figures are a little misleading, however, as the more powerful engine is coupled to a final drive 5 per cent higher. The Tii was fractionally slower in top and third up to about 60 mph than the 2002 but beyond that the extra 30 bhp is evident— the 70-90 mph acceleration time in third comes down from 11.3 to 8.1s. The rev counter is red-lined at 6400 rpm but the car will reach 60 mph in second without exceeding this speed. The engine is smooth and mechanically quiet up to around 5500 rpm

but it begins to get a little harsher beyond this.

Acceleration from rest is much better than that of the 2002; it reaches 50 mph half a second sooner and 60 mph in a second less. The slightly higher bottom gear doesn't affect the ease with which the BMW takes off nor its ability to romp away from rest on a 1-in-3 hill.

The maximum speed we've quoted is in fact our maximile figure — the speed attained after one mile's acceleration from rest. Normally we build up to the full maximum over one 2.8-mile lap and time the

next flyer, but the Tii started to fluff after less than a mile of the first flying lap by which time we had recorded a quarter-mile at 120 mph. By comparison with the 100 bhp 2002 the Tii should go 10 per cent faster on ideal gearing; this would give 117 mph which at 5950 rpm is just over the power peak at 5800 rpm.

It isn't possible to fit our petrol flow measuring apparatus to a fuel-injected engine but the factory claims 32 mpg at a steady 70 mph. This ties in well with our overall consumption of 24.0 mph which includes a large mileage at home and abroad.

At worst it was 22 mpg, at best 28 mpg. With a full 10.1 gallon fuel tank you can just scrape 250 miles when cruising at around 80 mph and using most of the considerable acceleration. But a bigger tank would be welcome.

Transmission

Although the synchromesh has been altered in the Tii box, the gearchange feels much like that of the 2002 — it is difficult to improve on something that is already very good. The ratios are well chosen and second is very useful for overtaking. While in

Above: comfortable seats with a good range of adjustment, and useful space for oddments atop the facia and in a centre console cubby. Right: reasonable access to the rear bench seat, though legroom is not very generous

Left: these cases filled the usefully sized boot. Below: massive intake pipes and air cleaner for the fuel-injected slant-four engine

Germany we tried the five-speed box that is optional in Europe and found that the ratios were unnecessarily close for the standard torquey engine. First was higher and fifth the same. On the standard box the change is very smooth and you can slice the lever around the gate confident that you will always get the right ratio and that the synchromesh will always be strong enough to allow easy engagement. The clutch was light and cushioned the drive well. We couldn't hear any noise from the body-mounted final drive unit but there was some gear whine in first.

Handling and brakes

To help cope with the extra performance a number of changes have been made to the running gear, including stiffer bodywork and dampers. The difference isn't immediately apparent (unless you've just driven a 2002), the stiffer damping being most noticeable on S bends as the car is easier to line up without uncomfortable lurching. The wheels now have 5J rims but still with 165 x 13 tyres to HR rating. On several different cars we tried Uniroyals, Continental and Michelin XAS: the Continentals were better than the Uniroyals on dry roads because they didn't squeal; the Michelins squealed but were good in the wet.

The Tii can out corner most saloons and has good steering response. There isn't too much roll and usually the handling is neutral. If you throw the car around it oversteers but in a very safe, controllable fashion. It oversteers if you ease the throttle in mid-corner, too, probably because of the semi-trailing arm rear suspension geometry. This is a safe feature and merely allows you to tighten the line without sudden steering movements.

Changes to the braking include bigger rear drums and two separately servoed systems; the pedal isn't too light, though. There was a bit of judder at the end of a long hard stop from high speed but the car passed our fade test with only a little smoke as protest. There was no increase in pedal pressure either then or after the water splash test. The centre mounted handbrake holds the car on a 1-in-3 slope and provides average emergency braking.

Comfort and controls

The seat slides through 12 reasonable positions (plus some more unreasonable forward ones) and the back rest has 18 angles, of which 10 can be used for driving. As a result most of our drivers found satisfactory settings without the high steering wheel being too uncomfortable for them to reach, though the driving position is not as good as that in the big BMWs. The pedals, too, are well placed, the organ-type throttle being easily blipped for heel and toe use. Adjustable head restraints cost extra.

For access to the rear seat there is a quick release knob on the squabs, and there is ample room for two adults in the back. The rake adjusting bar looks rather unpleasant at ankle level, though.

Stiffening the suspension hasn't improved the ride over indifferent surfaces though it is better damped for high speed undulations. The ride of the two-door BMWs isn't as good as it might be for an independent layout, as

Motor Road Test No. 58/71   BMW 2002Tii

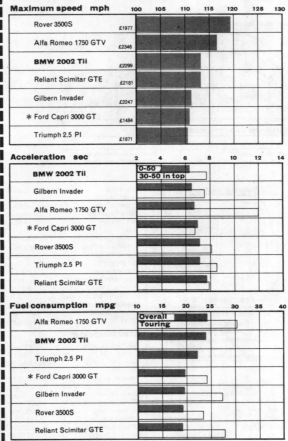

* before recent power increase

Make : BMW.
Model : 2002Tii.
Makers : BMW AG., Munich 13, W. Germany.
UK Concessionaires : BMW Concessionaires (GB) Ltd., BMW House, 361-365 Chiswick High Road, London W4.
Price : £1837.70 plus £461.30 equals £2299.00.

Performance tests carried out by *Motor's* staff at the Motor Industry Research Association proving ground, Lindley.
Test Data: World copyright reserved; no unauthorised reproduction in whole or in part.

Conditions
Weather: Cloudy with winds 7-18 mph.
Temperature: 46-55°F.
Barometer: 29.8in. Hg.
Surface: Dry tarmacadam.
Fuel: Super premium 100 octane (RM) 5-star rating.

Maximum Speeds
	mph	kph
Mean maximum (see text)	113.5	183
Best one-way ¼-mile	120.0	194
3rd gear	96	155
2nd gear } at 6500rpm	63	102
1st gear	27	44

"Maximile speed: (Timed quarter mile after 1 mile accelerating from rest)
| Mean | 113.5 | — |
| Best | 118.5 | — |

Acceleration Times
mph	sec
0-30	2.7
0-40	4.4
0-50	6.3
0-60	8.2
0-70	11.6

mph	sec
0-80	15.0
0-90	20.2
0-100	28.8
Standing quarter mile	16.5
Standing Kilometre	30.6

mph	Top sec	3rd sec
20-40	7.7	5.4
30-50	7.8	5.4
40-60	8.0	5.6
50-70	8.4	5.7
60-80	9.6	6.2
70-90	10.8	8.1
80-100	13.1	—

Fuel Consumption
Overall consumption . . . 24.0 mpg
(=11.8 litres/100km)
Total test distance . . . 3182 miles

Brakes
Pedal pressure, deceleration and equivalent stopping distance from 30 mph.
lb.	g.	ft.
25	0.32	94
50	0.75	40
65	0.96	31
Handbrake	0.32	94

Fade Test
20 stops at ½g deceleration at 1min. intervals from a speed midway between 40 mph and maximum speed (= 77 mph).

	lb.
Pedal force at beginning	38
Pedal force at 10th stop	42
Pedal force at 20th stop	35

Steering
	ft.
Turning circle between kerbs:	
Left	30.0
Right	29.2
Turns of steering wheel from lock to lock	3.6
Steering wheel deflection for 50ft diameter circle	1.1 turns

Clutch
Free pedal movement	= ¾in.
Additional movement to disengage clutch completely	=3¼in.
Maximum pedal load	=25lb.

Speedometer
Indicated	20	30	40	50	60	70
True	19	29	40	49	58	67½
Indicated			80	90	100	
True			77½	87	97½	

Distance recorder 2% fast.

Weight
Kerb weight (unladen with fuel for approximately 50 miles) 20.2 cwt.
Front/rear distribution 56½/43½
Weight laden as tested 23.9 cwt.

Motor Road Test No. 58/71 BMW 2002Tii

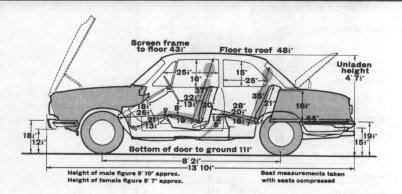

Screen frame to floor 43½"
Floor to roof 48¼"
Unladen height 4' 7½"

Height of male figure 5' 10" approx.
Height of female figure 5' 7" approx.
Bottom of door to ground 11½"
Seat measurements taken with seats compressed

Engine

Block material	Cast iron
Head material	Aluminium alloy
Cylinders	4 in line
Cooling system	Water pump, fan and thermostat
Bore and stroke	98mm (3.50in.) 80mm (3.15in.)
Cubic capacity	1990cc. (121.4 cu.in.)
Main bearings	5
Valves	Single ohc with rockers
Compression ratio	10:1
Carburation	Kugelfischer fuel injection
Fuel pump	Mechanical
Oil Filter	Full flow
Max. power (net)	130 bhp at 5800 rpm
Max. torque (net)	131 lb.ft. at 4500 rpm

Transmission

Clutch	Diaphragm sprung sdp
Internal gear box ratios	
Top gear	1.0
3rd gear	1.32
2nd gear	2.015
1st gear	3.767
Reverse	4.096
Synchromesh on all forward ratios	
Final drive	Hypoid bevel 3.45:1
Mph at 1000 rpm in:	
Top gear	19.6
third gear	14.8
second gear	9.7
first gear	5.2

Chassis and body

Construction	Unitary

Brakes

Type	Atc disc/drum with dual servoid systems
Dimensions	9.5in. dia. discs, 9in. dia. drums

Suspension and steering

Front	Independent with Macpherson struts and lower wishbone, anti-roll bar

Overall width 5' 1½"
Front track 4' 4½"
Rear track 4' 4½"

Ground clearances lowest point:—
(under front suspension) 5"
under engine 6½"
under exhaust system 8½"

Rear	Independent by semi-trailing arms with coil springs and anti-roll bar
Shock absorbers:	
Front:	In strut
Rear:	Telescopic
Steering type	ZF worm and roller
Tyres	165 HR x 13 Continental
Wheels	Pressed steel disc
Rim size	5J x 13

Coachwork and equipment

Starting handle	None
Tool kit contents	Three spanners, pliers, screwdriver, plug spanner
Jack	Screw type
Jacking points	One in each side at centre
Battery	12 volt negative earth 44 amp hrs capacity
Number of electrical fuses	11 + 1 (heated rear screen)
Headlamps	Two 6.7in. 45/40W

Indicators	Self-cancelling flashers
Reversing lamp	Yes
Screen wipers	Two-speed electric
Screen washers	Two-speed
Sun visors	Two, padded
Locks:	
With ignition key	Steering
With other keys	Doors and boot
Interior heater	Fresh air
Upholstery	Skai
Floor covering	Carpet
Alternative body styles	None
Maximum load	880 lb.
Maximum roof rack load	150 lb.
Major extras available	Heated rear window, alloy wheels, head rests, rally seats, 4 QH headlights

Maintenance

Fuel tank capacity	10.1 galls
Sump	7½ pints SAE 20/50
Gearbox	2.1 pints SAE 80
Rear axle	2.6 pints SAE 90
Steering gear	0.5 pints SAE 90
Coolant	12.3 pts. (2 drain taps)
Chassis lubrication	None
Maximum service interval	8000 miles
Ignition timing	24° btdc at 2200 rpm
Contact breaker gap	0.016in.
Sparking plug gap	0.027in.
Sparking plug type	Bosch W175T30
Tappet clearance (cold)	
Inlet	0.007in.
Exhaust	0.007in.
Valve timing:	
inlet opens	4° btdc
inlet closes	52° abdc
exhaust opens	52° bbdc
exhaust closes	4° atdc
Rear wheel toe-in	0-0.12in.
Front wheel toe-in	0-0.08in.
Camber angle	0-1°
Castor angle	4-4½°
King pin inclination	8½°
Tyre pressures:	
Front:	28 psi
Rear:	28 psi

1 clock. 2 heater fan. 3 cigarette lighter. 4 screen demister. 5 fuel gauge, temp. gauge on right. 6 oil and alternator warning lights. 7 speedometer with trip and total mileage recorders. 8 trip zero. 9 rev counter. 10 lighting switch. 11 two-speed wiper control. 12 side window demister slot. 13 rear screen heater. 14 hazard warning flasher. 15 indicator flasher stalk. 16 footwell air flow. 17 indicator and main beam tell-tales. 18 horn. 19 wiper washer stalk. 20 heater temperature control

the fairly high stance of the car requires stiffish springing for the handling that BMW owners expect. Surface breaks send a shudder through the frame as if there isn't enough compliance in the front suspension. At higher speeds it is much happier and the seats absorb road shocks as well, so passengers are never jerked around.

The interior is very airy with large areas of glass for good all-round visibility; you can also see the rear deck from the front seats which makes reversing easy. The rear bumper has a full width rubber facing and the edges and overriders are rubber faced at the front to guard against clumsy parkers.

The standard BMW lights give fair illumination with a typical Continental cut-off. One of the available extras is the system used on the 6-cylinder cars, with four QH lights and a modified front grille, at £65. These lights are extremely good.

Frameless windows are not the easiest to seal against wind noise. That on the two-door cars is not obtrusive until you are going over 80 mph. Up to that speed the car is pretty quiet as the engine seems hardly to be working. The interior air has positive outlets through the boot; opening the rear window increases the flow — and noise. The heater has controls for individual adjustment of volume to screen and interior with a third slide for temperature adjustment. Small slots at the end of the facia help keep the side windows demisted.

Fittings and furniture

Some people feel that a £2000 car should look rather more luxurious inside than does the sombre but functional black of the BMW. The three-dial instrument pod is well placed and informative and there is a clock in the centre. A shelf runs the full width of the facia with the instrument nacelle occupying part of it, leaving a small space on the right which takes a packet of cigarettes and little more.

Left of centre the tray is useful for papers and small objects but maps are best placed in the convenient console in front of the gearlever. There is a separate glove pocket in front of the passenger.

The carpeting and ambla/pvc seats are easily cleaned, as are the doors covered in the same material. The boot is very large, engulfing 10.8 cu.ft. of our Revelation cases. The spare wheel and tool kit are found under the floor.

Servicing and maintenance

The full-width bonnet is released by an over-centre lever on the passenger's side which is very easy to overlook after an oil check. But with its forward hinging action it is held down by its weight up to about 75 mph when underbonnet pressure lifts it slightly without any danger.

After initial servicing at 600 and 4000 miles, the BMW only needs garage visits every 8000 miles — an unusually long interval, so servicing is best left to the garage. Underbonnet accessibility is good enough for items that the private owner might want to check himself, like the distributor (which is just accessible against the bulkhead), the coil, plugs and reservoirs. A clear-topped fuse box is well sited on the top of the left wheel arch.

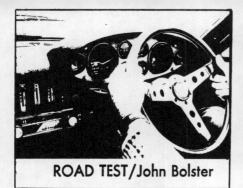

ROAD TEST/John Bolster

A well-appointed and practical car, the 2002tii is a very rapid form of transport.

BMW 2002 tii: A 2-litre saloon with quick acceleration

I always choose horses for courses, so when the French show came round I looked for something that was small enough for Paris, would idle for hours in traffic blocks, and would pass all the passionate Frenchmen on the *Autoroute du Nord*. From among the available machinery, I chose the fuel-injection BMW 2002.

The BMW, in all its forms, is very familiar to me. For the roads of Northern France, independent suspension of all four wheels is a minimum requirement and all BMWs have that. The tii has strong anti-roll bars at both ends and wide radial-ply tyres. It has the engine and gearbox in front, driving to a chassis-mounted hypoid unit at the rear, and the power unit is that well-known and almost indestructible four-cylinder, with a chain-driven overhead camshaft operating inclined valves through rockers.

Fuel injection is, admittedly, a complication as well as an expensive addition to an engine. At first glance, there might appear to be little advantage in the system over the multi-carburetter version of the same unit, for the gain in maximum power is not great. The point, however, is that the fuel injection engine gives more torque and it continues to give it over a wide band of revs. In practical terms, that means instant acceleration at any time, which is what fast road motoring is all about.

This characteristic is so marked that I wouldn't give a thank you for the optional 5-speed gearbox. With four well-spaced ratios, the fuel-injection BMW has all the gears it needs, and for this reason the acceleration is even better than would appear from the graph.

Gearchange points are not critical and if you put your foot down the car just goes, though wheelspin must be guarded against at the traffic lights.

With such vivid acceleration on tap, the little saloon cuts its way through traffic with considerable ease. It goes on accelerating up to about 112 mph, which is a speed that can be kept up indefinitely. Higher speeds take longer to reach, the shape of the body probably not attaining a particularly low drag co-efficient. However, 119 mph can be reached on the level, with a little more to come under favourable conditions. The high third gear gives splendid acceleration over a very wide range.

The engine is smooth for a four-cylinder and though it sounds efficient it is by no means noisy. The level of road noise is satis-

With its independent suspension all round, the 2002tii corners and accelerates very impressively.

factorily low on most surfaces but there is a good deal of wind noise. Although the suspension is well damped and there is remarkably little roll on corners, the ride is truly excellent on the bad French roads, the wheels having sufficient travel to absorb the undulations.

The BMW has high cornering power, showing up particularly well on the faster corners. It is well balanced, having perhaps a trace of initial understeer that can soon be cancelled by spirited handling. The steering does not have quite the feel of the road that a rack and pinion can give but it is satisfactorily direct and accurate. One can pay the brakes the compliment of saying that one never thinks about them because they always behave as they should.

In spite of its performance potential, the engine never fouls its plugs in traffic blocks. However, the test car was a slow starter from cold and did not always idle regularly. No doubt this was a question of simple adjustment but I am not familiar with the injection system on this car and decided not to interfere — I hope to take lessons in this sphere as I am driving so many injection cars nowadays. Apart from this slight mal-adjustment, the engine behave impeccably throughout.

Engines with fuel injection are usually economical of petrol and the 2002 tii is no exception. It would be a reasonable guess that the hard driver will get 25 mpg and his more timid brethren 28 mpg, with 30 mpg on the distaff side. On autoroutes, with lots of 110 mph motoring, the figure falls to 20 mpg, which is still outstandingly good. There are some large-engined cars which can also cruise at 110 mph but use so much fuel in doing it that it is scarcely a practical proposition, especially at the prices ruling in France.

During the time that I was in France, I never met another car that could equal the BMW for acceleration. I was overtaken once when my speedometer was showing 125 mph, but as my rival had three times my engine capacity, this was to be expected. In any case, I would not have cared to pay his petrol bill and I could out-accelerate and out-corner him easily. Certainly, I made the right choice of mount for this particular trip.

The BMW also served me well in England. Here, there is little need for sophisticated suspension but fierce acceleration will get you out of more trouble than any other quality. The sheer unexpectedness of the British driver can place sudden demands on the motorists around him; the vivid responsiveness of the 2002 tii may save him from his own folly on such occasions. It is equally good at dodging the well-lunched Frenchman in his 2CV, who suddenly asserts his priority from a hidden side turning, for in all countries the car of instant acceleration is the safest.

The BMW 2002 tii is a well-appointed and practical car. Though arranged for through-floor ventilation, it lacks the adjustable face-level current of air which the eyeball ventilators of the bigger BMWs provide; if the quarter-lights are used for extra ventilation, they are objectionably noisy. Other faults are few indeed and the car must be regarded as a very effective and rapid piece of transportation. You could buy a bigger vehicle for the money but not one that was a greater pleasure to drive.

The fascia of the 2002tii lacks face level fresh air ventilation (above). An addition to the well-known and well-proven four-cylinder engine is fuel injection.

SPECIFICATION AND PERFORMANCE DATA

Car tested : BMW tii 2-door saloon, price £2,299 including tax.
Engine : Four cylinders, 89 mm x 80 mm (1990 cc) ; chain-driven overhead camshaft operating inclined valves through rockers ; Kugelfischer fuel injection ; compression ratio, 10 to 1 ; 130 bhp (net) at 5,800 rpm.
Transmission : Single dry plate clutch ; 4-speed all-synchromesh gearbox with central change ; ratios 1.0, 1.32, 2.015, and 3.767 to 1 ; hypoid final drive, ratio 3.45 to 1.
Chassis : Combined steel body and chassis ; independent front suspension by coil spring damper struts and lower wishbones ; worm and roller steering ; independent rear suspension by trailing arms, coil springs, auxiliary rubber springs and telescopic dampers ; anti-roll torsion bars front and rear ; disc front and drum rear brakes ; bolt-on disc wheels fitted 165HR13 radial-ply tyres.
Equipment : 12-volt lighting and starting ; speedometer ; rev counter ; fuel and temperature gauges ; clock ; heating, demisting, and ventilation system ; 2-speed windscreen wipers and washers ; flashing direction indicators with hazard warning ; reversing lights ; radio (extra).
Dimensions : Wheelbase, 8 ft 2.4 in ; track 4 ft 4.4 in ; overall length, 13 ft 10.5 in ; width, 5 ft 2.6 in ; weight, 2,028 lb.
Performance : Maximum speed, 119 mph. Speeds in gears—third 91 mph, second 62 mph, first 34 mph. Standing quarter-mile, 16.9 s. Acceleration—0-30 mph, 3.4 s ; 0-50 mph, 6.6 s ; 0-60 mph, 8.9 s ; 0-80 mph, 17.6 s ; 0-100 mph, 26.8 s.
Fuel consumption : 20 to 30 mph (see text).

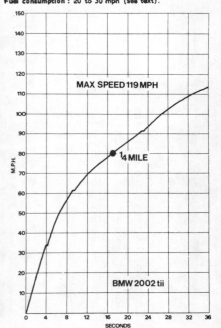

MAX SPEED 119 MPH

¼ MILE

MPH

BMW 2002 tii

SECONDS

BMW 2002tii

When comparing 2002s, the "ii's" have it/By Eric Dahlquist

Impression

The traffic signals work differently in Munich than America. Instead of the amber light warning when the red is about to come on, it goes the other way 'round—like the Christmas tree at the drags. So you go down Maximilian Strasse on Friday night and choose off other guys at the stop lights just like they used to do on Detroit's Woodward Avenue back in 1966. Only the cars are different—BMWs and Alfas and Mercedes and Opels—and the traffic polizei smile because they get to see free races. The new king of Maximilian Strasse is the BMW 2002tii. But then you're down on the stretch of Autobahn between the Austrian border and Munich, flat out, hitting right around 115 mph, trying to stave off the challenge of a new BMW Bavaria 3.0. With one third more displacement and six more mph on the top end, it's only a matter of time until the Bavaria slides by but the tii makes it strain—strain hard. The BMW 2002tii isn't King of the Autobahns—but it's close.

The old 2002, the sports sedan we got and loved in the 'States didn't have it after 90, at least, not like this one. But nobody really missed it because most American 2002's only saw 90 occasionally anyway. There isn't any place for full-bore work in the U.S. except Nevada and if the truth

be known, there aren't a lot of places left to do it in Germany either, so maybe that's why there is a 2002tii, a car small enough, nimble enough, and fast enough to play the old top speed game under the new restrictive rules but also be competitive in the cities. In 1969, the 2000tii was some of BMW's hot news at the Frankfurt Auto Show, a hot engine to bolster the sagging appeal of their 9-year-old intermediate. But in 1971, it's the crowning touch for their little super car, the 2002, a way to meet the emissions rap and save performance.

Someone commented earlier in the trip that the 2002tii may be wind sensitive over a hundred mph but that doesn't seem to be any great bother. You sit high in the car and the hood slope and large sweep of glass yield a kind of forward visibility available almost nowhere else except, perhaps, a bus. Arms out, grasping the pleasantly large steering wheel, the driver derives the sensation of ultimate control, of being well and truly the master of his fate. The tii feels so naturally right, the way all good automobiles ought to feel, completely comfortable through its entire speed range.

Based on the mini-racer 2002ti chassis, the tii has more robust front and rear brakes (disc/drum), generally stouter suspension components throughout (including anti-roll bars front and rear), and 1.4 inch wider track than the 2002's 52.4. At five inches, wheel rim width is broader by a

half inch although the significant items are new H rated Michelin XAS 130 mph radials, superceding the 2002's 112 mph S type. Later, on a drive through the foothills of the Bavarian Alps, we measured the suspension's quality on spiralled, undulating two-lane roads and did not find it wanting.

What all of this means is that the tii driver can devastate almost everything else on the road, hauling down into corners at Porsche 911-like velocities, having the same power reserve to throttle steer as well. Handling is generally neutral with a very small amount of designed-in understeer for high speed stability. Steering is, if anything, lighter than the excellent 2002. Impressive beyond anything else is the clever way BMW's engineers have achieved this on a wide range of road surface disparities with seemingly no sacrifice to ride, a feat even mighty General Motors seems helpless to accomplish. The one thing you can do with a BMW is load in passengers and roar down almost any road without fear of bottoming; adequately damped, realistic suspension travel is the key, folks. If the tii had any riding compromise, it is a certain low speed harshness over things like tar strips and this can be laid as much to the steel tire belts as suspension.

Right here, after three days of generally flogging the tii over the autobahns and rural byways of Bavaria, we were ready to say that it was maybe the most fun BMW or anybody has ever built into a

>>>>

The Kugelfischer-injected 2002tii engine belts out 140 hp @ 5800 rpm with the same authority as Chrysler's 426 King Kong hemi but with a lot less fuss. High performance, low pollution.

SPECIFICATIONS	
Engine	OHC 4-cylinder
Displacement	1990cc (121.3 cid)
Bore and Stroke	3.50 x 3.15 ins.
Horsepower (SAE Gross)	140 hp
	@ 5800 rpm
Torque (SAE Gross)	145 lbs.-ft.
	@ 4500 rpm
Compression Ratio	9.0/1
Transmission	4-speed manual
Final Drive Ratio	3.45/1
Steering Ratio	17.58/1
Front Suspension	McPherson strut with shock coils
Rear Suspension	Semi-trailing arms with coils, tube shocks
Body	Welded all-steel unit
Brakes	Disc front/drum rear, vacuum assisted
Wheelbase	98.4 ins.
Overall Length	166.5 ins.
Height	55.5 ins.
Width	62.6 ins.
Track Front/Rear	53.1 ins.
Weight	3.065 lbs.
PERFORMANCE	
Acceleration:	
0-60 mph	9.9 secs.
Top Speed	115 mph
Gas Mileage Range	22-25 mpg

BMW 2002 tii

car, certainly the best small sedan we've tried in its class. In Munich's old center with its narrow, crowded streets and heavy traffic, the tii was even better. You need a small, agile car here, one that can carry four people yet squirt, waterbug-like, through tight gaps in the swirling traffic. On the face of it, a 121.4 CID engine pumping out 140 hp at 5800 (145 lbs. ft. of torque at 4500 rpm) might be a bit edgy at low revs but Kugelfischer mechanical fuel metering is so precise as to cancel the inherent slow-speed nervousness of the high-lift, long overlap, camshafts and tuned intake manifold runners. So, the tii surfaces as the German version of the original tri-power GTO Pontiac.

As far as quality goes, this BMW, all BMWs, are in a class by themselves. The paint flows like a competition orange mirror across the car, broken on the flanks only by inch-and-a-half wide, metal-backed plastic inserts intended to reduce parking damage. Everything fits properly. The doors shut with the solid, time-worn Teutonic authority Americans wistfully recall from Detroit twenty years ago. The seats are comfortable, fully adjustable and covered with a simulated leather material looking like it will be the last thing on the machine to wear out.

If the 2002 tii has a fault, it is the conspicuous lack of a modern flow-through ventilation system incorporating adjustable face-level registers. True, by judicious manipulation of the vent wings and rear windows, a habitable temperature can be maintained, but at the expense of increased wind noise. And, with the front seats all the way back for tall drivers, rear passenger legroom suffers somewhat, though it is certainly no worse than American two-doors a third larger in size.

And there is one other thing too, though it is a suggestion rather than a complaint. On the way back from BMW's new proving ground we had a brief but spirited tussle with a brand new 2-liter Alfa Berlina. We won, happily, but it brought to mind the idea that the two cars are close in specification—2-liter engine, mechanical fuel injection, weight, size, price—except that the Alfa has a five-speed transmission as standard equipment. BMW offers an optional ZF 5-speed but it is a rare option and they are wondering whether to abandon it altogether and concentrate on other things. Certainly, the 2002 tii's flexibility is such that it doesn't really need a 5-speed and in fact they have gone up from the 2002's 3.64:1 final drive to 3.45, giving the machine an even longer-legged capability. Still, a 5-speed is a certain psychological filip for the kind of person who will buy the tii, in the same way a bicycle freak covets a 15-speed over a 10-speed.

On balance, 5-speed or no, the tii is one of the benchmarks in sedan touring car design, superbly executed and disappointing in only a few minor ways. One dark cloud, however, may loom on its horizon. With the German Deutschmark revalued and the new U.S. port-of-entry import surcharge, the price of all German cars is escalated significantly from what it was six months ago. At the time we were there, the factory was still deliberating on the tii's final U.S. sticker, somewhere said to be in the neighborhood of $4100, or around $400 more than the old 2002. Excellence doesn't come cheap. /MT

BMW's seating position and visibility are unexcelled. Note that brake and accelerator pedal are equal height for easy heel and toeing. Car could use better ventilation system.

The mountain marvel

A look at the BMW 2002 TII sedan with fuel injection

Anybody who knows a better all-around mountaineering sedan than the new BMW 2002 TII must have a hot line to the devil.

Following nearly 2000, mostly alpine, miles in this fuel-injected missile I would be more than willing to admit that its ventilation is laughable for instance. Or that the famous 2002 chassis is getting towards the end of its string for flat-out motoring with 130 hp in the nose.

But it remains the most nimble hairpin charger around with Kugelfischer injection which all but turns 7500 foot pass roads into sea-level freeways. The TII has more punch than a TI with less fuss. This is the engine announced nearly two years ago. They waited until it was really right.

Meanwhile BMW was lining up a few cosmetic changes in line with customer murmurs. These apply to all two-door BMWs: things like the elastic plastic (looks like rubber) stripe down each side and ditto insets in the bumpers. And the finally-reclining seats or more readable dials. In the TII you get a rev counter, heated rear window and leatherette steering wheel as well.

The body, a 320,000 best seller in five output versions since 1966, is part of the pleasure of seeking out smaller passes. Vision remains outstanding five years after it was first designed.

The English market these cars as coupes which is closer to the truth than sedan though you can carry a couple in back on short trips. Two and their luggage have really rich space, however, with the bonus of good small storage and touches like the cross-ribbed dash shelf which prevents the sunglasses sliding about.

The good-size trunk does get warmer from their exhaust than seems necessary, be it noted. And the door windows don't wind clear down despite muscle-bound handles. It takes an NFL lineman to work the knobs for their wind wings. So there are a few things left for the Munich firm to fix.

BMW also claims better air extraction in the 1971 version thanks to vents above the rear window. Forget it. This car was a sauna south of the alps, not to mention noisier than hell with the windows open as they had to be for survival.

Along with better dials and more knee padding BMW finally fitted three-speed wipers and moved their switch to a wand under the steering wheel, literally at your fingertips. That TII wheel has a thin rim and a little better grip than plastic but I still wanted gloves on hot, sticky days.

Hillclimbing by car is greatly eased by the light, direct steering and quick, precise gearbox action. Their optional five-speed box with top still direct would make it even nicer. A limited slip differential would smack of paradise. In any case a slightly longer than 2002-normal final drive ratio (3.45) gives the TII an easy freeway gait.

This is a 119 mph sedan after all, capable of 16 second quarter mile runs on a mere 120 cubes. What's more we drove it virtually flat out in all gears for two weeks, including five of the steepest (up to 16%) and highest (over 7500 feet) passes in the Alps and still got overall fuel consumption of 18.8 mpg, plus 1.5 quarts of oil in 1950 miles.

Using the car for family runs as well as high altitude work would make 25 mpg a cinch. The injection system, keyed to throttle setting, revolutions and engine temperature is very little thirstier than that single carb on the normal 2002.

With two and plenty of luggage aboard the car would still pull uphill cleanly from 2500 revs in top. It was always a cinch to start provided you remembered to stay off the throttle pedal until it fired when hot. Compared to the temperamental TI with two dual-body carbs which has been discontinued, the TII with Kugelfischer injection not only has more power and a torque band better matched to its gears, but it is far easier to drive around town as well.

Cooling is the chief remaining engine problem. Ever since the first two-liter model introduced in January of 1968 they have faced marginal cooling. When you try to use these 147 horses for any length of time, say down a hot Italian autostrada, the temperature needle will go all over red.

After all, 6000 in top is a true 115 mph and the TII just won't take that for more than 20 or 30 minutes at a time when temperatures get up around the 90 mark. This information is brought to you courtesy of the Nevada desert club.

Pushed right along up a winding road the BMW remains nearly neutral until you use all that new power to hang the tail out at any angle desired. The car shows a good deal of roll by modern standards and this serves to warn the less than ultra-expert driver that he is approaching oversteer. Those who like to charge will still find a BMW ideal.

On the other hand a chassis which first appeared with over a third less power to set the handling standards five years ago is bound to show its age by now. BMW did beef up the suspension members front and rear for this added poke. The relative softness (by sporty sedan standards, that is) only bothered us in very tight descending hairpins when you could rub a tire on the fender.

We did manage to get some brake smell on our faster downhill rushes but there was never any pedal loss and the pads continued to work without evidence of glazing.

Brake circuits are set up on a double-dual system. If one circuit fails it leaves 75% of your brake power, if the other goes out, the worst conceivable case, a driver still has 60% of his very good brakes. This is a soothing thought at the high speeds which seem so natural to a TII.

Factors like this give the new BMW its special charm on unknown, winding roads. You can hustle along, achieving amazingly good point to point averages, and yet hoard a large margin of handling safety for the unexpected.

This 2002 TII proved to be very much an automobile and engine worth waiting for.

BMW 2002 T11 2-Door Sedan
Data in Brief

PERFORMANCE AND MAINTENANCE

Acceleration:		Gears:
0-30 mph	3.5 secs.	I
0-45 mph	5.7 secs.	I, II
0-60 mph	9.0 secs.	I, II
0-75 mph	13.7 secs.	I, II, III
0-¼ mile	16.1 secs.	

Ideal cruise	90 mph
Top speed	119 mph
Average economy (city)	17.5 mpg
Average economy (country)	20 mpg
Fuel required	Super
Oil change (miles)	3500
Lubrication (miles)	3500
Type tools required	Metric

SPECIFICATIONS AS TESTED

Engine	121.4 cu. in. injected inline 4
Bore & stroke	3.5×3.15 ins.
Compression ratio	10 to one
Horsepower	147 (SAE gross) @ 5800 rpms
Torque	150.5 lbs.-ft. @ 4500 rpms
Transmission	4-speed, manual
**Steering	3.5 turns, lock to lock 31.5 ft., curb to curb
**Brakes	disc front, drum rear
Suspension	spring leg front angled wishbone coil rear
Tires	165 HR 13 radial
Dimensions (ins.)	Wheelbase 98.4 length 166.6, width 62.6, height 55.5 front track 53.1, rear track 53.1 ground clearance 6.3, weight 2180 lbs.
Capacities	Fuel 11.9 gals. oil 4.5 qts., coolant 7.4 qts. trunk 15.8 cu. ft.

10,000 miles Long Term Test

BMW 2002 AUTOMATIC

By David Thomas

Automatic transmission ideal for city driving, yet detracts very little from sporting appeal of this compact saloon. Rapid brake-pad wear and leaking final-drive only significant problems encountered during 10,000 hard miles. Unusually easy to maintain in pristine condition.

"THE World's Best 2-litre" proclaimed the sticker in XNJ 998J's rear window. In spite of being a BMW addict, I was ready to dismiss this as so much advertising ballyhoo. Now, having lived with the car for 10,000 miles, I'm not so sure!

From my own point of view, what is there to rival a 2002 in this capacity class? Family considerations dictate a practical four-seater, yet my personal preference is for something compact and sporting. The situation is further complicated by my insistence on reasonable standards of refinement and quietness. I can think of no other automatic which fits the bill. In manual form, the injection 2002 Tii is an attractive alternative — albeit at the disadvantage of a £400 increase in price. Having fond memories of a long-term Alfa Romeo 1750 Berlina, this (in current 2000 form) would also join my list of "possibles".

Performance

All too often, automatic transmission spells considerable penalties in terms of ultimate performance and overall economy. Not so with the 2002, whose ZF unit seems more efficient than most of its contemporaries. To underline

the model's potential in automatic form, I will relate a somewhat amusing tale of an encounter which was sparked off by the aforementioned sticker. Early one morning, while waiting at an isolated set of traffic signals, a sporting vee-eight arrived alongside. The driver called my attention and, pointing at his own car, remarked "The world's best 3-litre!" On the green, he proceeded to demonstrate just what this meant in terms of performance. The temptation was too great, and the 2002 joined in the fray! To its surprising credit, it emerged the clear victor — a feat few automatic "fours" could hope to emulate.

Since *Autocar* has not previously published figures for a 2002 in automatic guise, some further comment may not be amiss. Mileage at the time of the car's visit to MIRA was around 6,000; as always, it was running extremely well.

Top speed averaged 103 mph, with 106 mph coming up in the faster direction (wind gusting to 10 mph). At the latter speed, the ludicrously optimistic speedometer showed 117 mph — all but round the clock! Why *do* BMW (along with certain other German manufacturers) always seem to fall foul of this one? In contrast, the tachometer seemed pretty accurate, indicating just a shade over the theoretical (no converter-slip) revs under steady-speed conditions.

Confirming impressions gained on the road, acceleration times were most impressive. Sufficient torque is available at the rear wheels

to induce wheelspin on getaway, resulting in a 0-30 mph time of only 3.6 sec. Aided by this decidedly brisk step-off, the 2002 reaches 60 mph in 10.6 sec and the quarter-mile mark in 18.1 sec. These times are appreciably faster than those returned by *manual* versions of most rivals. The Rover 2000 TC, for example, achieved 3.9, 12.2 and 18.5 sec. With its electronic-injection engine, the Volvo 144 GL managed 4.1, 11.6 and 18.3 sec. Triumph 2000 times were 4.5, 14.9 and 19.7 sec. To be fair, these are more spacious, four-door models. A more realistic comparison is provided by the Capri 2000 GT. In manual form, this clocked 3.5, 10.6 and 18.0 sec — pretty much the same as the 2002 *automatic*. Fast through-the-gears times are meaningless unless backed by good transmission response. The 2002's ZF unit cannot be faulted on this score. Provision is made for automatic down-changing on part-throttle, with the result that the driver rarely feels it necessary to over-ride the control mechanism. In fact, two of my colleagues thought the unit over-sensitive to throttle movement, but I disagree on this point. For the record, the maximum speeds at which kickdown changes can be effected are 62 (top-to-intermediate) and 34 (intermediate-to-low). Automatic up-changes (with the pedal in the kick-down position) take place at 40 and 68 mph, with the tachometer indicating around 5,500 rpm in both cases. There is little or nothing to be gained by exceeding these revs, although another 900 rpm is available before the needle reaches the red.

In circumstances where it is beneficial to use the selector lever, such as the approach to a tightish corner, the unit's response is unusually rapid. This holds true whether one is changing down or up. One minor criticism concerns the abruptness of the over-run change into low when holding intermediate. At all other times, change-quality is good.

Petrol consumption

Unfortunately, no steady-speed fuel consumption checks were carried out. However, making due allowance for the 5.3 per cent odometer error (over-reading), the consumption averaged exactly 23 mpg over the 10,000-mile test period. Periodic checks show that it remained in the 21.5-23.5 mpg bracket for the first 9,000 miles. Thereafter, following a belated routine service by MLG of Chiswick (see later), it improved to 25.7 mpg. The latter figure included a gentle drive to MIRA and back, which resulted in a best-ever figure of 27.4 mpg. Summing up, it would seem that a briskly driven model in good tune should return 23-26 mpg.

No oil used

No matter how hard the 2002 was driven, no measurable quantity of oil was used. In addition, the power-unit remained almost spotlessly clean.

Taking delivery

Having dealt with the subject of performance and economy, let us now take a look at the day-to-day running of the car while in *Autocar's* hands.

On arrival at Dorset House, the odometer showed 87 miles. First chore was topping-up with four-star fuel as a prelude to our regular check on consumption. Thanks to the generous size of the cap and filler-neck, this involves no risk of blow-back. Total capacity is 10 gal — barely adequate for long-distance journeys.

Oil levels (engine and transmission) were checked and a quick tour of inspection made.

☞

1. *After 10,000 miles and a year in London, the car's dark blue paint was unmarked*
2. *One of the delightful features of the 2002 is its slim pillars and large glass area. The front grille (inset) is painted matt black*
3. *The engine stayed as clean as the exterior with no visible oil leaks*
4. *The test car had pvc seats, although there is now a cloth option for the central panels*
5. *It is the rather cramped back seat which justifies the name "coupé" more than the overall styling*
6. *The spare wheel lives in a well under the boot floor, with tools and jack neatly clamped around it*

XNJ 998J

BMW 2002 AUTOMATIC LONG TERM TEST . . .

The only "fault" spotted was incorrect setting of the air-intake valve; this was duly switched from "S" to "W", which feeds pre-heated air to the carburettor (it was late November).

On the way home that evening, it soon became obvious that both factory and concessionaire had missed some minor faults. Worst of these was an abnormally fast tickover (about 1,200 rpm in neutral); another was misalignment of the headlamps (set much too high). A few minutes' work in a lay-by improved matters no end — thanks to the accessible thumb-screws (beneath easily removed covers) for headlamp adjustment. Other points noted were a tendency for the brakes to squeal when applied gently and failure of the indicator stalk to self-cancel. Other than this, it showed every promise of being a delightful car.

Getting acquainted

Starting from cold the following morning was a first-turn affair, but it was soon evident that the automatic choke was providing much too rich a mixture during the warm-up period. The bi-metallic spring used in this device features water and electric heating; having satisfied myself that the latter was working, I was content to leave well alone for the time being.

One of the first things that impressed me was the excellence of the ride and freedom from road noise. There was little doubt in my mind that the car represented a significant improvement on our previous long-term 2002 (a manual model). This impression was to last throughout my period of "ownership".

Less pleasing was the behaviour of the heating and ventilation system. Water-valve control is employed on this model. In addition to its characteristic sluggish response, the system failed to maintain a reasonably constant temperature within the car. The situation was further aggravated by the absence of face-level

vents. Another problem was ineffective extraction, leading to misting up in humid weather. On the credit side, the two-speed blower was unobtrusive and the heated rear window (an extra-cost option) very effective.

1,000-mile service

Soon it was time for the first service, the work being entrusted to P. & L. Motors, Enterprise Garage, Upminster. In addition to the routine tasks involved, they were asked to attend to the non-cancelling indicator switch, check the headlamp and choke settings, and fit a screen-pillar radio aerial. Faults found by the garage amounted to two over-tight tappets, excessive contact-breaker dwell (74 deg instead of the specified 60 deg), and the presence of a stray piece of polythene sheet (approx 15 ×2 in) in the air-cleaner housing. Non-cancelling of the indicator was found to be caused by a faulty steering-column collar, for which a replacement had been ordered. Both headlamp alignment and choke-setting were given a clean bill of health. Cost of materials (oil, filter and cam-cover gasket) amounted to £2.70; no labour charge was made for this work. Price of the radio aerial was £3.30, a modest £1.50 being charged for the considerable work involved in fitting it.

Automatic choke still troublesome

The car had obviously benefited from the vetting it received at the 1,000-mile mark. Although quite new still, it felt very peppy.

Shortly afterwards, I delivered it to the Radiomobile fitting centre at Cricklewood in order to have a radio fitted. No tailor-made fitting kit was available, but they made a first-class job of the installation. The set

Above: Instruments include a rev counter and the horn is worked by neat push bars in the wheel spokes

performed very well, but I suspect that it would have benefited from the use of a better quality aerial (possibly a roof-mounted one).

Despite the garage's assurance that the choke was in order, warm-up was still proving troublesome. On very cold mornings, over-richness could actually bring the car to a halt. This was sufficient provocation to make me re-set the unit on a trial-and-error basis. Somewhat to my surprise, this proved quite effective. Even so, I failed to achieve that ideal setting which results in the engine being fed exactly the right mixture at all times. Oddly, there was no improvement in economy, but I was happy enough with the 22-23 mpg being returned at this time.

Although the next service was scheduled for 4,000 miles, the clock showed nearer 4,700 at the time. Again P & L Motors carried out the work. Apart from fitting the new steering-column collar under warranty, this was strictly routine. Materials (oil and air filter, plus oil) amounted to £3.51¼ and the labour to £4.00.

Selector lever problems

At around 6,000 miles, difficulty was experienced in getting the transmission selector lever to clear the neutral and park "guards" on the quadrant. As the car was urgently needed by our Editorial Director, something had to be done! On dismantling, the problem was found to have been caused by "stripping" of what clearly had been an under-sized thread on the

1. Reclining backrests are standard and the tip-up arrangement does not interfere with the setting
2. The Radiomobile installation fills most of the central locker, but there is still room for maps underneath
3. This patch of wear on the carpet seems to indicate that the driver's heel mat is too short
4. Because of the full-width front bonnet the radio aerial must be roof or pillar mounted

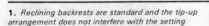

1

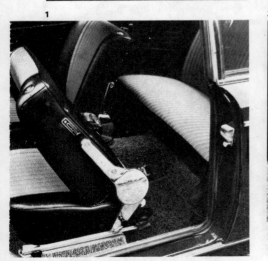

2

3

stem of the pawl. This rendered the T-handle button ineffective. As a temporary measure, the unit was reassembled without the offending part. As soon as the car was returned, a replacement (cost 50p) was fitted. In normal circumstances, of course, this work would have been covered by warranty.

Worn-out brake pads

Shortly afterwards, colleague Martin Lewis used the car to cover the Senior Service Hill Rally. On his return, he complained that the brakes were pulling to the right. Sure enough, they were. It didn't take long to find the cause — the left-hand brake pads were completely worn out, and those on the right very nearly so!

Brake-pad inspection forms part of the 4,000-mile service. The relevant instruction reads "Check *overall* (my italics) brake pad thickness and renew if less than 7 mm (0.28 in.)". This can be very misleading; what it doesn't make clear is that the pad backing plates are virtually in contact with the retaining clips at this stage — in other words, the pads are worn out.

In our case, some 8 mm had been worn away from each pad in 7,000 miles, equivalent to 4.6 mm in 4,000 miles. At this rate of wear, overall pad thickness would have to be 11.6 mm (12 mm for all practical purposes) before these items could be considered fit for a further 4,000 miles. The moral is obvious — inspect the pads yourself or make quite sure that the garage man understands the problem. In any event, you will know what to look for if the brakes start pulling!

This episode would normally have added £9.77 to the maintenance bill — £8.27 for the pads themselves, the remainder for labour. In our case, labour was our own, but the relevant charge has been added.

Change of garage

Around this time, I moved house from Upminster to Marlow. Although I had been very pleased with the treatment I'd received at the hands of P & L Motors, it now became more convenient to have the car serviced at MLG of Chiswick. Belatedly (at 9,000 miles), it was presented for its next service, another straightforward one (no extra jobs). In fact, MLG discovered that the stop-lights were inoperative — the result of a faulty switch. They also spotted a bad oil leak past the final-drive pinion seal but, at my request, left this job until a later date. Materials (stop-light switch, plugs, contact-breaker, oil and air filter, engine and EP oils) amounted to £5.55. Since

this is a major service, labour charges totalled a hefty £13.75.

Performance was now better than ever and, as indicated earlier, economy had improved markedly. Some 400 miles later, I revisited MLG for renewal of the pinion seal. Materials, seal and lock-washer cost 89p, labour amounting to £7.50.

With this problem disposed of, the car was in peak condition. However, to my great dismay, my term of "ownership" was nearing its end. How I wish I could have bought it for my wife (that, at least would have been my excuse!). Paintwork was unmarked, as was the bright-work. Apart from a threadbare patch on the driver's carpet, the inside was indistinguishable from new. This was not the result of loving care and attention — it simply happens to be an extraordinarily easy car to keep in good shape.

Tyres (Continental radials) were approaching two-thirds worn at this stage. Had I kept the car, I wouldn't have been sorry to see these go. Their wet-road adhesion was never very good,

and I have the feeling that a set of Dunlop SP Sports would have been very worth-while.

Summing up

What a delightful little car the 2002 had been! I loved its Jekyll and Hyde character — unobtrusive and well-mannered on the one hand, a real road-burner on the other. Its handling, being more-or-less neutral, was exactly to my taste. Its compactness and superb visibility made it a traffic car *par excellence*. Good road-insulation was a very strong point.

Nothing is perfect, of course. There was that accursed heater to contend with! Another criticism concerned the rapid brake-pad wear and tendency to fade under hard usage. The frameless windows caused a fair amount of wind noise at around maximum speed. That's just about it on the debit side!

To repeat my earlier question, what is there to rival a 2002 in this capacity class? Having re-lived the pleasures of "owning" XNJ 998J I have only one answer a 2002 Tii. □

PERFORMANCE CHECK

Maximum speeds

		mph		kph		rpm	
Gear	R/T	Staff	R/T	Staff	R/T	Staff	
Top (mean)	107	103	172	166	5,800	5,600	
(best)	110	106	177	171	5,960	5,750	
3rd (Inter)	89	77	143	124	6,500	6,400	
2nd (Low)	59	46	95	74	6,500	6,400	
1st	31		50		6,500		

Standing ¼-mile, R/T: 17.4 sec 77 mph   Standing kilometre, R/T: 32.8 sec 96 mph
Staff: 18.1 sec 77 mph   Staff: 33.5 sec 92 mph

Acceleration, R/T:	3.5	5.3	7.6	10.6	14.2	18.2	26.4	37.2
Staff:	3.6	5.5	7.8	10.6	14.6	20.4	30.2	
Time in seconds	0							
True speed mph	30	40	50	60	70	80	90	100
Indicated speed MPH, R/T:	33	43	53	63	73	83	93	104
Indicated speed MPH, Staff:	27	41	54	65	77	88	99	111

Speed range, Gear Ratios and Time in seconds

Mph	Top		3rd	Inter	2nd	Low
	R/T	Staff	R/T	Staff	R/T	Staff
10-30	—	—	6.4	—	3.8	2.6
20-40	8.1	—	5.6	—	3.5	3.3
30-50	7.6	—	5.5	4.9	3.7	—
40-60	8.4	7.7	5.8	5.3	5.1	—
50-70	8.5	8.2	6.2	6.9	—	—
60-80	10.2	10.5	8.6	—	—	—
70-90	13.2	16.1	—	—	—	—
80-100	17.9		—	—	—	—

Fuel consumption
Overall mpg, **R/T:** 25.5 mpg (11.1 litres/100km)
Staff: 23.0 mph (12.3 litres/100km)
NOTE: "R/T" denotes performance figures for BMW 2002 tested in *AUTOCAR* of 16 May 1968.

COST and LIFE of EXPENDABLE ITEMS

Item	Life in Miles	Cost per 10,000 Miles
		£ p.
One gallon of 4-star fuel average cost today 34p	23.0	147.83
One pint of top-up oil, average cost today 18p	Service interval	Nil
Front disc brake pads (set of 4)	7,000	11.81
Rear brake linings (set of 4)	17,000	2.66
Tyres (front pair)	16,000	11.90
Tyres (rear pair)	18,000	10.58 (1)
Service (main interval and actual costs incurred)	4,000	48.32 (2)
Total		233.10
Approx standing charges per year		
Depreciation		386.00
Insurance		38.00 (3)
Tax		
Total		682.10

Approx cost per mile = 6.8p
NOTES: (1) Logical course would be to renew all four tyres at 16,000 miles, increasing total cost (for 10,000 miles) by £1.32.
(2) Includes cost of renewing brake pads at 7,000 miles and final-drive pinnion seal at 9,000 miles.
(3) Insurance quotation is for a 30-year-old driver living in Marlow. No-claims bonus of 60 per cent. Excess of £25 on accidental damage.

TURBOCHARGED BMW 2002

What the factory does for an experiment a performance-minded dateline dealer does for you

JOE RUSZ PHOTOS

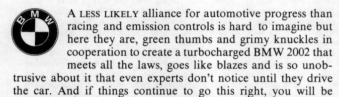

A LESS LIKELY alliance for automotive progress than racing and emission controls is hard to imagine but here they are, green thumbs and grimy knuckles in cooperation to create a turbocharged BMW 2002 that meets all the laws, goes like blazes and is so unobtrusive about it that even experts don't notice until they drive the car. And if things continue to go this right, you will be able to buy one.

This worthwhile piece of work comes from Vasek Polak. That makes the racing portion of the combo perfectly clear. Polak is a former driver, known now as the owner/sponsor/entrant of the Porsche 917-10 which Milt Minter drives in the Can-Am and which R&T drove in the October issue. Polak is also a dealer for both Porsche and BMW. As a businessman he knows that he does well by supplying what the public needs. And he knows that what he sells must meet the laws, which in California prohibit the removal or modification of emission controls. (He's also a human being, that is, he breathes air and wouldn't want to produce smog even without considering the law.)

When Polak started this project he had several advantages: BMW and Porsche both had their engineers working on turbocharging for racing and for high performance production cars of the future, as witnessed by the Penske Porsche 917 and the show BMW Turbo in this issue. Enter a prime pair of sources for encouragement and advice. Polak had decided to install a turbocharged engine in his 917, which gave motivation and an in-house sort of a cross-fertilization as the techniques and procedures learned on one project could be applied to the other.

Polak's crew plucked a 2002tii out of stock, ordered an Eberspacher turbocharger—like the ones used on the 917, but smaller—and set to work.

The resulting installation looks neat and simple. Polak snorts at that, saying that it took six months of hard work and experiment to come up with such a neat and simple installation. The turbocharger is mounted on the lower right front of the engine block. The exhaust is routed from the stock manifold through the turbine wheel, then beneath the car to a small fiberglass-packed muffler just beneath the rear bumper. It's not much of a muffler, but most of the exhaust pressure is used up spinning the impeller so not much muffler is needed. The noise level goes many decibels above that of a stock 2002 tii in a deep, pleasant way—noisy but not raucous and not especially noticeable most of the time.

The air intake and filter are at the right side of the radiator, with the air piped through the turbocharger and across the engine via a steel pipe to the stock air horn for the fuel injection. From that point into the engine it's all straight production 2002tii, untouched by human hands. The other changes are minor; the oii pressure gauge fitting is tapped and oil supplied from there to the impeller and drained back into the oil pan, there's a pipe from the blower pressure relief valve into the air intake upstream of the impeller and the crankcase is ventilated into the relief pipe, which is under negative pressure from the intake pipe.

Nice and simple. It can be thus because the 2002tii engine isn't simple. It's built strong from the start, designed to hold up under maximum use because that's what it gets at home. And the fuel injection is complex, as it must be. But because the injection regulates fuel volume and strength by measuring pressure in the inlet tract between throttle butterfly and valve, and because all the changes, specifically the capacity for positive pressure on the other side of the butterfly, are made away from the injection's sphere of influence, why, the injection doesn't have to be changed at all. So it isn't. Unlike turbocharged engines with carburetors there is no need for pressurized float bowls and throttle shafts, or secondary fuel pumps and electric relays, etc. And the emissions levels aren't changed, nor is the equipment. Polak fitted colder spark plugs to protect against detonation at full power. The distributor has a cutout which limits the engine to 6400 rpm because the turbocharger would otherwise push past the engine's limit, and the blow-off valve is set at 6.5 psi for the same reason. But within those limits Polak reckons the engine to be no more than just stressed,

TURBOCHARGED BMW 2002

and he hasn't changed pistons or lowered the compression ratio. In fact the test car's engine has never had the cylinder head removed.

When the work was completed, the car was put on a chassis dynometer, where it produced 124 bhp at the rear wheels at 6000 rpm. Before turbocharging, the car had 72 bhp at the same engine speed.

One is inclined to doubt this impressive figure on first acquaintance with the car. The engine starts quickly and idles and sounds just like a normal 2002tii except for the deeper exhaust tone. And in normal driving the car feels showroom stock. With a light foot on the pedal and the normal shift points, there's not as much as a hint of added power.

But the power comes on with a bang. As the figures show, using full power through the gears cuts several seconds off all the times to speeds, with the cuts getting deeper as speed goes up. The start is virtually unchanged, as there's no time for the impeller to speed up and provide boost until about 3000 rpm. Nor would brutal tricks like revving the engine and dropping the clutch work: there's no boost unless the throttle butterfly is nearly wide open.

There is no dreaded turbocharger lag as such. Rather, with wide open throttle at low rpm the car accelerates like an unblown 2002tii, briskly. When the impeller is spinning at a useful speed the needle on the gauge flicks over to six and the car surges forward; like a racing engine when it comes into its band of useful power, the difference being that there is no flat spot, no stumbling and banging, at less than the useful speed.

Once again we wish that the standard test procedure called for measurement of acceleration from a steady speed, from 30 mph to 80 mph, say, in third gear. A normal passing situation, more important than leaping from stoplight to stoplight, and a test in which the turbocharged BMW would do even better than it does on the standard test.

And speaking of standard tests, the turbocharged car went farther per gallon than did our test production 2002tii. The mpg test is a rigid procedure, calling for accelerations to set speeds, cruising at steady speeds for set distances, etc. Under these conditions the turbocharged car did better than the production car, presumably because the test conditions were more easily met by the more powerful engine. If the turbocharger was called into service often—and why have it if you don't use it?—then the fuel consumption would of course increase.

This was our third recent experience with turbocharged versions of production cars, and it was the most impressive of the three by a wide margin. The Vega truck (Jan. '72 R&T) proved to be a good performer when not hampered by derangement of its elaborate fuel pressure controls and when caught between changes of sparkplugs, for which its appetite was

insatiable. We had a turbocharged Datsun 240Z on hand for the technical article about turbocharging in the May '72 issue, but it blew a head gasket before any figures could be recorded. Turbocharging works. It can also be troublesome. Polak's car has been tested and driven several thousand miles without incident and it performed without flaw during the 10 days and several hundred miles we had it. Still, the history of the technique makes durability and servicing something to think about.

What of the future? Polak has applied to have his system certified for sale in California, which requires that any change to the engine not increase the emission levels. As another step, he's concerned that the stock injection won't provide enough fuel for sustained operation at wide open throttle. Likely the fuel-power mixture will be richened or the pressure relief valve will be set at 5 psi, to decrease the amount of air being pumped into the engine. This would cut the rear wheel power down to 102 bhp at 6000 rpm but Polak thinks the gain in safety margin would be worth the lessened power.

Whichever, the cost will not be cheap. Polak estimates that the complete job, all parts and the work done in his shop by his mechanics, will be close to $1500. That's a lot and he's not eager to simply sell the kits for home conversion. It's possible that Polak and the BMW factory could arrive at some sort of franchise arrangement with certain other BMW dealers stocking and installing the turbochargers. But that's at least one step beyond the present plans and Polak can't offer any definite timetable.

Too early for a line to form, then, but when it does, the place to be in line at is Vasek Polak Motors, 199 Pacific Coast Highway, Hermosa Beach, Calif. 90245.

Comparison Data Turbocharged BMW 2002tii vs production 2002tii		
	Turbocharged	Production
Acceleration to speed:		
0-30 mph	3.5 sec	3.9
0-40	4.9	5.9
0-50	6.7	7.7
0-60	9.0	9.8
0-70	12.1	13.9
0-80	16.1	17.9
0-90	21.5	n.a.
0-100	29.6	32.0
Miles per gal.	24.5 mpg	22.7 mpg
Interior noise, dBA:		
Maximum, 1st gear	83	82
Constant 70 mph	86	76

Remodelled BMW 2002 Tii

The BMW 2002 has been manufactured for quite a number of years. As is well known, it is derived from the small and relatively light bodyshell of the 1600, fitted with the 2-litre engine. The power unit, like all BMWs, has inclined valves operated by a chain-driven overhead camshaft and rockers. The Tii model has an up-rated engine with fuel injection, developing 130 bhp.

The subject of the present test is the latest version which has been re-styled front and rear while the interior has been remodelled, with additional sound insulation. The mechanical specification remains the same, apart from a fractionally wider track. There is independent suspension front and rear, with MacPherson and semi-trailing arm geometry respectively, plus anti-roll bars at both ends. ZF-Gemmer worm and roller steering is still used and the disc front and drum rear brakes have twin servos.

Since I last tested this model, the price has risen by no less than £900. One doesn't get a lot of motor car for all that money but the compact size is an advantage and the acceleration is outstanding in any company. However, in spite of the new trim the interior is still a bit spartan for this price class and the absence of face-level eyeball ventilators is astonishing, the swivelling quarter-lights creating a great deal of wind noise. More luxurious seats would be appreciated, too.

The 2-litre BMW engine must be one of the best four-cylinder units ever built. It has none of the roughness at low speeds which plagues most of the larger fours and is outstandingly flexible. The former starting problems of the injection engine have been completely overcome, the machinery springing instantly to life on the coldest mornings, and the theoretical advantages of fuel injection in saving petrol are realised. In my previous test of the Tii, I was able to average 20 mpg when cruising at 110 mph whenever possible, in France. This time, I proved that the car will achieve well over 40 mpg at a steady 50 mph, which means that a clever driver will get 35 mpg on country journeys, perhaps

Suspension is independent all-round.

reduced to 25 mpg in thick town traffic.

A few spot performance checks showed that the capabilities of the latest car are virtually identical with those of the earlier model tested. To avoid wasting fuel, therefore, I have used some of the figures previously obtained to complete the data panel, rather than going through the repeated full-throttle tests that I normally carry out. BMW cars always have pleasant gearboxes with nicely spaced ratios, which allows the efficient power unit to give its best performance.

The suspension feels fairly hard at low speeds but is outstandingly good at coping with really bad roads. At high speeds, the car rides the bumps very well and the absence of roll on corners contributes to the comfort of the passengers. The road noise is very moderate, though the wind noise increases somewhat as the speed rises.

The BMW goes through corners in a most satisfactory manner, with moderate understeer and a tail that can be brought round under power on occasion. The steering gear ratio is about right and the spokes of the wheel are arranged to give a clear view of the instruments. The front disc brakes have 4-piston calipers and automatic pad wear compensation, in conjunction with substantial drums at the rear. The results are truly excellent, with extremely potent retardation and freedom from fading.

The engine could not be called silent, though its sound level is moderate except at maximum revs. Like all BMW engines, it has a hum that sounds efficient but it never seems to be highly stressed. With fuel injection, the already good low-speed torque becomes

Latest cars have a re-styled front and rear and more comfortable interior.

Two litre engine uses Kugelfischer injection.

Above: familiar, fascia is still rather spartan. Below: moderate understeer prevails.

Fuel injection provides good low speed torque and helps fuel consumption.

outstanding, permitting top gear to be used a great deal when conserving petrol. The torque is sufficient to promote wheelspin rather easily on wet roads, but the car remains very controllable under these conditions.

The body shape is inconspicuous, which can be quite an advantage. However, the car is unmistakably a BMW and its looks show plenty of character. The 2002 may be used as a full 4-seater, though it is best for the people in front to avoid pushing their seats right back. The luggage boot is surprisingly roomy for a car of such moderate size.

Though sheer performance takes second place at the moment, it is pleasant to know that the maximum speed is not far short of 120 mph and a reading of 125 mph is easily obtained on the slightly optimistic speedometer. More important, perhaps, is the smooth performance in top gear between 20 and 30 mph, an area where many four-cylinder cars thump and rumble until the driver is forced to change down and waste precious fuel.

There remains the question whether or not fuel injection justifies its cost in a road car. That it can give excellent fuel economy is certain and by its use a four-cylinder engine may be given much of the flexibility of a six. Though it may never be used for the more basic types of car, its virtues make it more than worth while for a machine of the calibre of the BMW.

Though this is an expensive little car, it is one of those rare dual-purpose vehicles which combines the handling and performance of a competition car with the perfect manners of a town carriage. The changes in the latest model are very slight and this is basically quite an old design, but it is still right on top for speed, acceleration, and fuel economy. To many, the racing background of the BMW adds greatly to its appeal, too.

SPECIFICATION AND PERFORMANCE DATA

Car tested: BMW 2002 Tii 2-door saloon, price £3,199 including car tax and VAT.

Engine: Four cylinders 89 mm x 80 mm (1990 cc). Compression ratio 9.5 to 1. 130 bhp at 5800 rpm (net). Chain-driven overhead camshaft operating inclined overhead valves through rockers. Kugelfischer mechanical fuel injection.

Transmission: Single dry plate clutch. 4-speed all-synchromesh gearbox with central change, ratios 1.0, 1.32, 2.02, and 3.764 to 1. Hypoid final drive, ratio 3.64 to 1.

Chassis: Combined steel body and chassis. Independent front suspension by coil spring damper struts and lower wishbones. Worm and roller steering. Independent rear suspension by semi-trailing arms, coil springs, auxiliary rubber springs, and telescopic dampers. Anti-roll torsion bars front and rear. Twin servo assisted disc front and drum rear brakes. Bolt-on disc wheels, fitted 165 HR 13 radial ply tyres.

Equipment: 12-volt lighting and starting. Speedometer. Rev counter. Fuel and temperature gauges. Clock. Heating, demisting and ventilation system with heated rear window. 2-speed windscreen wipers and washers. Flashing direction indicators with hazard warning. Reversing lights. Radio (extra).

Dimensions: Wheelbase 8 ft 2.4 ins. Track 4 ft 4.8 ins. Overall length 13 ft 10.5 ins. Width 5 ft 2.6 ins. Weight 2226 lbs.

Performance: Maximum speed 119 mph. Speeds in gears: Third 91 mph, second 62 mph, first 34 mph. Standing quarter-mile 16.9 s. Acceleration: 0-30 mph 3.4 s, 0-50 mph 6.6 s, 0-60 mph 8.9 s, 0-80 mph 17.6 s, 0-100 mph 26.8 s.

Fuel consumption: 20 to 35 mpg.

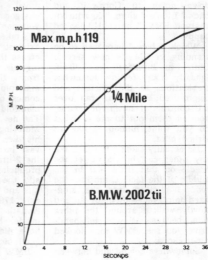

Max m.p.h 119

¼ Mile

B.M.W. 2002 tii

MPH / SECONDS

Well blow me down...

Mike McCarthy travels to Cornwall and back courtesy of a Turbocharged BMW and a Gas Turbine Herald

"Are you busy next week?" asked the Ass Ed (sorry, Asst Ed) casually.

"Yes," I said, quick as a flash (I know how his casual questions can lead to all sorts of nastiness).

"Doing what?" he asked.

As ever in times of dire emergency my mind was an absolute blank. I stood and stared at him.

"Right," he said, "You can drive down to Cornwall and back." I looked glum. "In a turbocharged BMW," he said. I looked happy.

Which is how I happened to be standing in BMW's new service centre in Brentford at 8.30 am (ghastly hour) feeling somewhat trepidatious as the efficient and bright-eyed BMW man ran over the controls (I mean, of course, pointed them out to me — what do you want, humour?) like an airline pilot.

He actually said: "It's just like any other car, but don't let the needle on that little dial in the middle of the facia climb into the red." I climbed into the king-sized hairdryer — then got out and slowly walked around the other side, because it was left-hand-drive you see. BMW man looked supercilious.

Somewhere behind and between the plastic beard in front, the cauliflower spats on the side that hide fat, fat tyres and the black plastic spoiler on the boot lid (which for some reason makes the car look like a small truck) there is a BMW 2002 that we know and love of old. Except that the technocrats at BMW (I'm sure they are bright-eyed and efficient too) have added a fairly novel option — a turbosupercharger. As everyone knows (if you don't you don't read *Motor*) this takes surplus energy from the exhaust gases and uses it to increase the pressure of the incoming air. So instead of suffering from the well-known disease manifold depression the car becomes quite Fascist and causes manifold oppression, as it were. The net result is what we of the Motoring Press (he said, full of his own self-importance) call "a vast increase in power." In fact the 2-litre engine started out life producing a reasonable 100 bhp; add the turbo and a few other bits and it kicks out an unreasonable 170 very DIN horsepower. And the only way you tell from inside that it is potent is that little dial — and a red (for danger?) facia panel.

BMW gave me a sheet of paper with a drawing of the dial on top, and in capital letters underneath FOR MAXIMUM MOTORING. Now the dial has nothing so vulgar as numbers on it, so you can't talk about "There I was, on 5 lb boost" or whatever. Instead there are three sectors, the first white and quite large, the second tiny and green, and the third red and very large. As the sheet says, the needle stays in the white sector for normal driving. Things get more exciting when it goes on to say that when the needle is in the green sector maximum turbocharging occurs. The ultimate comes when it says, again in capitals, IF THE NEEDLE MOVES INTO THE RED SECTOR, LIFT OFF — the pressure relief valve is stuck. It's obviously intended for some sort of game, like

a pin-ball machine: you must keep it above the white but below the red. The reassurance note that a sticking relief valve is unlikely did not reassure me at all, since I am the eternal pessimist.

Anyway, I turned the key in the ignition waiting for a loud wailing and howling — the original banshee cry, beloved of aged motoring writers, and which is always mentioned whenever the Mercedes SSKL is talked about. It fired immediately, but sounded like any other BMW 2002, if anything a little quieter. Disappointing. It must be true, I thought, a turbocharger does act like an additional silencer. I gingerly executed a three-point turn in the confines of the reception area; I didn't want to disappear out through the receptionist's little glass box. It

4.5 grands worth of diminutive Turbocharged 2002 (top); if you want one you'd better hurry, they're importing fewer than 200. Left: pity this is in monochrome. The instrument surround is bright red — a warning, perhaps, to keep your eyes open!

This is what 170 German horsepower looks like (left) and yes, I couldn't find the turbocharger either ! The innocuous dial on the right, next to the clock, tells you (as if you wouldn't know) that it's all happening

behaved impeccably. Good grief, I thought, it's actually quite tractable. (Tractable to me means that it doesn't make me angry because of the noise/temperamental engine/ peculiar transmission/ odd controls/ sheer difficulty that a number of tuned cars display. I'm a great one for creature comforts.)

Left down the A4, past the Firestone factory. No chance to use more than 2000 or so rpm : too much traffic. Burble, burble, it went, nice and docile. No problem. I relaxed, unsticking my (by now) clammy hand from the steering wheel. I headed west, out through the dormitory suburbs to the M3. No fuss, no dramas, but also no heavy right foot. After getting lost a couple of times — why do they always put direction signs up when the best route is obvious, but never, never at critical T-junctions ? — I saw the lower reaches of the M3, stretching away into the distance.

At 2000 rpm nothing much happens. The tacho needle just climbing relatively slowly to about 2700 to 2800 rpm. At that point a soft whistling begins, getting slightly louder and higher in frequency as engine revs rise. Then the needle on that little gauge rushes over to the green bit (up to now it had been hovering forlornly around the bottom end of the white bit) and suddenly you're moving. Not just quickly, but like the proverbial cat with the scalded tail. The needle on the tacho just about bends itself on the stop, you pop the clutch, slip the gearlever into third, and it all happens again, except that this time you don't drop the revs and keep the turbocharger spinning, so again there's that superb push in the backside. By this time prudence, not to mention an almost pathological fear of the Q-car police mini-van (would you believe ?) that has been known to creep around that neck of the woods dictated a return to insanity and 50 mph —

well, 50 or so. Time to look around the car a bit. Ride—harsh, I suppose, but I've known worse on cooking family saloons. Steering is light and delicate (this car must have the high ratio box that Hardly referred to when he wrote about the 2002 Turbo back last September), and the right amount of feel for me. Noise is reasonable.

Off the M3 on to the dreary and depressing A303, possibly the most worked upon road in Britain. Once more no fuss, no boiling or plug fouling, no snatch or jerk. Remarkable.

Through Exeter, with a stop for petrol (only four star—hope that's all right) and coffee — or tea, I still don't know which. It was lukewarm and sickeningly sweet.

Away from Exeter and across Dartmoor on the B something-or-other. No traffic apart from the odd sheep or two — safe behind hedges, I might hastily add — and a twisty road that the well-known seaside snapshot photographer and Jaguar-owner Paul Skilleter quoth highly of. This, I say grinning inanely to myself, is where they mean you to keep that little needle firmly in the green sector. And I tried, how I tried. Superb, incredible fun, but then a few damp patches cooled my fervour and the big Pirellis. They did not like the wet.

The Hardly said that " the handling will certainly suit the Achim Warmbolds (who ?) and other loose-surface German heroes with oversteer being virtually on top — (sorry) tap." And he's right. Play it wrong, like getting the turbocharger to sing at the wrong point, and whoops ! It's tail-first into the flora and fauna.

Driving a turbocharged car is not at all like the pop-pop, spit-spit, backfire, hiccup then away you go bit that you get with the "cammy" overcarburettered modified cars that we sometimes drive for " Motoring Plus." It's smooth, very smooth. A hard shove is all

you feel with no definite " now it's in, now it's not " point. On the other hand the turbocharger is not working very hard at low load and revs, but is spinning it's little heart out (at 100,000 rpm, would you believe) at full load and speed. So the faster you go, the faster you go, if you know what I mean. The original BRMs, with centrifugal superchargers, suffered from the same characteristic, and caused Messrs Fangio and Moss, among others, to execute some strange manoeuvres. I think BMW may have to look a little carefully at who wants to buy it . . . but they are going to change the tyres for some more appealing to the British temperament.

I was woken the next morning suffering from the late-night syndrome—the party sat up until two, telling of how brilliant and brave we were. I managed to put on a superior air to the others, because I " had driven the car before," so could sneer while they searched for the ignition switch, or reversed over the rose bushes. It was a very grey day, as they say, and pouring with rain. The idea was to go off two by two, and make our way to St Ives. A certain member of the motoring press who, up to now, I had regarded as a friend, paired up with me along with a nervous member of BMW's press corps. My friend drove.

I knew there was something I had to tell — George, shall we call him, but my brain hurt. I remembered some 10 minutes later as we clouted a bank and dropped into a ditch, all wheels locked. " These tyres aren't very good in the wet," I said. We got out, except George, who sat with episcopalian unconcern behind the steering wheel turning it this way and that as we heaved and strained. A gentleman farmer came past in gumboots, and obligingly climbing into the ditch with us to heave and strain. With a loud

squelch the car came out of the ditch. The only damage was a set of muddy handprints on what had up to then been pristine silver paint. Not a scratch, otherwise. Why does it never happen to me that way ?

From there on we settled down to an amicable game of " You frighten me, I'll frighten you." We stopped at Goonhilly so that George could snap away happily with his box Brownie. I had forgotten mine. We got lost many times. Neither of us could navigate very well.

After lunch in St Ives we all played musical cars : those who had driven the Turbo took over 3.3Ls, the other new car for us to thrash, I mean try. By this time my brain was working again, and I realised that really I am cut out for the life of a millionaire. It's my way of life. Wafting along with all creature comforts, being courteous to the hoi poloi even when they get in the way, and discussing lofty sentiments like the best way of cooking sole bonne femme or whether left foot braking on an automatic was good or bad.

The intention was for me to drive one of the 3.3Ls back to London. Some quick calculations showed that no way was I going to be there before midnight, so I nastily pulled rank and suggested that a seat on the plane flying back would not go amiss. BMW acquiesced. For some reason the receptionist at the airport at Newquay insisted that I had to call myself " Miss Ann Hope," which was an embarrassment but it did mean that I was travelling back to London in a Herald — which you might have gathered by now is of the flying sort.

And that is a description of the sort of hard times that we motoring journalists have to put up with. Life is not all caviar and champagne, you know. They sometimes put Guinness in as well.

Hand built in limited numbers the BMW 2002 is only available in left-hand-drive. Progress is unbelievably smooth on the road.

BMW Turbo—flexible racer

For many years, engineers have been trying to design a car which would combine the traffic manners of a low-compression hack with the open-road performance of a competition machine. High-density induction is the obvious answer and Mercedes-Benz built cars in the nineteen-twenties and thirties with a supercharger which could be put in action by merely engaging a clutch. Unfortunately, a blower driven from the crankshaft consumes a lot of horsepower, so a relatively small gain in performance was accompanied by a large increase in fuel consumption.

Yet the idea is immensely attractive and the problem has now been solved by harnessing the normally wasted energy of the exhaust gases to drive the supercharger. The extremely high revolutions of the exhaust-driven turbine suit the centrifugal type of supercharger, which is far more efficient than positive-displacement compressors and needs no wasteful step-up gears in this instance. Fuel injection overcomes carburetter pressuris-

ing problems and the turbocharger can work as effectively with petrol engines as it has for a long time with diesels.

The BMW Turbo was originally a competition car, but its racing achievements are too well known to require discussion. The subject of the present test is a production car, though at this stage hand-built in limited numbers and only available with left-hand steering. I tested it simply as a fast touring vehicle and found that it has an enormous potential as the ideal high-performance car of the future. It has the same sort of speed and acceleration as the hottest versions of the 3-litre BMW, for instance, but its small size is a great advantage on British roads. Above all, its fuel economy is incomparably better, which is what modern motoring is all about.

For commuting, the engine is generally kept below 4000 rpm, when the static compression ratio of 6.9 to 1 is representative of the actual figure, ensuring extreme flexibility on the high gears. If the revs are allowed to enter the

The Turbo suffers from too much "go faster" decoration making it dangerously conspicuous.

interesting part of the spectrum, there is a positive boost of 7.8 lb, which puts the effective compression ratio up to about 9.5, the same as the Tii, which is the HUCR (highest useful compression ratio). Now power is required from the engine and the higher volumetric efficiency increases the output from 130 to 170 bhp at the same revs.

On the road, the results are outstanding, the engine being unbelievably smooth, quiet and flexible for a four-cylinder unit. There is a suggestion of whistling wind occasionally before any real boost is developed, but most of the time the Turbo is quieter than a normal 2002, for the turbine acts as a most effective exhaust silencer.

The engine is deliberately de-tuned to give a long life with complete reliability and an ignition cut-out avoids any risk of over-revving. This is an essential piece of equipment because the engine accelerates so fast under full boost that it would be all too easy to go right into the red.

On the test car, the cut-out began to function above an indicated 136 mph, which is about 130 mph against the watch. For me, the gearbox was rather too far away and the synchromesh baulked on fast changes, but I did a 0-60 mph in 6.7 s with quite a leisurely change from first to second. Similarly, I did the standstill to 100 mph acceleration in well under 20 s, with a minimum of wheelspin and unhurried gearchanges. The driving position is excellent, apart from the too remote gearlever, and the seats give good lateral location.

The behaviour of the Michelin tyres was outstanding on wet roads and one can really use all the power all the time, almost irrespective of surface conditions. On a previous occasion, I did experience some brake fade with a Turbo, but I failed to worry the brakes during this test. The car is well balanced on corners, the big Michelins giving some extra cornering power compared with the standard 2002, but the ride has not been stiffened up and the Turbo is perfectly comfortable for shopping trips.

It would be possible to criticise the Turbo because full boost is not instantly available at virtually zero revs. In practice, this need not apply, for it is normally possible to foresee when full acceleration will be required and get things turning over nicely in preparation. There is a knack which is soon acquired but during hard driving the revs can be kept up

Below: The BMW's compact size is a great advantage on congested British roads.

Under the bonnet turbocharger installation boosts power to 170 bhp DIN.

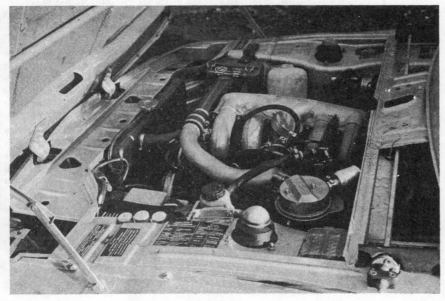

sufficiently so that there is no appreciable delay in response.

In my opinion—and there will be those who disagree—the Turbo has too much "go-faster" decoration. It could be driven faster on the road if it were less conspicuous, the coloured stripes performing no useful function while the flared guards over the wide tyres could be blended into the body sides more neatly. Similarly, the front and rear spoilers evidently do their job efficiently, judging by the high-speed stability of the car, but I am sure that they could be just as effective if they were less noticeable. Some owners may wish to emphasise the car's racing background, but the police may find it rather too interesting.

The BMW 2002 has been with us for a long time but the addition of the turbo-charger has made it one of the most effective and economical ultra-fast touring cars that has yet been produced. I had an overall average of 23.5 mpg, including taking the performance figures, and most owners will do far better than this, probably approaching 30 mpg on occasion.

Personally, I don't mind a "left-hooker," but I'm sure there is sufficient demand in England to justify the production of some right-hand-drive examples. Surely it's time that some eyeball ventilators were added, too, for we have all grown out of swivelling quarter lights. Perhaps if the production were increased, the car could be sold at a more realistic price, for it's a pretty expensive 2-litre, even though it is a 130 mph car.

The BMW 2002 Turbo has six-cylinder flexibility with only a four-cylinder thirst. It can be driven all day in London without ever wetting a sparking plug and on the open road it can see off almost anything. It handles remarkably well and gives a comfortable ride. I like it!

SPECIFICATION AND PERFORMANCE DATA

Car tested: BMW 2002 Turbo 2-door saloon, price £4220.84 including car tax and VAT.

Engine: Four-cylinders 89 x 80 mm (1990 cc). Compression ratio 6.9 to 1, 170 bhp (DIN) at 5800 rpm. Inclined valves operated by chain-driven overhead-camshaft and rockers. Schafer mechanical fuel injection with exhaust-driven turbo-supercharger.

Transmission: Single dry plate clutch. 4-speed all-synchromesh gearbox with central change, ratios 1.0, 1.279, 1.861 and 3.351 to 1. Hypoid final drive, ratio 3.36 to 1. 40 per cent self-locking differential.

Chassis: Combined steel body and chassis. Independent suspension of all four wheels by coil springs and telescopic dampers, with MacPherson front and semi-trailing arm rear geometry. Anti-roll bars both ends. ZF-Gammer worm and roller steering. Servo-assisted dual-circuit disc/drum brakes. Bolt-on steel wheels fitted 185/70 VR 13 tyres (light-alloy wheels extra).

Equipment: 12-volt lighting and starting. Speedometer. Rev-counter. Fuel, temperature and blower-pressure gauges. Clock. Heating and demisting system. Flashing direction indicators. 2-speed windscreen wipers and washers. Reversing lights.

Dimensions: Wheelbase 8 ft 2 in. Track 4 ft 5.5 in. Overall length 13 ft 10 in. Width 5 ft 6 in. Weight 2281 lb.

Performance: Maximum speed 130 mph. Speeds in gears: Third 95 mph, second 62 mph, first 33 mph. Standing quarter-mile 15.2 s. Acceleration: 0-30 mph 2.2 s, 0-50 mph 5.4 s, 0-60 mph 6.7 s, 0-80 mph 12.2 s, 0-100 mph 19.5 s.

Fuel consumption: 23 to 29 mpg.

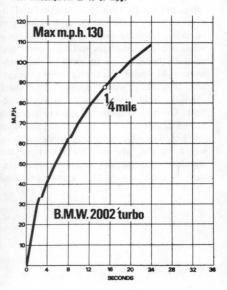

Max m.p.h. 130

¼ mile

B.M.W. 2002 turbo

Continued from page 15

speed (which doubles as cruising speed) is a shade over a hundred, and nothing in the chassis, running gear, or engine ever gives the impression that it's being worked too hard. It's like effortless, no kidding. It couldn't come down the side of a mountain any more gracefully if Gower Champion choreographed the whole trip.

Maybe the neatest part of the whole deal is the fact that the 2002 was originally proposed as a kind of second-choice, American anti-smog version of the wailing 1600 TI they were selling in Germany, but the second-choice version turns out to be better than the original. The 2002 is faster 0-60, and faster at the top end as well. Not to mention the fact that it's a whole lot smoother and quieter.

How they can do all that good stuff and then screw it up with one of those incredible Blaupunkt radios is a little hard to imagine, but that's what they did. The rule with Blaupunkt and Becker seems to be,

"The Bigger and More Complicated and Expensive Our Radios Are, The Lousier The Reception." The 2002 had a lovely-looking AM/FM affair neatly slipped into its console—easily a hundred-and-fifty bucks worth of radio—and I couldn't pick up a Manhattan station from the far end of the Brooklyn Bridge. Honestly. It was maybe the dumbest radio anybody ever stuck in an automobile, like all Blaupunkt and Becker radios, yet the German car makers—for reasons unknown—continue to use them.

It's a great mystery. Motorola, Bendix, Delco, and Philco can all sell you foolproof, first-class radios for about 75 bones—the Japanese can knock one off for about 98 cents—but the best German car radio you can buy throws up its hands in despair if you expect it to pull in a station more than three-quarters of a mile away.

Fortunately, the BMW is fast enough that you can keep picking up new stations as the old ones fade away. What you really want to do in this case, though, is install a good domestic stereo tape system. Maybe a little kitchen, too. The car is nice enough that you'll probably want to spend an occasional weekend in it—especially when you're fighting with your wife, or there's nothing good on television.

A final word of advice. The crazy-mad little BMW 2002 is every bit as good as I say it is—maybe better. If the 1600 was the best $2500 sedan *C/D* ever tested, the 2002 is most certainly the best $2850 sedan in the whole cotton-picking world. Besides the model-number was increased by 25%, but the price increase for the larger engine only amounted to 14%, and if *that* ain't a fair deal . . .

Feel free to test-drive one, but please don't tell any of those ten million squares who are planning to buy something else. They deserve whatever they get. Now turn your hymnals to Number 2002 and we'll sing two choruses of Whispering Bomb. . .●

Continued from page 36

All of this is to say that, as a sports car, the 2002 is more than just agreeable. As a sedan it's not disagreeable but it's not as comfortable as its price would indicate. We are not enamored with the driving position. The large diameter steering wheel is positioned more toward horizontal than conventional Detroit practice, and if you position the seat far enough forward so that the top of the wheel is within easy reach, you find that the control pedals are too close, particularly the accelerator. Since the seat is high you are forced into maintaining an unnatural and tiring angle between the gas-pedal foot and its attached leg. Also, the seat backs do not support you in such a way that would be comfortable for long distances. The seats themselves are mildly contoured buckets and do a remarkably good job of restraining you laterally, partially because the deeply textured insert discourages sliding around and partially because the softness of the cushions make them effectively more bucketlike than they would appear. The seat/shoulder belt arrangement, however, reflects German contempt for fussy attempts at self-preservation. Both straps join, with an unfathomable adjusting system, at a single buckle, and the fixed end of the shoulder strap mounts, below the rear window in such a way that is sure to cause high compressive loads on your spine in the event of a crash. We wouldn't wear the shoulder strap on a bet.

While the front seats have plenty of space in every direction for two adults, leg room in the rear is a dear commodity. We have no complaints about head and shoulder space, and because the side windows swing out rather than roll down, the side padding in the elbow area has been moved out toward the exterior sheetmetal to give a surprising amount of lateral passenger space. In general, the interior gives the impression of good materials and workmanship applied to a conservative design.

It's this quality, fortified with sophisticated engineering, that makes the premium German cars, Porsche, Mercedes-Benz and BMW, highly desirable to the discerning buyer. Considering the German's reputation for attention to detail, we find it unthinkable that the 2002, after two years in production, still has an overheating problem. Both of the test cars, if allowed to idle for 10 minutes, even in 30°F weather, would have their temperature gauges registering in the red zone. If it's that bad in the winter, we suspect summer driving in slow traffic would be intolerable. The importer had even installed a higher capacity cooling fan in the automatic transmission car, but its most significant contribution was an unpleasant roar at cruising speeds.

Overheating isn't the only unpleasantry associated with owning a 2002 as you will probably find out at your dealer's parts counter. Because we've been hearing comments about the high price of BMW parts (Porsche and Mercedes-Benz as well) we checked the prices of a few—a muffler, head gasket, clutch assembly, taillight lens, front fender and front bumper—that we felt an average owner would most likely have to replace. Then we compared this list with that of other similarly priced cars: Fiat 124 coupe, Triumph TR6, Volvo 142, Peugeot 504 and a Chevelle V-8. The total for the BMW was significantly higher than for any other car. Because of differences in design—for example, the 2002 has a 3-piece front bumper and you might get by with replacing only part of it—you can't project the entire parts price structure from this short list. Still, we would certainly caution against abusing your clutch (over $100) or breaking a taillight lens (almost $17).

To speak further of prices would be to belabor the point. In the things that the 2002 does best—harassing Triumphs, petrifying your passengers and awakening every dormant Fangio trait in your psyche—it can't be beat. Moreover, it's our firm belief that those things are cheap at any price. And since all of this subversion is camouflaged by the most Puritan of sedan bodies your wife won't have a clue until it's too late. ●

BMW 2002 Turbo

1,990 c.c.

Exhilarating performance without any temperament and little loss of economy over standard 2002Tii. Taut ride and excellent handling and brakes give startling journey time potential. Poor ventilation and fairly high noise level familiar shortcomings of 2002 design. No conventional performance competitors at the price. Regrettably, available only in left hand drive form.

Some roll is noticeable when cornering hard but general ride and handling inspire the greatest confidence

FEW WAYS of increasing the power of an engine look simpler in principle than turbo-charging. Harnessing the exhaust gases with a small impeller that is used to blow air into the engine to increase the density of the charge seems so logical, that one wonders why it is not employed more often. There are however, some snags. The turbochargers themselves cost a lot of money, and there are few companies producing them. There are also abundant problems in the installation of such a device, not all of which are overcome even in the BMW's case. The biggest problem concerns the induction system's ability to meter fuel appropriately, regardless of whether it is being drawn into the engine as the result of manifold depression, or whether the charge is being forced into the engine as a result of pressure from the turbocharger. In this, the BMW turbo is conspicuously successful, but in respect of the accommodation of the necessary large-bore exhaust system, the design is not as good, as there are a number of annoying vibration periods that result from poor location of the system. However, problems of this nature are readily soluble and we would hope that only early production examples suffer these annoyances.

BMW first gave notice of their interest in turbo-charging when they campaigned cars so equipped in the Touring Car Challenge way back in 1969. In the 2002 saloon, they knew that they had a chassis with a proven success record in saloon car racing; all that was needed was more power!

The success of the project culminated in winning the European Touring Car Challenge, and in those days, Porsche 911s raced in the same class, so BMW's win was no mean achievement. Having proved their point by winning the Championship, the emphasis in BMW's racing programme moved on to developing the bigger saloons and coupés into race-winning cars, and turbocharging seemed to have died a death. Then, in September 1973, what should be the star of the Frankfurt Show but the 2002 turbo—now developed as a road car with plans for the building of at least 2,000 examples.

Compared to the car as seen at the time of the original announcement, the Road Test example is mechanically identical; only the external decorations have been toned down since the first car appeared with "turbo" in large letters in mirror image on the front air dam. As sold in the UK, the 2002 turbo has just a restrained side flash in BMW's racing colours with "turbo" set in it and a matching colourful flash across the front air dam that helps to disguise the extreme depth of the front of the car. On the tail of the car there is restrained identity lettering, but the most obvious external features are the add-on glass fibre wing extensions that hide wheels of greater offset than the normal 2002 wheels. At the rear of the car there is a full-width soft rubber lip on the trailing edge of the boot and of course at the front, the deep front air dam and the absence of a bumper completely change the appearance of the nose.

In the class of genuine 4-seater sports coupés/saloons such as the Triumph Dolomite Sprint, the Fiat 124 Coupé, the Ford RS2000 and the Alfa Romeo 2000GTV, the normal 2002Tii is most competitive already. By increasing the performance so dramatically as in the turbo's case, BMW have moved the car into a very different echelon of rivals. In fact, the first comparable performer to the 2002 turbo is the Porsche 911 and that is nearly £2,000 more to buy, and one must go up as far as the the Porsche 911S before finding one that is appreciably quicker than the 2002 turbo.

Power output from the 1,990 c.c. engine is no less than 170 bhp (DIN) at 5,800 rpm and the maximum torque figure is 117 lb. ft. at a not unconservative 4,000 rpm. The explanation for the increased torque is that the effective cubic capacity of the engine is increased by the effect of the improved charge density that the turbocharger confers, and, of course, torque is directly related to capacity. Thus there is no lack of flexibility in the turbo-charged car and it only feels less tractable than

AUTO TEST

BMW 2002 Turbo

the normal 2002tii at very low revs because it is higher-geared. Thus, in town or during slow running in traffic, the 2002 turbo shows no special shortcomings and indeed, the excellent gearchange and ready response of the engine enable smart progress to be made in broken traffic.

The maximum pressure that the turbocharger is allowed to create in the inlet manifold is 1.55 atm (approx 7 psi above ambient pressure) and a valve opens automatically when this pressure is reached. Although adjustable, this valve is set by the factory and if it is touched other than by a dealer, the warranty is invalidated.

From 4,000 rpm onwards, pressure in the inlet manifold is at 1.55 atm, the torque is at its maximum, and the power is building up quickly to its peak. On the road, a steadily increasing surge is felt as 4,000 rpm is exceeded and this continues to build up as the revs rise. Thus it can be judged that for optimum performance it is best to keep the engine turning in the range 4,000 to 6,000 rpm, and the well-chosen close-ratio gears enable this to be done successfully.

Performance

Nose-heavy weight distribution and relatively narrow tyres for the power output mean that it is easy to get appreciable wheelspin when attempting to get optimum acceleration times through the gears. After much experiment it was found that dropping the clutch suddenly at 4,800 rpm produced just the right amount of wheelspin to avoid dropping the engine speed below 4,000 rpm while at the same time avoiding an excess of wheelspin that would have wasted time. With this treatment, the car leapt from rest to 30 mph in 3.0 sec, and there was just a brief squeak of wheelspin when taking 2nd gear in which the turbo raced on to 60 mph in just 7.3 sec. The rev limiter allows a maximum in 2nd gear of 63 mph when 3rd gear can be taken and held to 6,400 rpm, giving 98 mph. The time to 100 mph would have been slightly quicker had the cutout not operated just before reaching this speed, but even so, a time of 20.7 sec from rest to 100 mph is fast by any car's standards.

Not surprisingly, acceleration tails off from 100 mph onwards, but the turbo is just among the elite of high performance cars capable of reaching 120 mph in under half-a-minute. Acceleration in each gear shows more obviously how the effect of the increasing assistance of the turbocharger can

be felt. In third gear, for instance, the standard 2002Tii is faster for each 20 mph increment up to 50 mph, giving a time of 5.6 sec from 30-50 mph against 6.2 sec for the turbo. The times from 40-60 mph are similar at 5.7 sec for the Tii against 5.5 sec for the turbo, but then the latter just marches away as its times gets less and the Tii's get longer. Both 50-70 mph and 60-80 mph are covered by the turbo in 5.0 sec and 70-90 mph is covered in 6.0 sec. Proof that it is worth hanging onto third gear even until the rev-limiter operates is given by reference to the acceleration times in top gear. They show the equivalent 70-90 mph time in top gear to be 7.7 sec and in practice this means, that on the road one can sprint past and away from

most cars and such acceleration in either third or top gear nullifies the disadvantage of the left-hand-drive. About the only speed range at which the turbo is at a disadvantage is when following traffic at around 55-60 mph when little useful acceleration is left in second gear and third gear acceleration is still building towards its optimum. This can be overcome by hanging back slightly on the approach to a likely overtaking place and then rushing up to overtake in anticipation of a clear road. The use of such dodges and the turbo's re-

serves of acceleration in any gear, give the potential of remarkably short journey times.

Roadholding and ride

Such considerable qualities of acceleration are limited if they are not matched by good roadholding, and fortunately in the turbo's case, this is of a very high standard. Nose-heavy weight distribution and fairly stiff front end roll control mean that the turbo, like the basic 2002Tii is set up to give initial understeer. However, with so much available power, a transi-

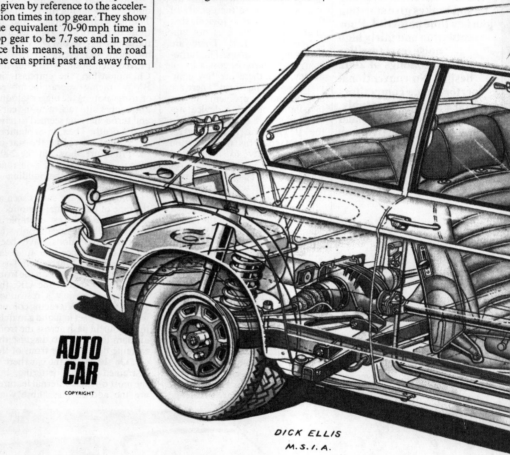

DICK ELLIS
M.S.I.A.

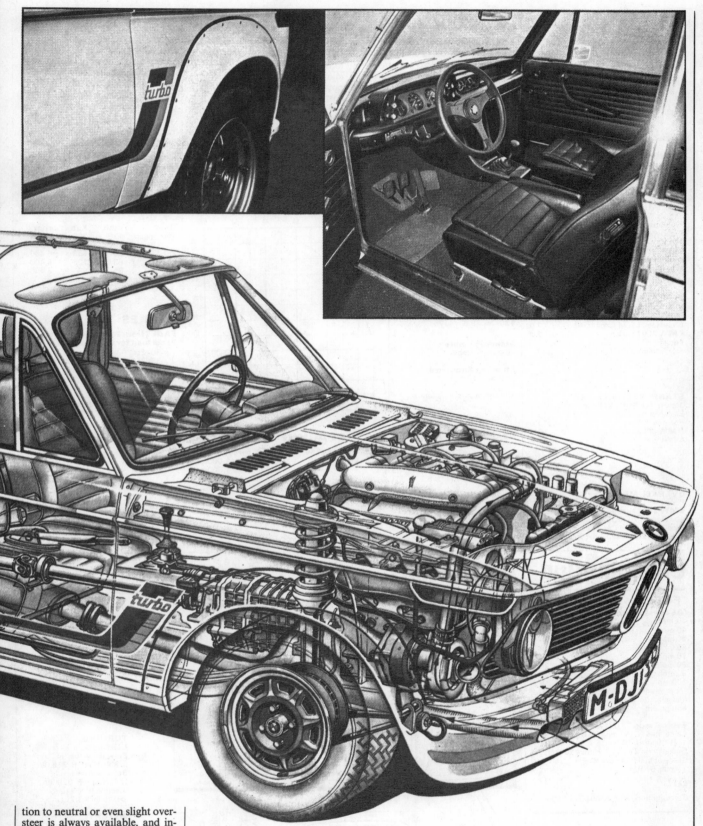

tion to neutral or even slight over-steer is always available, and indeed at slow speeds especially on wet roads, some caution must be taken to avoid too much over-steer. The accurate and lightweight ZF-Gemmer worm-and-roller steering allows plenty of feel of what is happening at the front of the car, and in addition, the steering is free from kickback on rougher surfaces. The steering ratio is the same as that of the normal 2002Tii at 3.7 turns lock-to-lock for a compact turning circle a little over a mean 32 feet. For serious road or competition use, higher ratio steering would be a help and as the steering effort required is low, even at parking speeds, a higher ratio would probably be a significant all-round advantage. The only further point that might be made in the context

Dick Ellis' cutaway of the BMW 2002 turbo shows the installation of the turbocharger immediately below the heat shield that surrounds the exhaust manifold. The arrows show how the air is taken into the compressor and sent along thin wall piping to the plenum chamber atop the engine. The air taken in through the hole in the glass fibre front air dam is used to cool the turbocharger. As suspension differences compared with the standard 2002Tii are confined to different settings only, the only visible sign of the 2002 turbo's improved road performance is the ventilated front disc brakes. In the other colour pictures on this page can be seen the distinguishing details of the turbo, such as the red instrument surround, detachable glass fibre wing spats, the soft rubber spoiler on the bootlid and the effective bucket seats that have head restraints as standard

BMW 2002 Turbo

of handling concerns the effect of the peakiness of the power output. Effectively, this means that as one is accelerating through a long corner, one is getting a steadily increasing amount of power, tending to tighten the line more and more and this effect is more marked than in a car of similar power output but possessing a flatter power curve.

The springing, damping and roll resistance of the turbo are all firmer than the normal 2002Tii which moves the point at which the semi-trailing arms begin to jack up to higher speeds. When allied to the turbo's limited slip differential, the firmer suspension gives more predictable control of the handling at the car's limit of cornering power as, unlike the normal 2002Tii, the inside rear wheel does not lift and spin with consequent loss of speed. Even if

---

Comparisons

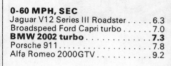

MAXIMUM SPEED MPH
Jaguar V12 Series III
  Roadster . . . . (£3,743) 143
Broadspeed Ford Capri
  turbo . . . . (£3,419) 140
BMW 2002 turbo . . . . (£4,221) 130*
Porsche 911 . . . . (£6,124) 130*
Alfa Romeo 2000GTV . . (£2,945) 120
Manufacturer's claim

0-60 MPH, SEC
Jaguar V12 Series III Roadster 6.3
Broadspeed Ford Capri turbo 7.0
BMW 2002 turbo **7.3**
Porsche 911 . . . . 7.8
Alfa Romeo 2000GTV 9.2

STANDING ¼-MILE, SEC
Jaguar V12 Series III Roadster 14.9
Broadspeed Ford Capri turbo 15.4
Porsche 911 . . . . 15.8
BMW 2002 turbo **16.0**
Alfa Romeo 2000GTV 16.4

OVERALL MPG
Porsche 911 . . . . 23.2
BMW 2002 turbo **21.7**
Alfa Romeo 2000GTV 21.1
Broadspeed Ford Capri turbo 17.1
Jaguar V12 Series III Roadster . . . 15.0

Performance

ACCELERATION

True speed mph	Time in Secs	Car Speedo mph
30	3.0	33
40	4.3	43
50	5.7	53
60	7.3	64
70	9.8	74
80	12.5	84
90	15.7	94
100	20.7	104
110	27.2	114
120	39.8	125

Standing ¼-mile
16.0 sec 91 mph

Standing Kilometre
28.9 sec 112 mph

Mileage recorder: accurate

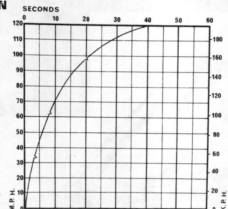

GEAR RATIOS AND TIME IN SEC

mph	Top (3.36)	3rd (4.44)	2nd (6.79)
10–30	—	7.7	4.2
20–40	10.0	7.0	3.8
30–50	9.1	6.2	3.3
40–60	8.6	5.5	3.1
50–70	8.4	5.0	—
60–80	7.7	5.0	—
70–90	7.7	6.0	—
80–100	8.5	—	—
90–110	11.3	—	—
100–120	18.6	—	—

GEARING
(with 185/70VR 13 in. tyres)
Top . . . . 20.36 mph per 1,000rpm
3rd . . . . 15.41 mph per 1,000rpm
2nd . . . . 10.08 mph per 1,000rpm
1st . . . . 5.41 mph per 1,000rpm

MAXIMUM SPEEDS

Gear	mph	kph	rpm
Top (mean)	130*	209	6,400
(best)	130*	209	6,400
3rd	98	158	6,400
2nd	63	101	6,400
1st	35	56	6,400

*Manufacturer's claimed maximum

BRAKES
FADE (from 70 mph in neutral)
Pedal load for 0.5 g stops in lb

1	30–25	6	35
2	35–25	7	30–35
3	35–30	8	35
4	35	9	35
5	35	10	40–30

RESPONSE from 30mph in neutral

Load	g	Distance
20lb	0.20	150ft
40lb	0.51	59ft
60lb	0.86	35ft
80lb	0.96	31.4ft
Handbrake	0.30	100ft

Max. Gradient 1 in 3

CLUTCH
Pedal 42lb and 5in

Consumption

*FUEL
(At constant speed—mpg)*

30 mph	41.6
40 mph	38.2
50 mph	34.0
60 mph	29.7
70 mph	27.0
80 mph	24.0
90 mph	21.4
100 mph	18.9

*N.B. Manufacturer's claimed figures— fuel injection incompatible with *Autocar* equipment*

Typical mpg 23.0 (12.3 litres/100km)
Calculated (DIN) mpg 24.6
  (11.5 litres/100km)
Overall mpg 21.7 (13.0 litres/100km)
Grade of fuel Premium, 4-star
  (min. 97 RM)

OIL
Consumption (SAE 20W/50) 1,500mpp

TEST CONDITIONS
Weather: Dry, clear and fine
Wind: 5-10 mph
Temperature: 21 deg C (70 deg F)
Barometer: 29.7 in. hg.
Humidity: 62 per cent.
Surface: Dry concrete and asphalt.
Test distance: 1,700 miles

Figures taken by our own staff at the Motor Industry Research Association proving ground at Nuneaton.

Dimensions

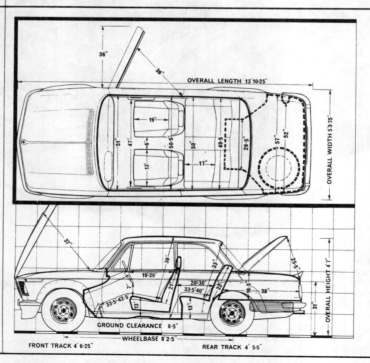

STANDARD GARAGE
16ft × 8ft 6in.

TURNING CIRCLES:
Between kerbs
L, 33ft 11in.; R, 31ft 0in.
Between walls
L, 35ft 2in.; R, 32ft 3in.
Steering wheel turns, lock to lock 3.7

WEIGHT:
Kerb Weight 21.7 cwt
(2,429lb–1,103kg).
(with oil, water and half full fuel tank).
Distribution, per cent.
F, 54.7; R, 45.3
Laden as tested:
24.6cwt (2,754lb–1,251kg).

the driver lifts off; the feeling that the normal 2002Tii gave of being "on tiptoe" is absent in the turbo version and one can give only unreserved praise to the car for its handling. A certain contributor to the high cornering potential is the aerodynamic aid that the front dam and rear spoiler give, for in addition to contributing to good straightline stability, they ensure no loss of precision as cornering speeds increase.

In the search for good handling, the ride may suffer but in the turbo's case, this is only marginally worse than the high standard set by the 2002Tii at low speeds, and praise is due to BMW for finding that elusive compromise between ride and handling. Praise is due too for the Michelin XWX tyres with which the test car was fitted, for there are no conditions of dry or wet road under which these tyres give any cause for complaint.

Brakes

We have criticised previous 2002 BMWs for the speed sensitivity of their brakes and also a tendency to go "soggy" when used frequently and hard. The adoption of ventilated front discs and the introduction of a pressure-limiting valve into the rear circuit has removed these criticisms, and the system is now well up to the standard of the rest of the car. An added bonus is that the softer pad material that the ventilated front disc brakes use improves the initial response of the brakes compared to the normal 2002Tii and less than 30lb

---

Specification
BMW 2002 turbo

FRONT ENGINE, REAR-WHEEL DRIVE

ENGINE
Cylinders	4, in-line
Main bearings	5
Cooling system	Water; pump, fan, thermostat
Bore	89mm (3.504in.)
Stroke	80mm (3.150in.)
Displacement	1,990 c.c. (121.4 cu. in.)
Valve gear	Single overhead camshaft and rockers
Compression ratio	6.9 to 1. Min. octane rating: 98RM
Induction	Schafer mechanical injection with exhaust gas-driven KKK/BLO turbocharger
Fuel pump	Kugelfischer high pressure type PL04
Oil filter	Full-flow, replaceable cartridge
Max. power	170 bhp (DIN) at 5,800 rpm
Max. torque	117 lb. ft. (DIN) at 4,000 rpm

TRANSMISSION
Clutch	Fichtel and Sachs, diaphragm spring, 7.9 in. dia.

Gearbox	*4-speed, all-synchromesh, optional 5-speed	
Gear ratios	Top 1.00	
	Fourth 1.24	*Fourth 1.00
	Third 1.58	Third 1.28
	Second 2.16	Second 1.86
	First 3.37	First 3.35
	Reverse 3.65	Reverse 4.00
Final drive	Hypoid bevel, 3.36 :1	
Mph at 1,000rpm in top gear	20.36	

CHASSIS and BODY
Construction	Integral with steel body

SUSPENSION
Front	Independent; MacPherson struts, lower wishbones, coil springs, telescopic dampers, anti-roll bar
Rear	Independent; semi-trailing arms, coil springs, telescopic dampers, anti-roll bar

STEERING
Type	ZF-Gemmer worm and roller
Wheel dia.	15 in.

BRAKES
Make and type	ATE ventilated disc front, drum rear, pressure limiting valve in rear circuit
Servo	ATE vacuum
Dimensions	F, 10.08 in. dia. R, 9.8 in. dia. 1.57 in. wide shoes
Swept area	F, 210.4 sq. in., R, 88.6 sq. in. Total 299 sq. in. (244 sq. in./ton laden)

WHEELS
Type	Pressed steel disc 5½J in. wide rim
Tyres—make	*Michelin XWX/Pirelli CN36SM
—type	radial ply tubed
—size	185/70VR 13

EQUIPMENT
Battery	12 volt 44 Ah.
Alternator	53 amp a.c.
Headlamps	110/120 watt (total)
Reversing lamp	Standard
Electric fuses	12
Screen wipers	Two-speed, wash/wipe facility
Screen washer	Standard, electric
Interior heater	Standard, water valve type
Heated backlight	Standard
Safety belts	Standard, inertia reel, static in rear
Interior trim	Cloth seats, pvc headlining
Floor covering	Carpet
Jack	Screw-pillar type
Jacking points	2 each side beneath sills
Windscreen	Laminated
Underbody protection	Tectyl underbody sealing to floor pan and wheel arches.

MAINTENANCE
Fuel tank	15.4 Imp. gallons (70 litres)
Cooling system	11 pints (inc. heater)
Engine sump	7½ pints (4.4 litres) SAE 20W/50 Change oil every 2,000 miles Change filter every 2,000 miles.
Gearbox	1.8 pints. SAE 80EP. Change every 16,000 miles.
Final drive	1.7 pints. SAE 90 (Hypoid) Change every 8,000 miles
Grease	No points
Valve clearance	Inlet 0.006—0.008 in. (hot) Exhaust 0.006—0.008 in. (hot)
Contact breaker	0.016 in. gap; 62 ±3 deg. dwell
Ignition timing	25 deg. BTDC (stroboscopic at 2,500 rpm)
Spark plug	Type: Bosch W200 T 30. Gap 0.24 in.
Tyre pressures	F, 30; R, 30 psi (normal driving) F, 30; R, 33 psi (high speed and full load)
Max. payload	892 lb (405 kg)

*Fitted to test car

SPEEDOMETER	DIPPING MIRROR
IGNITION LIGHT	REV COUNTER
OIL PRESSURE WARNING LIGHT	TRIP RESET
	CIGAR LIGHTER
WATER TEMPERATURE GAUGE	REAR WINDOW DEMISTER
LAMPS & PANEL LAMP	
FUEL GAUGE	CLOCK
	TURBOCHARGER BOOST GAUGE
FOGLAMP PROVISION	2 SPEED WIPERS & SCREENWASH
INDICATORS TELL-TALE	
MAIN BEAM TELL-TALE	HEATER CONTROL & BLOWER
	GLOVE LOCKER
BONNET RELEASE	IGNITION STARTER & STEERING LOCK
	REAR FOGLAMP & TELL-TALE PROVISION
HEATER & AIR CONTROL	ASH TRAY
INDICATORS DIPSWITCH & HEADLAMP FLASHER	HAZARD SWITCH & TELL-TALE
HANDBRAKE TELL-TALE	HANDBRAKE
HORN	

Servicing

	2,000 miles	4,000 miles	8,000 miles
Time Allowed (hours)	1.17	1.33	3.40
Cost at £3.30 per hour	£3.86	£4.39	£11.22
Engine oil	£2.00	£2.00	£2.00
Gearbox oil	—	—	£1.00
Oil filter	£1.79	£1.79	£1.79
Air filter	—	—	£15.24
Contact Breaker Points	—	—	£0.77
Sparking Plugs	—	—	£1.59
Total Cost:	**£7.65**	**£8.18**	**£33.61**

Routine Replacements:	Time hours	Labour	Spares	TOTAL
Brake Pads—Front (2 wheels)	0.50	£1.65	£5.59	£7.24
Brake Shoes—Rear (2 wheels)	1.00	£3.30	£19.44	£22.74
Exhaust System	1.00	£3.30	£71.55	£74.85
Clutch (centre+driven plate)	2.50	£8.25	£87.80	£96.05
Dampers—Front (pair)	2.50	£8.25	£54.75	£63.00
Dampers—Rear (pair)	1.00	£3.30	£26.20	£29.50
Replace Drive Shaft	0.50	£1.65	£54.77	£56.42
Replace Alternator	0.50	£1.65	£50.16	£51.81
Replace Starter	1.00	£3.30	£106.13	£109.43

BMW 2002 Turbo

pedal pressure is required for normal check braking. The accelerated brake fade test did not reveal any tendency for the braking efficiency to fall off, and indeed, the optimum braking figure of 0.96g given by the brakes when cold was repeatable at the same pedal pressure immediately after the last fade test application had been done. The handbrake gave a useful 0.30g which would be sufficient to stop the car on its own from 30mph in 100ft. As would be expected, the turbo had no difficulty in restarting on a 1-in-3 hill, rushing away with wheelspin after holding securely on the convenient and efficient handbrake.

Fuel consumption

With an overall consumption of 21.7mpg, the turbo is only beaten among the world's outstanding performance cars by the remarkable Porsche 911 which managed 23.2mpg overall. Inevitably, this figure includes a great deal of very hard driving, for this is what the car is all about. The best figure obtained was 24mpg on a long journey including much motorway and this is the sort of consumption that most owners are likely to get with some regularity. The turbo's fuel tank holds 15.4 gal so there is a really useful range of over 350 miles available. Although the Kügelfischer high pressure injection pump is not compatible with our Petrometa test equipment, the BMW claimed figures have been used in the data panel since the calculated DIN consumption figure is acceptable enough to indicate that these figures are accurate. The fuel tank fills well to the neck without blowback.

Comfort and controls

Immediate differences inside a turbo compared with other 2002 models are the bucket seats, a red surround to the instruments and the turbocharger boost gauge; otherwise, the interior is the same as the current 2002Tii.

The bucket seats are a deliberately tight fit for people of average build upwards (or outwards). Thus they give excellent lateral support which the high cornering forces demand. The backrests are finely adjustable for rake, and there is more than adequate rearward movement. However, with the front seats right back, little kneeroom remains for rear seat passengers and some compromise is necessary. For the driver, the seating position

The fuel injection plenum chamber, a multiplicity of pipework and various controls for varying atmospheric pressures and changing mixture strength with throttle opening mean a confusing under bonnet scene. However, items requiring routine maintenance are all within easy reach. To the engine's right are the air filter and generous water reservoir and the coil is tucked away on the bulkhead, well away from spray and dirt

has to be quite high as, on this left-hand-drive model, the pedals are floor-pivoted (as opposed to top-hung on the right-hand-drive BMWs that are imported). The pedals themselves are comfortable to operate, and there is space to rest the left foot beside the clutch and adequate spacing of brake and accelerator to allow heel-and-toe operation. The smart leather-rimmed steering wheel has a thick, hard rim and is undished. Ahead through the wheel is a full display of round instruments.

All the controls are within easy reach of the driver and as the car is fitted with inertia reel seat belts as standard, the controls are also accessible to a front seat passenger. Heating and ventilation controls are sited on the facia rail either side of the steering column. A poor feature is that the heat control is on the driver's left, making it difficult for the front seat passenger to operate, although the volume and heater fan control are accessible to both in the centre of the car.

The turbo was given all the improvements for 1974 cars that were announced at the 1973 Earls Court Motor Show which include slight revision to the rear seat cushion to provide more legroom than hitherto and the door trims are colour-keyed to the remainder of the interior trim.

Living with the 2002 turbo

Usually in the case of the highest performance version of a particular model, there is some clue either from the exhaust noise or the more exotic appearance to give a clue as to the car's status. In the turbo's case, the exhaust is in fact quieter than the standard car as a result of

the very big bore system that must be used to avoid back pressure on the turbocharger. The exhaust is made in special heat-resistant material to combat the very high temperatures that result from the turbocharger installation. So the only clues are the external bodywork changes and of course, the blistering performance.

The increased performance is gained at a quite reasonable increase in fuel consumption and the only penalty that one has to pay is in the more frequent service attention that the car requires. The very high temperatures in the turbocharger require that the engine oil be changed more frequently for fear that the oil's qualities will be destroyed more rapidly. Thus, the oil and filter must be changed every 2,000 miles and as the filter requires a special tool for removal, this has to be done by an authorised dealer. Apart from this requirement, only a change of rear axle oil at 8,000-mile intervals is an exception to normal servicing procedure for similar cars. BMW insist that any attention to the turbocharger and the mechanical fuel injection be carried out by authorised dealers only but emphasise that once set up accurately, the Schafer (Kugelfischer) fuel injection should be free of problem. Certainly in the case of the Road Test car, it always started first turn, and ran without temperament thereafter, providing exemplary drive-away characteristics. All the controls are light and all work well with a feeling of solidity. The gearchange especially has short definite movements back and forth and across the gate.

Some of the test staff felt that a longer gearlever would be an improvement in providing greater leverage to make the change even faster and to help to overcome synchromesh resistance when changing down into first gear on the move—an operation that occurs often on very winding roads when seeking optimum performance. The clutch is not too heavy in its operation, and the driving position allows a good leverage on the pedal. Its take-up is progressive and as the transmission is free of snatch or wind up, smooth progress is easily possible.

Access to items requiring routine maintenance is good beneath the big forward hinged bonnet, and even the dipstick can be easily unravelled from the mass of pipework and trunking that surrounds it. The combined reservoir for the brakes and clutch is brought to the nearside front wing top for easy visual checking and for replenishment if necessary.

The boot size is less than that of the normal 2002 as the greater capacity of the tank means that the floor is higher. However, the shape is still regular and a big suitcase can still be fitted in.

Conclusions

One unwelcome feature of most high performance cars is their size, as in general, the big engines used demand plenty of space. In the BMW turbo's case, like Porsche, tremendous performance is available in a handy package, and it is surprising how much this helps in making good progress in broken traffic.

In this country, a disadvantage that will weigh heavily against the car is the fact that it is only available in left-hand-drive form, which is heartily disliked by insurance companies if they do not already dislike the performance potential. Where the car is most likely to fail in marketing terms is in being the top of a range that starts with quite mundane examples in a performance sense and already possesses a similar model that appeals to the discriminating sporting motorist. However, the 2002 turbo is most civilised and sacrifices nothing in the provision of so much performance at a price unmatched by any rivals. It is a pity that something as simple as excessive heat in the region of the steering box should be the reason why an acceptable right-hand-drive version is not available. □

MANUFACTURER: *Bayerische Motorenwerke AG, Munchen 13, West Germany.*

UK CONCESSIONAIRES: *BMW Concessionaires (GB) Ltd., BMW House, 361-365 Chiswick High Road, London W4.*

PRICES

Basic	£3,607.55	Insurance	Group 7
Special Car Tax	£300.63		
VAT	£312.66	**EXTRAS (inc. VAT)**	
Total (in GB)	**£4,220.84**	Five speed gearbox	£255.04
Seat Belts	£32.25	Steel sliding sunroof	£125.25
Licence	£25.00	*Fitted to test car*	
Delivery charge (London)	£17.22		
Number plates	£5.00		
Total on the Road (exc. insurance)	**£4,300.31**	**TOTAL AS TESTED ON THE ROAD**	**£4,300.31**

BMW 1600 & 2002, 1967-1976

They are great fun and appreciating quickly

BY THOS L. BRYANT

I N THE 10-year span covered in this Used Car Classic, we probably devoted as many or more pages to the BMW 1600/ 2002 series as to any other model. And from the very beginning it was obvious that these are exceptional sport sedans. In the first road test of the 1600 (May 1967), we talked about the car's "excellent handling and stability," and concluded, "At the risk of becoming tiresome, let us say just once more that the BMW 1600 is a great automobile at the price" (then just a little more than $2600 on the west coast).

The 1600 was a pacesetter car for BMW, reviving the firm's flagging financial position and introducing significant numbers of Americans to the joys of the marque. The single-overhead-cam 4-cylinder engine displaced 1573 cc and was rated at 96 bhp at 5800 rpm, with 91 lb-ft of torque at 3000. Our original road test report described it as "one of the smoothest 4-cylinder engines we've encountered and there is just enough roar on acceleration to make it sound meaningful. It winds smoothly right through the rev range and is still pulling eagerly at the 6000-rpm redline." We were also impressed with the appearance of the engine, appreciating its aluminum cam cover, clean castings of the head and block and the obvious care taken in installation. Fuel delivery was by a single Solex downdraft carburetor.

Just a year later (May 1968), we published a road test of the 2002, which was essentially the same car but with a 2-liter (1990-cc) engine. The 2002 was meant as a replacement for the 1600 TI, the dual-carburetor, highly tuned version that boasted 118 bhp at 6200 rpm. It seemed clear that BMW foresaw that the TI model was going to have difficulty conforming to the coming U.S. emission standards, but that the 2-liter engine from the 2000 TI sedan would fill the bill. With its exterior dimensions being virtually the same as those of the 1600 engine, there were no installation problems.

The 2002 was somewhat disappointing to our road testers of the day who found it "Noisier and not much quicker than 1600 . . . usual BMW traits of quality, handling, ride . . . modern sports car performance for four passengers at a reasonable price." The 2002's performance was obviously affected by the air injection and carburetor/distributor changes needed for the fledgling emission standards, and 0-60 mph acceleration was accomplished in 11.3 seconds, compared to 11.6 sec for the previous year's 1600. We did point out, however, that the 1600 with similar emission controls probably would not be that quick. Nevertheless, the initial 2002 did not gain the editors' nod over the 1600, and the road test report ended: "Our conclusion, then, is that the 1600 remains the best value in the BMW line." This reflected the roughly $300 difference in price between the two at the time.

In October 1969 we revealed the results of an Owner Survey on the 1600 and 2002 (more about that report later). We didn't road test either model in 1970 (unbeknownst to us at the time 1970 was the last year in the U.S. for the 1600), but in 1971 there was much to report. In our August issue the BMW 2002 was named the Best Sedan, $2200-4000, in our list of the Best Cars in the World, 1971. The description of the car that appeared in that article is worth repeating: "The BMW 2002 is not just a sedan for transportation but a car for the enthusiast who needs space for four people. A family sports car, you might say. And while the 2002 is not big on carrying capacity, it will carry a family if need be and when it's not busy with such mundane chores, it provides the driver with great motoring. Its 2-liter engine is torquey and smooth if not quiet, its gearbox is a delight to operate, its suspension supple, yet competent, and its brakes reassuring. For a long time we've said that BMW has the best set of mechanicals in the world for a medium-priced sports car, sitting right here in this upright sedan."

By October of that year, BMW had introduced the 2002tii version into the U.S. and that called for an examination. The tii was the high-performance 2002, with Kugelfischer mechanical fuel injection instead of the single carburetor. The compression ratio was down to 9.0:1 compared to the 10.0:1 of the earlier 2002 models because of the toughening emission-control standards, but the tii did offer impressive horsepower and torque gains over the carbureted version: 140 bhp at 5800 versus 113 at 5800, and 145 lb-ft torque at 4500 compared to 116 at 3000. It was obvious, however, that the fuel-injected engine had to be wound rather tightly to get the most out of its capabilities.

The fuel delivery system was not the only change, as the tii also was fitted with different gearbox ratios for the standard 4-speed as well as having a 5-speed transmission available as an option. The 4-speed's ratios were slightly taller than those of the normal 2002, as was the final drive (3.45:1 versus 3.64), making the tii a car more readily suited to high-speed cruising. The 5-speed model came with a 4.11:1 final drive.

The other differences also played a part in giving the tii a more sporting character: larger brakes, 1.4-in. greater track width with wider wheels (5.0 in. instead of 4½ in.) and Michelin XAS radial tires with an H speed rating in place of the S-rated tires; and slightly beefier chassis components.

In our performance testing of the fuel-injected 2002, we found that it was not significantly quicker to 60 mph or through the standing-start quarter mile than the normal model. The 0-60 time for the tii was 9.8 sec and the quarter mile was covered in 17.3 sec at 78.5 mph—these times were 0.6 and 0.3 sec quicker, respectively, than for the carbureted 2002 of the day. The road testers reported that the tii used for that acceleration testing was not as thoroughly broken in as they would have liked, and mentioned too that there was "particular difficulty getting the 2002tii 'off the line' smoothly (BMW rear suspension always lets the wheels patter badly anyway) and when the wheels finally settled down the engine bogged."

The tii's handling garnered its share of praise in that road test, complementing high marks for the car's responsive engine, nice gearbox and good controls: "Then comes handling, and for a rather tall sedan the 2002tii is quite good. Its steering seems somewhat lighter than previous 2002s we've driven, despite the new car's greater weight; it's still not the lightest thing going but is very precise and quite quick enough. The tii comes with anti-roll bars front and rear, which keep body roll down to a moderate level, and the wider track, wider wheels and slightly stiffer tires all conspire to make the tii significantly better-handling than a 2002."

Our next encounter with the 2002 occurred in May 1972 when we compared the tii version with the Alfa Romeo 1750 Berlina and the newly introduced Mazda RX-2; a test designed to discover if the new Japanese sedan could compete with two of Europe's most successful sport sedans (we concluded it could). We were dismayed at the price increases that had shoved the small BMW sedan from a $2500 car when introduced as the 1600 in 1967 to $3803 for the 2002 and $4360 for the tii version. Nonetheless, the BMW continued as a favorite of ours, and it

Teutonic simplicity marks the interior design of the 1600/2002.

BRIEF SPECIFICATIONS

	1967 1600	1968 2002	1971 2002tii	1974 2002tii
Curb weight, lb	2050	2210	2310	2420
Wheelbase, in.	98.4	98.4	98.4	98.4
Track, f/r	52.4/52.4	52.4/52.4	53.8/53.8	53.8/53.8
Length	164.5	166.5	166.5	176.0
Width	62.6	62.6	62.6	62.6
Height	54.0	54.0	55.5	55.5
Engine type	sohc 4	sohc 4	sohc 4	sohc 4
Bore x stroke, in.	3.30 x 2.79	3.50 x 3.15	3.50 x 3.15	3.50 x 3.15
Displacement, cc	1573	1990	1990	1990
Horsepower @ rpm	96 @ 5800	113 @ 5800	140 @ 5800	125 @ 5500
Torque @ rpm	91 @ 3000	116 @ 3000	145 @ 4500	127 @ 4000

PERFORMANCE DATA
From Contemporary Tests

	1967 1600	1968 2002	1971 2002tii	1974 2002tii
0-60 mph, sec	11.6	11.3	9.8	9.5
Standing ¼ mi, sec	18.2	17.9	17.3	17.7
Avg fuel consumption, mpg	25	22-27	22.7	23.5
Road test date	5-67	5-68	10-71	6-74

TYPICAL ASKING PRICES*

1967-1970 1600	$1500-2500
1968-1970 2002	$2000-4000
1971-1973 2002	$2750-4500
1971-1973 2002tii	$3000-5000
1974-1976 2002	$4000-6000
1974-1976 2002tii	$4500-8000

*Prices are estimates based on cars that are in reasonably good condition but not restored to like-new. Cars in excellent condition will, of course, command higher prices, while poorly maintained cars will be cheaper than the range given here.

earned first-place votes in the comparison for handling, ride, gearbox, outward vision, body structure, interior and exterior styling, and overall finish, as well as being rated best overall "by a comfortable margin."

The 1972 emission controls were tough on imported cars because unleaded fuel became the order of the day: "The familiar and popular BMW was such a victim," we reported in a brief test in January 1973 when we examined the changes for the new year that would help alleviate the unpleasant side effects in driveability that had begun to plague the carburetor-equipped model. The 1972 car's compression ratio had fallen to 8.3:1 and the air pump for emission control was engendering backfiring on deceleration, exhaust back pressure, and extreme underhood temperatures.

To help correct these symptoms, BMW adapted its tri-spherical turbulence-inducing combustion chamber (used in the 6-cylinder BMW engines) to the 2002's engine—"The chamber apparently gives good emission characteristics, power output and fuel economy," we noted in the update. "Our test car ran with practically no symptoms of lean carburetion and went as well as the 2002 we tested for our June 1968 issue with a 10.5-sec 0–60 mph time and a 17.8-sec quarter mile. The 1968 car had done 10.4 and 17.6 respectively, and differences that small aren't significant," we concluded.

In June 1974 the 2002tii again figured in a comparison test—sports cars versus sports sedans—as it went up against the Jensen-Healey. The report noted that the 2002, in carburetor and fuel injection models, had received an extensive facelift that year. The grille was redesigned and new larger taillights were the immediately obvious alterations along with some improvements to the interior trim. Perhaps the most significant alteration of the 1974 2002, however, was the newly required bumpers to meet U.S. safety standards. Although they were cleanly designed and made of aluminum, they still added 9.5 in. to the car's overall length and more than 100 lb of weight—and BMW purists, of course, thought them unsightly, to say the least.

Our assessment of the 2002tii, however, was that its "character remains essentially the same: a practical, fairly roomy car for four people and their luggage with very sporting engine, suspension and brakes, exceptional solidity of construction and an unmistakably German precision about its controls. This is a car which tells you in no uncertain terms what it's doing but stops just short of making you uncomfortable in the process—a combination that pleases a lot of enthusiastic, fast drivers."

In its confrontation with the Jensen-Healey, the 2002tii got the nod in 0–60 mph acceleration (9.5 sec compared to 9.7) but the British sports car won the quarter mile with a time of 17.4 sec at 80.5 mph compared to the German sedan's 17.7 sec at 81.0. On the winding road portion of the test, the Jensen-Healey "does

The BMW 2-liter engine is impressive in looks as well as performance.

have the greater capabilities," we concluded, although "the BMW is still highly satisfying and sporty to drive. . ."

It's interesting to me that perhaps the best summary of the 2002 came in the form of a eulogy when we presented the initial road test of its successor, the 320i, in the December 1976 R&T: "Despite a base price that had risen to more than $6500, the 2002 was a brisk seller even in its final days. It was out of date in some important areas, particularly ventilation, but its reputation for reliability combined with ride, sporty performance and handling were hard to beat. It was the ideal car for the practical enthusiast who refused to give up the joy of driving simply because his automotive requirements dictated room for more than two people and generous trunk."

Buying a Used BMW 1600/2002

ONE OF our earliest Owner Survey reports featured the 1600 and 2002 (October 1969), and we received nearly 1000 responses to our Used Car Classic Questionnaire (September 1979) from BMW owners, so we have a considerable amount of background information on points to examine when choosing one of these cars.

First, from the Owner Survey report, there were two problem areas mentioned by more than 10 percent of the owners: clutch throwout bearing and emission-control-system ills. The clutch troubles were cited by 13 percent and usually required one or more replacements. The emission control complaints were voiced by 17 percent of the 1968–1969 model owners (the 1967 1600s had none) and generally dealt with poor driveability rather than actual failures, although the air pump's anti-backfire "gulp" valve did fail on some cars—this item was mentioned by a number of people who completed the Used Car Classic questionnaire too for models from 1968 through 1971.

Other problems listed in our Owner Survey included easily broken interior fittings—specifically window winders—mentioned by 10 percent, while 8 percent reported failed door latches, and 7 percent listed problems with three items: speedometers, wiper motors or gearbox (usually synchronizers). Mufflers were mentioned by 25 percent of the 1967 1600 owners but didn't make the 5-percent minimum figure for the 1968–1969 models; however, our Used Car Classic questionnaire results showed mufflers and exhaust system problems were mentioned for every year from 1967 through 1975. Overheating was mentioned by 22 percent of the 2002 owners in the Owner Survey but didn't seem to afflict the 1600 significantly, although in our 1979 questionnaire, overheating and radiator troubles were commented on by owners of 1600s and 2002s for each model year except 1973 and 1975–1976.

Other problems that surfaced in our review of the Used Car Classic questionnaires included front-end shimmy related to tie-rods (1967 through 1971), gearbox output shaft and flange wear (1969, 1972 through 1975, with 1973 models seeming to suffer most in this area), and cylinder head leaks resulting from overheating and warpage of the aluminum head (1970 through 1972 models). Carburetion problems and/or dissatisfaction surfaced most commonly on 1971 through 1973 models, and again on 1975–1976 2002s, probably reflecting driveability complaints related to emission standards.

In pointing out things to look for when buying a used 1600 or 2002, many owners also cited rust around the front turn signal housings, wheel wells, rocker panels, the rear shock towers and along the bottoms of the doors. Owners of early 1600s found the 6-volt electrical system a trial, and almost everyone was resigned to the gearbox synchros going bad, especially in 1st and 2nd.

It may seem that I've listed more problem areas for BMWs than is common with previous Used Car Classic articles, but I suspect this is actually a case of simply having more input from more owners than ever before. Most BMW drivers wrote glowing comments about the joys of their 1600 or 2002. Even though the 2002 has not been out of production for very long, it has already begun to assume cult-car status, as many BMW fans find the newer models are not perhaps as sporting, and because many enthusiasts have simply been priced out of the market for a new model. As one New York owner wrote on his questionnaire, "Please don't buy these cars! I need a lifetime supply and can't afford the new BMW junk." Or, in the words of an Orlando, Florida owner: "Being an avid car enthusiast, I have owned and driven many diverse specimens and still consider the 2002 to be the greatest all-around car *ever*, and worthy of any necessary expense."

That brings up a final point about buying a used BMW 1600 or 2002. The price of parts is high and getting higher the longer the cars are out of production. Also, BMW specialists generally charge relatively high labor prices for their expertise. So the potential buyer should keep in mind that service, parts and repairs will generally not come cheaply, and factor that into any budget plans before purchase.

Driving Impressions

DAVID ANDERSON is a Los Angeles attorney who is a BMW *aficionado* of the first order. He drives a 1972 2002tii that he bought new and on which he has rolled up 128,000 miles. He also owned a 1968 1600 that he bought used in 1969 and kept and enjoyed for 10 years—clearly not a man given to changing cars willy-nilly. His 2002tii is what I think a Used Car Classic example should be: clean, well cared for, mechanically excellent and, most importantly, used daily for driving pleasure.

Anderson admits to driving his BMW quite hard; it's his belief that's what cars of this sort are designed for, and the best way to enjoy them. His engine developed worn rocker shafts at 87,000 miles, so David had it rebuilt, blueprinted and balanced by Hyde Park BMW in Los Angeles just over 40,000 miles ago. Along with Koni shocks and adjustable anti-roll bars, at 105,000 miles on the odometer he invested in a new set of springs and was impressed with the restoration of the supple ride and handling characteristics for which the car is famous. He has also been running different distributor advance springs (either BMW 1600 or Corvette distributor springs, he says) and finds this modification improves performance and fuel mileage both. One of the first things he did was replace the radiator core with an American-made one to give greater cooling capacity and prevent chronic

overheating for which 1600s and 2002s are famous. He has also put in a Recaro seat at the driver's position, and runs Phoenix Stahlflex 205/60-13 tires on 6.0-in. alloy rims. Anderson feels the wider wheels and tires give his car that extra bite in cornering and braking, and after driving the car I heartily agree. David also tipped me off that there is an aluminum disc in the front shock towers of 1974–1976 2002s to raise the front end in compliance with U.S. bumper height rules. Removing those discs, Anderson says, results in better handling.

Anderson's 2002tii is an exciting car to drive. It has the taut feel of a well made, well maintained car, and the engine and chassis are both first-class in response. The engine revs freely right up to (and through) the 6500-rpm redline without missing a beat. The acceleration is not blindingly quick but the 2002tii is no slouch getting up to speed. David's car, like many if not most 1600s and 2002s, suffers from bad gearbox synchros, especially noticeable in making the 1–2 shift. But, as he says, there's really no known cure for this that will last any length of time. You can redo them, but it doesn't take very long for them to go bad again, so you simply learn to live with this condition. Other than the synchros, however, the gearbox is a delight to use, and has a strong, positive feel.

The handling is stimulating and made me want to press on with more and more daring. The 2002tii is a car that feels comfortable right from the start and I didn't have any sensation of needing time to get used to any idiosyncrasies beyond the characteristic oversteer when the car nears its limits. David's wheel/tire combination seems a perfect choice to me, as driving at speed down a winding lane with a touch of water and sand here and there was a lark, with the speed limited only by body roll (not inordinate) and common sense.

David Anderson's philosophy about his 2002tii is that it's a car built to offer maximum driving pleasure. He believes that it's a car that requires the finest maintenance and he's quite fastidious about it, both mechanically and cosmetically. He admits that it isn't an inexpensive car to keep in tip-top shape, but it gives him so much driving fun that it's worth it. Also he can't think of a new car that offers near the pleasure he derives from his 2002tii. That's understandable—it is an exceptional automobile.

PRACTICAL CLASSICS BUYING FEATURE

Buying a BMW 2002

*John Williams discovers that BMW motoring
need not be expensive.*

The BMW 2002 was first launched in the United Kingdom in May 1968. It combined the two door four seater coupe bodywork of the 1502 and 1602 models with the 1990cc engine of the 2000 saloons, and this proved to be a very rapid combination and certainly a drivers car. At £1,597 the BMW was not cheap, being about £120 dearer than the Rover 2000 which was more luxurious but rather slower, and only £170 cheaper than the Jaguar 3.4S which offered a great deal more luxury, and slightly more performance, although admittedly at a higher price in terms of petrol consumption.

Above:

This single carburettor version of the BMW 2002 has plain pressed steel wheels which are disguised by large chromed hubcaps and wheel trims. Pre-1974 models had narrow, 13 x 4J wheels.

In due course alternative body styles became available. The BMW 2002 Touring (1971-75) had a hatchback style and was quite a useful dual purpose vehicle. The 2002 Cabriolet was made for only a short period in 1973-74 and is now quite rare.

The BMW does not possess the 'personality' which tends to be attributed to those cars which are trimmed in leather and walnut, but the interior is comfortable and a lot more spacious than the compact exterior styling suggests. This impression is reinforced by the lightness of the interior due to the large window areas. There are reclining front seats, and the back of each front seat tilts well forward to allow easy access to the rear. Pre-1971 cars had plastic upholstery which at least had the virtue of being easy to clean. In 1971 the seats were redesigned to incorporate cloth inserts but retain the plastic panels around the edges. The cloth inserts have proved to be unsatisfactory, being both difficult to keep clean and unable to withstand very much wear and tear. Replacement seat covers are available from BMW at about £70 per seat — plus the labour charge for fitting. From late 1974 velour upholstery was used, and although this

is quite easily damaged it has not been as troublesome as the earlier cloth inserts.

Some cars were fitted with a winding steel sunroof by the factory, and this well made and remarkably trouble free option would be worth having.

POWER UNIT

The engine is a four cylinder single overhead camshaft unit of 1990cc. Various fuel systems were used and this article is mainly concerned with the single carburettor version and the 2002 Tii (from September 1971) which was fitted with Kugelfischer fuel injection. There was also the 2002 Ti which had twin Solex carburettors, but few of these are to be found in this country. The 2002 Turbo (1974-75) with its Schaver fuel injection and turbocharger is a very interesting and exremely quick variation on the 2002 theme, reflecting BMW's active involvement in saloon car racing, and several German specialists (particularly Alpina) offered further performance versions of the 2002.

Engines are unlikely to require major attention at less than 60,000-70,000 mile intervals, and they can last to well over

Buying a BMW 2002

100,000 miles. When major attention is required it is not usually the pistons and bores which are showing signs of wear, but rather the crankshaft and (five) main bearings. Lack of proper maintenance causes an unnecessary amount of wear in the rocker shafts and rocker arm bushes, and this wear is certainly present if there is very much tappet noise. For some reason many owners seem to think that because it is a BMW it will go on forever without attention, whereas it is absolutely essential for the engine oil to be changed every 4,000 miles before it gets a chance to thicken and become sludgy. Failure to attend to this important point inevitably causes the wear already mentioned, and continued neglect leads to excessive wear on the crankshaft and a steady increase in the cost of repairs — the two rocker shafts are £18 each. Given proper attention these components can last a very long time.

BMW FACTS

May 1968: BMW 2002 Coupe introduced in the UK. 4 cylinder 80 x 89mm 1990cc ohc engine. Single carburettor. 100 bhp at 5500 rpm. Maximum speed 106 mph, overall fuel consumption 24 mpg.

June 1971: 2002 Tii available in the UK. Fitted with Kugelfischer mechanical fuel injection. Stronger bodyshell and suspension, and larger brakes, wheels and tyres.

Sept 1971: 2002 Touring available in the UK. This was an estate version.

Feb 1973: 2002 Cabriolet available in the UK. This was an open tourer version with a removable roof panel (which packed into the boot) and a collapsible fabric rear panel with a plastic window.

Sept 1973: 2002 Turbo option available in the UK. 170 bhp at 5800 rpm.

Dec 1975: 2002 production discontinued.

TRANSMISSION

The standard gearbox was a four speed manual unit and a three speed automatic transmission was available from 1969. A five speed manual box was an alternative option, and it is still possible to obtain a kit for converting the four speed box to five speed (at a price). There was a weak point in the gearboxes prior to about 1974. It was the method by which the tail flange on the main shaft was supposed to be locked onto that shaft. Unfortunately it did not work very well, and the flange frequenty came adrift. The early sympton of this was a tendency for the car to jump out of second gear, and if this was ignored for long enough, drive would be lost completely, the shaft ruined and a replacement gearbox needed. It took the factory a long time to put matters

This is a 1975 Turbo. This very fast motor car has 5½-inch wheels, ventilated front discs, Bilstein shock absorbers and struts, a limited slip differential, and a high axle ratio to give 20 mph per 1000 rpm (and, like it's predecessors it goes into the red at about 6400 rpm). There is a rear spoiler, flared wheel arches, and Mahle alloy wheels, but the fins on the front wings are not standard. ▼

The neat lines of the coupe bodywork. The nearest car is a 1974 Tii. Notice that the wheelnuts are now exposed and there are very small

hubcaps incorporating the BMW badge, on 13 x 5J rims.

The 2002 Tii was one of several BMWs which were present and in use during our April 25th Test Day at Goodwood (see the report elsewhere in this issue).

What to pay

An unusual variant like the Cabriolet will be expensive, and almost £3000 was being asked in a recent advertisement. On the other hand a good 1972 Tii Coupe should be obtainable for about £1000. An older car in fair condition but requiring a little work would be priced at about £500. It is possible to find, say, a pre 1974 model which is in particular need of an engine overhaul but is otherwise a fairly sound car. If you are willing to tackle the engine work, such cars can be bought for around £300.

The driving controls in an automatic transmission single carburettor 2002. There are fuel and temperature gauges, and the speedometer reads up to 120 mph. The tachometer reads up to 8000 rpm, but goes into the red at about 6400 rpm. An automatic choke is standard equipment.

There is a useful amount of boot capacity, and note that the centre car is a pre 1974 model with the round rear lamp units. In 1974 the oblong rear lamp units were first fitted, and it is partly because of this that genuine bargains can be found amongst the earlier "out of fashion" cars.

right and it was not until 1974, about 18 months before the end of production, that the gearbox was improved.

Differentials tend to be noisy, indicating some wear in the crown wheel and pinion, but an occasional problem is their tendency to break up the planet gears. Not that this is necessarily noticeable from the driver's point of view — cars have been known to keep going for many miles with this damage.

STEERING AND SUSPENSION

The steering is of the recirculating ball type and the car has a very useful turning circle. There is hardly any 'play' in the steering except at extreme lock, and whilst the steering may seem somewhat heavy to those of delicate build in slow manoeuvring situations, it does require less effort and maintains a very steady course at speed.

The suspension is independent all round with MacPherson struts, coil springs and anti roll bar at the front, and semi-trailing arms with coil springs, shock absorbers and anti-roll bar at the rear. The rear suspension together with the differential, flexible driveshafts and hubs, is mounted on a subframe which is in turn rubber mounted to the body. There are disc brakes at the front and drums at the rear, and the fuel injection models have larger discs and drums. Twin servos are fitted to all these models.

BODYWORK

The bodywork is of unitary construction and this (together with suspension components) was strengthened in time for the Ti and Tii models. Any steel car body has particular areas which tend to be the first to display rust damage, and to list these areas is not to imply that other parts of the car do not rust as well. The front wings (which bolt on but are welded

The back of each front seat can be released by a lever (which can be seen on the side of the drivers seat in this picture) giving access to the rear seat.

Buying a BMW 2002

One of the many nice features of these engines is the method by which the valve clearances are adjusted. This is one of the aluminium rocker arms incorporating an eccentric. Adjustment is achieved by revolving the eccentric to the required position and then locking it in that position with the hexagonal nut.

The spare wheel does not intrude into the boot space as it lives in a deep well below the wooden platform which acts as a boot floor. It is easy to ignore the wheel well, and once corrosion starts the proximity of the nearside rear wheel tends to accelerate the process. Check this area — severe damage as shown in this picture is unusual but it does happen.

Production Details

Year	Model	Production
1966-71	BMW 1600-2	210,451
1967-68	BMW 1600 Ti	8,835
1967-71	BMW 1600 Cabriolet	1,682
1971-72	BMW 1600 Touring	4,379
1971-75	BMW 1602	56,351
1971-75	BMW 1802/A	83,351
1971-74	BMW 1800 Touring	4,075
1968-75	BMW 2002	302,349
1969-75	BMW 2002 Automatic	34,558
1968-71	BMW 2002 Ti	16,448
1971-75	BMW 2002 Tii	38,703
1971-75	BMW 2002 Cabriolet	2,517
1971-74	BMW 2000 Touring	14,980
1971-74	BMW 2000 A Touring	989
1971-74	BMW 2000 Tii Touring	5,783
1973-74	BMW 2002 Turbo	1,672
1975-77	BMW 1502	71,564

to the front panel) are likely to show the first evidence of rust, particularly along the vertical edge just ahead of the doors and also around the indicator light units. Blockage of the drain holes in the bottom skin of the front panel (below the front bumper) causes rot in this area. Sills have tended to last quite well although earlier cars are now showing their age, and it is worth checking the extent of any damage in the rear part of each sill, which is incorporated in the rear wheel arch. Factory made sill panels do not include this area, and replacement panels have to be obtained from independent suppliers. Rear wheel arches also tend to rust but repair sections are available. The boot floor and spare wheel well tend to be ignored because they are hidden beneath a wooden platform in the boot, and although serious damage is not usual, rust can spread very quickly if the wheel well drain hole is not kept clear.

BACK TO BACK

QUICK QUARTET

The sporting saloon vogue made its mark in the seventies. Four of them — models from Ford, BMW, Vauxhall and Triumph — are compared by Mike Walsh

Modern suspension and engine developments have blurred the distinction between sports cars and saloons, to the extent that many four-seater closed cars can out-perform and out-corner most sporting soft-topped rivals of similar capacity. To pin-point the beginning of this trend in production development is difficult, but the Riley 1.5 was certainly one of the first. The advent of the cheeky Mini Cooper created a new breed of performance driver, the working class lad who could chase and embarrass the hardy sports car fraternity without burning too much of a hole in his pocket.

Today, mass-produced convertible sports cars have long since vanished, leaving the market to exclusive, hand-built thoroughbreds. But the development of the sporting saloon has never ceased, both on road and track. After the Mini Cooper, Ford were the first to exploit the market potential of the 'go faster' saloon. In fact, a corporate decision from Detroit in the early sixties led Ford of Europe to develop a performance image and thus provide immortal classics like the GT and Lotus Cortina — they were fast, versatile, immensely practical and relatively cheap.

By the seventies, the market had become intensely competitive, with almost every major manufacturer producing performance versions of family saloons, some more hybrid than others. Saloon car racing and rallying on national and international levels gained greater prominence, and success here was quickly exploited.

The four cars chosen for this group test were all developments of an existing saloon model, though the Firenza coupé is more distinctive than the other three, particularly in its styling.

The BMW 2002Tii is the oldest of the bunch, and in many respects the most conservative. The formula of front-mounted engine and rear wheel drive in a high quality package is unchanged in present BMWs. The 2002, in fact, was the idea of American BMW importer Max Hoffman, who suggested that BMW match their lightest body shell with their largest four cylinder engine as a way of coping with federal smog controls which strangled the 1600 Ti engine. The result proved an instant winner.

The basic 2-litre engine is a tough iron block with an aluminium head, and is mounted at a 30 degree tilt. This trusty design with five sturdy main bearings has a single chain-driven overhead camshaft, operating inclined valves via twin rocker shafts. September 1971 saw the arrival of the 2002 Tii, the extra 'i' representing injection by the excellent Kugelfischer system. Power increased by 10bhp over the twin

carburettor model's 120bhp. The fuel-injected engine required revised valve timing, and a slight increase in compression to 9.5:1. Road testers were unanimous in their praise for the unit, and *Motor* found the engine 'quite happy to rev beyond 6000rpm in the lower ratios without getting rough'. They also discovered that the injection engine gave better overall fuel consumption than the carburettor model.

Transmission choices, in theory, were wide, though restricted for right-hand drive cars, and five-speed 'boxes were a rarity in Britain. Most of the mechanicals were standard throughout the 2002 range, with Macpherson strut front suspension, and a trailing arm independent rear end with front and rear anti-roll bars. To help cope with the extra performance the body shell was stiffened and harder dampers fitted. The steel wheel width rose from 4½ to 5ins. The first examples arrived in Britain in June 1971, and little alteration was made through the model's four year production life. Minor changes were made to the interior trim in 1974 for the Lux designation, and this model is the most desirable of the range.

The 2002 had an honourable career as a race and rally car both in factory and private hands. The injected racing unit, producing 210bhp, was invincible in the 2-litre class of the European Touring Car Championship, and powered Dieter Quester to four outright wins in 1969. Simply, the original 2002 in 1969 set such high standards that the fuel injected model produced saloon car performance that has only recently been eclipsed by latter day Golf GTIs.

'A BMW eater from Triumph?' was a common speculative headline when the Dolomite Sprint was launched, and even the French enthused over its character. *Motor* concluded: 'At £1740 it's hard to see what else but a Sprint can be best for anyone in the market for a fast entertaining prestige saloon that's as strong in character and comfort as its sporting pretentions. It seems to us quite outstanding value for money without a rival in sight.' With such appraisals from the press, how could Triumph go wrong? The answer — common to the Stag and TR6 — was inadequate quality control and poor technical back-up. This quickly tarnished the model's reputation, and sales.

Advanced engine

Much of the 'Dolly's' delight is in its advanced engine, developed by Spen King in consultation with Walter Hassan and Harry Mundy. The Triumph/Saab slant-four was bored out to 1998cc and equipped with a special four valve alloy cylinder head. The 16 valves were operated by a single eight-lobe overhead camshaft, the inlets directly by bucket tappets and exhausts indirectly by short rockers. The rockers are inclined at 35 degrees, with just enough room for spark plugs at the bottom of deep tunnels. The new design was equipped with two sidedraught SU carbs and produced an excellent 127bhp at 5700rpm, thus providing a very tough competitor to BMW.

To take the extra power, beefier transmission from the Stag and TR6 was used, and the suspension was given stiffer spring rates. The steering was slightly lower geared to reduce the effort from fatter tyres on 5½ins rims. The brakes were only slightly modified to incorporate TR6 drums at the rear, but this was inadequate, proving to be a constant problem for road testers and race drivers. For such performance the chassis needed ventilated discs, not to mention dual circuit hydraulics.

Like the BMW, the styling was borrowed from an existing car, but in Triumph's case the rather humdrum 1500 saloon range, styled by Giovanni Michelotti. It seems odd, looking back, that Triumph converted a front-wheel drive, all independent suspension lightweight saloon, into a rear-drive, high performance, live axle slingshot. After such extensive mechanical development, it was a great disappointment that the same basic body was retained. BMW already had an exclusive image, but this Triumph suffered from its similarity to cheaper models. The only external changes for the Sprint were alloy wheels, a vinyl roof and a new front spoiler. However, the lavish cabin with matt teak veneer for the dash and door caps, deep carpets, and shapely brushed nylon seats matched the Sprint's exclusive pretensions.

BMW 2002Tii: controllable handling, but vague steering

BMW cockpit is comfortable, but some thought it spartan

BMW single ohc 130bhp four-cylinder is smooth and quiet

Triumph Dolomite Sprint: good on paper, but many failings

Dolly Sprint interior offers wooden dash and good seats

An interesting engine, with 16 valves and single camshaft